Palgrave Studies in Governance, Leadership and Responsibility

The fall-out from many high profile crises in governance and leadership in recent decades, from banking to healthcare, continues to be felt around the world. Major reports have questioned the values and behaviour, not just of individual organizations but of professionals, industries and political leadership. These reports raise questions about business corporations and also public service institutions. In response this new series aims to explore the broad principles of governance and leadership and how these are embodied in different contexts, opening up the possibility of developing new theories and approaches that are fuelled by interdisciplinary approaches. The purpose of the series is to highlight critical reflection and empirical research which can enable dialogue across sectors, focusing on theory, value and the practice of governance, leadership and responsibility.

Written from a global context, the series is unique in bringing leadership and governance together. The King III report connects these two fields by identifying leadership as one of the three principles of effective governance however most courses in business schools have traditionally treated these as separate subjects. Increasingly, and in particular with the case of executive education, business schools are recognizing the need to develop and produce responsible leaders. The series will therefore encourage critical exploration between these two areas and as such explore sociological and philosophical perspectives.

Esther Poveda-Pareja ·
Bartolomé Marco-Lajara ·
Mercedes Úbeda-García ·
Encarnación Manresa-Marhuenda
Editors

The Strategic Paradigm of CSR and Sustainability

A Public-Private Approach

palgrave
macmillan

Editors
Esther Poveda-Pareja
Business Administration Department
University of Alicante
San Vicente del Raspeig, Spain

Bartolomé Marco-Lajara
Business Administration Department
University of Alicante
San Vicente del Raspeig, Spain

Mercedes Úbeda-García
Business Administration Department
University of Alicante
San Vicente del Raspeig, Spain

Encarnación Manresa-Marhuenda
Business Administration Department
University of Alicante
San Vicente del Raspeig, Spain

ISSN 2662-1304 ISSN 2662-1312 (electronic)
Palgrave Studies in Governance, Leadership and Responsibility
ISBN 978-3-031-58888-4 ISBN 978-3-031-58889-1 (eBook)
https://doi.org/10.1007/978-3-031-58889-1

This Palgrave Macmillan imprint is published by the registered company Springer Nature Switzerland AG
The registered company address is: Gewerbestrasse 11, 6330 Cham, Switzerland

Contents

Notes on Contributors

José Antonio Belso-Martínez, Ph.D. is Full Professor of Applied Economics at the University Miguel Hernández (Spain). His research has focused on several topics such as: clusters, networks, internationalization, innovation and policy. He has published in leading academic journals such as: *Economic Geography, Regional Studies, Urban Studies, Cities, Entrepreneurship and Regional Development, Journal of Knowledge Management, Journal of Business Research, Journal of Small Business Management, European Planning Studies*, among others. His research has been awarded by the top Spanish scientific societies (Spanish Association of Regional Science, International Association of Applied Economics-ASEPELT and Foundation of Savings Banks-FUNCAS.

Daniel Catalá-Pérez is Professor of Management at the Universitat Politecnica de Valencia (UPV), Spain. Ph.D. in Business Management and Administration, his research interests include public-private collaboration and how this management formula contributes to the value creation in both, public and private sectors. He is also the chairman of the Spanish Evaluation Society and therefore he is interested in the evaluation of public policies, even applying private sector evaluation techniques. He participates in the Innoecotur project, analysing the role of public sector as promoter of circular economy strategies for the hospitality industry.

Francisco Javier García Corral graduated in Law and Master in Sustainable Local Development and Co-Development from the University of Almería, is finishing his Ph.D. in Economics, Business and Law in the area of Public and Business Law. He is an external Professor and member of the Applied Economics Group of Almeria (SEJ 147), actively participating in its project "Village branding". His research has focused on sustainable local development and the use of complementary forms of payment.

Blanca de-Miguel-Molina is Professor in the Department of Business Organisation at Universidad Politècnica de Valencia (Spain). Ph.D. in Business Management and Administration, her research interests include the involvement of companies in the local communities where they operate, and industries analysis, including creative industries. She participates in the Innoecotur project, analysing the needs of tourism firms in their transition to the circular economy.

María de-Miguel-Molina is Professor of Management at Universitat Politecnica de Valencia (UPV), Valencia, Spain. Ph.D. in Management, her Doctoral Thesis studied the hazardous industrial activities and the environmental public policies to control them. Her research interests include Public Policy & Strategy, Human-centred approach. At the moment she participates in the InnoEcoTur project, where circular economy strategies are proposed for the hospitality industry.

Jaime de Pablo Valenciano, Ph.D. in Economics (University of Almería) and Economics Degree (Alcalá de Henares University, Madrid). He has more than 30 years of experience as Full Professor at the School of Economics and Business. He has been Guest Professor in numerous universities, such as the Catholic University of Chile (Chile), University of Santiago de Guayaquil (Ecuador), Andean University (Sucre-Bolivia), Kiev (Germany), Hame Polytecnic (Finland), Beira (Portugal), Quebec (Canada) and Miami (United States). Since 2020, he is responsible for the project "Village branding". The aim of the project is to study the problem of depopulation in rural municipalities.

Manuel Expósito-Langa, Ph.D. is Associate Professor of Management at the Polytechnic University of Valencia (Spain). His research has focused on several topics such as: clusters, industrial districts, social capital, networks and innovation. He has published in leading academic journals such as: *Industry & Innovation, International Entrepreneurship and Management Journal, Entrepreneurship and Regional Development, Regional Studies, Papers in Regional Science, European Planning Studies, Journal of Small Management, European Journal of International Management or Journal of Organizational Change Management*, among others. Nominated among the best papers at the Copenhagen Business School's biannual awards in 2013.

Juan Milán García is Assistant Ph.D. Professor in the Applied Economics area at the University of Almería, Spain. He has published many articles in leading academic journals including Journal of Cleaner Production, Globalization and Health, Marine Pollution Bulletin or Frontiers in Marine Science. His research interests include Local Development and Bibliometrics Methodology, and he is taking part in a project known as "Village branding", whose main objective is to reduce the depopulation rate of rural areas.

Beatriz Garcia-Ortega is Professor of Business Management at Universitat Politècnica de València (UPV), Valencia, Spain. Her Ph.D. in Management addressed Corporate Social Responsibility (CSR) in the mining industry from the perspective of the social impacts of their companies and community involvement. Her research interests are the role of companies, their CSR actions, and overall strategy in their relationship with society and their contribution to it in terms of their well-being, sustainability and progress. The research is carried out fundamentally from the perspective of the message that companies convey, with special attention to the communication of their senior executives and their ethical approach, with several publications in relevant academic journals and international conferences.

Dr. Encarnación Manresa-Marhuenda is Associate Professor of Business Organization since 2002 and Director of the Strategic Management Division at University of Alicante. Graduated in Economic Studies with honours (2001) and Ph.D. Degree in Business Studies at the University of Alicante (2005). She is author of several book chapters, papers published in national and international academic journals and speaker in conferences on Management and Business topics. Her research interests are on the area of Strategic Management, Corporate Strategy, Environmental and Innovation Economics, Human Resources Management, International Business and Higher Education, among others. She has participated in several European, national and regional, public- and private-funded projects.

Dr. Bartolomé Marco-Lajara is Professor of Business Organization at the University of Alicante (Spain). He holds a Ph.D. in Economics and his doctoral dissertation is focused on strategic alliances management. His research interests are on Strategic Management and Tourism Management. He is author of several books, book chapters and international articles related to teaching methodology and the areas above mentioned. On the other hand, he is member of the Tourism Research Institute at the University of Alicante since its foundation. He has participated in many public- and private-funded projects, being the main researcher in many of them. He was assistant dean of the Economics Faculty at the University of Alicante during eight years, holding now the position of Head of the Department of Business Organization at this University.

José Luis Caparrós Martínez is Associate Professor at the University of Almería and the International University of La Rioja. He has been working since 2001 in the Department of Environment of the Andalusian Regional Government, in works related to the management and conservation of biodiversity and sustainable rural development.

He holds a Ph.D. in Economics and a degree in Environmental Sciences. His research interests focus on science-management interfaces, in which scientists and managers work together to propose solutions to the different environmental challenges and problems of our society. He has published articles in leading academic journals including *Globalization and Health, Water, and Global Ecology and Conservation.*

Dr. Daria Morozova is a Lecturer of Fashion and Marketing at Glasgow Caledonian University (UK). Her research interests include sustainable and ethical consumption of fashion, creative entrepreneurship and, recently, technofashion such as wearables and virtual clothes. Her Ph.D. (Aalborg University, Denmark) was focused on wearable technology and its implications for different forms of sustainability, including a social aspect. Her works have been published in *Journal of Consumer Culture, International Journal of Consumer Studies and Cultural Studies.*

Carlos A. García Meseguer is Industrial Engineer specialized in management and environmental field, at the present working as responsible of the valorization & technological transfer area in a research institute at Universitat Politècnica de València, as well as manager of research projects. He has experience in participating in cooperation programme like TEMPUS, ERASMUS+, H2020, FP7, etc. In the past, he collaborated with the regional government in the process of management and evaluation of regional programme calls to obtain funding for researches project carried out by the industry. He is also doing his Ph.D. in Circular Economy & innovation policies.

Luis Antonio Millán-Tudela is Assistant Professor in the Department of Management at University of Alicante. MBA and Bachelor of Mechanical Engineering, his research focuses on business longevity, and more specifically on the factors that influence the survival of companies. This activity is developed within the research group "Dirección Estratégica, conocimiento e innovación en una economía global (DECI-GLOBAL)". He also teaches subjects in the area of management in different degrees related to business administration.

Dr. Ángel Peiró-Signes is a Professor of Strategy and Operations Management at the Business School, Polytechnical University of Valencia (Spain). He holds a Ph.D. in Business Administration and Management, B.S. degrees in industrial, organizational and materials engineering and Master degree in Business Administration.

His research interests include environmental orientation and eco-innovation in companies. Professor Peiró-Signes was a visiting scholar at the Center for Hospitality Research, CHR, at Cornell University 2011–2012, at the Bath Centre for Healthcare Innovation and Improvement, Bath University, UK, and at the Cornell Institute for Healthy Futures in 2016 and 2018.

His research has been published in top-rated journals as *Cornell Hospitality Quarterly, Journal of Cleaner Production, Corporate Social Responsibility and Environmental Management, Science and Engineering Ethics or Business Strategy and the Environment*, among others.

Dr. Lin Peng holds a Ph.D. in Human Resource Management and is an assistant researcher at Training Academy for Executive Leadership, Ministry of Emergency Management. Her research interests are mainly focused on corporate social responsibility, human resource management, emergency management. She is author of articles related to these topics and has presented papers, and has taken part in projects related to these topics.

Dr. Esther Poveda-Pareja holds a Ph.D. in Economics, Business and Society and is an Assistant Professor of Business Organization at the University of Alicante. Her research interests are mainly focused on corporate social responsibility and strategic management (concretely in agglomeration economies and tourism management). She is author of articles and book chapters related to these topics and has presented papers in national and international conferences. She has taken part in public and private projects related to these topics.

Inmaculada Martín-Rojo is Professor of Business Organization at the University of Málaga. She has carried out research stays at universities such as Sapienza (Rome) and Harvard (UU.EE.), and has taught at Spanish and foreign universities. She is director of masters, courses and seminars on the tourism sector held at Menéndez Pelayo International University and University of Málaga. She has written many books and papers in scientific journals on management of tourist companies. She combines his academic work with advising companies and institution.

Joaquín Sánchez-Planelles works as Project Manager at the Ângela Impact Economy consultancy and holds a Ph.D. in Business Administration and Management from the Polytechnic University of Valencia. Much of his professional career has been spent in the field of consulting. Both his professional career as a researcher are focused on helping companies to integrate sustainability into their business models.

He has several academic publications and collaborations with research projects. He has developed methodologies that allow knowing the most appropriate sustainable practices to be implemented by organizations.

He has a degree in Environmental Sciences from the University of Barcelona and a Master's Degree in Business Management, Product and Services from the Polytechnic University of Valencia.

Dr. Marival Segarra-Oña is a Professor of Innovation and Competitiveness at the Business School, Polytechnical University of Valencia (Spain). She holds a Ph.D. in Management and BS degrees in industrial and mechanical engineering.

Her research interests include sustainability and eco-innovation applied to industrial and service sectors and its link with the social innovation area.

Professor Segarra-Oña was a visiting scholar at the Center for Hospitality Research, CHR, at Cornell University 2011–2012, at the Bath Centre for Healthcare Innovation and Improvement, Bath University, UK, and at the Cornell Institute for Healthy Futures in 2016 and 2018.

Her research has been published in top-rated journals as *Cornell Hospitality Quarterly, Journal of Cleaner Production, Corporate Social Responsibility and Environmental Management, Science and Engineering Ethics or Business Strategy and the Environment*, among others.

María Belén Silva-Cárdenas with ten years of work experience as a Business Engineer, she became a specialist in marketing and strategy for small and medium businesses to help companies create value through innovation and communication in diverse markets, especially in Real Estate and Hospitality.

In 2019, she initiated her career as a researcher on sustainability and started studies as a Master's in Business, Product, and Service Management at the Polytechnic University of Valencia (UPV), which finished successfully, with distinction. During these years, she has focused her research on the SDGs, Eco-innovation and Circular Economy, including through her Master Thesis and participating as a collaborator at a research group for a four years project on Circular Economy applied to the Touristic sector, Innoecotur, led by the UPV.

Yolanda Trujillo-Adriá works as an Open Innovation expert at Valenciaport Foundation and holds a B.S. degree in Aerospace Engineering and a master's degree in Business Management from the Polytechnic University of Valencia. She is currently a Ph.D. Candidate in Management at Polytechnic University of Valencia, developing her research in circular economy and innovation for the transport sector, with a special interest on the influence of transport in tourism.

Professionally, she has developed her career on the transport field working for aeronautical, railway, ports and construction companies on innovation and sustainability, while researching about the integration of circular economy models in the field.

Dr. Mercedes Úbeda-García is a University Full Professor of Business Organization at the University of Alicante. She is a member of the Tourism Research Institute of the University of Alicante. Her main lines of research are related to Human Resources Management, Corporate Social Responsibility and Organizational Ambidexterity, in the tourism sector. She has participated in various international, national and regional public research projects related to tourism. She is the author of books and book chapters related to her lines of research, as well as numerous articles published in international journals such as: *Corporate Social Responsibility and Environmental Management, Journal of Sustainable Tourism, Business Ethics: A European Review, Tourism Management, Cornell Hospitality Quarterly, Current Issues in Tourism, International Journal of Hospitality Management, International Journal of Contemporary Hospitality Management, Regional Studies, Journal of Business Research, International Journal of Human Resource Management, Journal of Intellectual Capital, Personnel Review*, among others.

Jeanneth Marcela Valdivieso-Uvidia, MBA, is a Ph.D. candidate in the Ph.D. programme in Business Administration and Management at the Polytechnic University of Valencia. Her research, of a multisectoral nature and under the strategic management approach, includes topics such as green innovation, green absorptive capacity and sustainable performance in companies in the Valencian Community (Spain). He has a research stay at the Escuela Superior Politécnica de Chimborazo (Ecuador). He has also participated as a speaker at conferences such as the International Conference on Regional Science.

Rosa María Martínez Vázquez is Ph.D. Professor in the Applied Economics area at the University of Almería, Spain. She has published many articles in leading academic journals including Marine Pollution Bulletin, Environment Science Europe or Frontiers in Marine Science. Her research interests include Local Development, nautical tourism and Bibliometrics Methodology, and she is taking part in a project known as "Village branding", whose main objective is to reduce the depopulation rate of rural areas.

Dr. Yufei Wang holds a Ph.D. in Business Administration and is an Assistant Professor of Business Administration at Zhejiang Sci-Tech University. Her research interests are mainly focus on corporate social responsibility, corporate environmental strategy and green innovation, especially the influencing mechanism of CSR and green innovation. She is author of articles and book chapters related to these topics and has published papers in national and international journals.

List of Figures

Sustainable Tourism: Toward a Circular Economy with Transportation as a Key Factor

Strategic Planning for a Smart Sustainable City Model: The Importance of Public Administration and Enterprises Cooperation

Implementation of the Sustainable Development Goals (SDGS) in Municipalities with Less Than 2,500 Inhabitants: The Agenda Marca Pueblo Project

List of Tables

Agglomeration Environments to Enhance CSR Strategies: A Tourism District Approach Towards Sustainability

Sustainable Tourism: Toward a Circular Economy with Transportation as a Key Factor

Regulation Wave in the Fashion Industry: Media Framing of Legalised CSR

Strategic Planning for a Smart Sustainable City Model: The Importance of Public Administration and Enterprises Cooperation

Implementation of the Sustainable Development Goals (SDGS) in Municipalities with Less Than 2,500 Inhabitants: The Agenda Marca Pueblo Project

Introduction

Esther Poveda-Pareja, Bartolomé Marco-Lajara,
Mercedes Úbeda-García,
and Encarnación Manresa-Marhuenda

Over the last few decades, environmental and social phenomena have occurred in which the effects of harmful actions on the part of companies and citizens can be glimpsed. Some examples are the increase in global temperature or the high levels of toxic emissions (Azcárate et al., 2019), the scant progress in terms of gender equality from 2015 to the

E. Poveda-Pareja (✉) · B. Marco-Lajara · M. Úbeda-García ·
E. Manresa-Marhuenda
Business Administration Department, University of Alicante, San Vicente del Raspeig, Spain
e-mail: esther.poveda@ua.es

B. Marco-Lajara
e-mail: bartolome.marco@ua.es

M. Úbeda-García
e-mail: mercedes.ubeda@ua.es

E. Manresa-Marhuenda
e-mail: encarnacion.manresa@ua.es

E. Poveda-Pareja et al. (eds.), *The Strategic Paradigm of CSR and Sustainability*,
Palgrave Studies in Governance, Leadership and Responsibility,
https://doi.org/10.1007/978-3-031-58889-1_1

present day, as shown by indicators such as the Gender Index of the Sustainable Development Goals [hereinafter SDGs] (EM2030, 2022) or the currently low levels of labour progress, where inequalities between countries are very high and have been exacerbated by the effects of the pandemic (International Labor Organization [ILO], 2022). In addition, high levels of poverty still exist nowadays, affecting 10% of the world's population (United Nations [UN], 2022).

This has provoked the mobilisation of governments and official institutions over decades in the design of regulations to alleviate them, such as compacts, conferences, treaties, alliances, among other variants, which have been put into practice during the last years (e.g. Earth Summit, Conference for Sustainable and Environmental Development, UN Conference on the Human Environment, World Conference on Sustainable Tourism, World Conference on Sustainable Development, among others), including the establishment of global goals in the pursuit of sustainable development (Millennium Development Goals [MDGs] and SDGs).

However, it has been found that despite significant efforts, the desired levels of sustainability have not yet been achieved, even after the pandemic resulting from COVID-19, which was seen as a turning point that would promote environmental and social awareness among citizens and companies. In fact, despite the efforts to promote corporate social action by different institutions over the last three decades, Lee (2011) highlights the existence of very disparate positions on CSR, ranging from those companies that are more inclusive to those that show no interest in this type of practice. In this sense, the analysis of the CSR and sustainability strategy is key to understand which factors still prevent full compliance with the standards required by supranational institutions.

Within this analysis, it is important for business management researchers to focus on the shortcomings that cause business practices not to have the expected effects on global sustainable indicators. On the one hand, it is worth noting that the very delimitation in the conceptualisation of CSR and sustainability is a subject of debate in the academic field of business strategy (Bansal & Song, 2017; Lankoski, 2016; Rasche et al., 2017; Van Marrewijk & Werre, 2003), as it has been observed that concepts, such as CSR and corporate sustainability, among other alternatives, are used interchangeably when in fact they differ in terms of their origin, theoretical influence, level of action and approach. As a result, companies may not be able to consistently meet sustainability requirements when developing such strategies.

In general terms, CSR is broadly understood to describe how the company should act while sustainability refers to the way in which this can be achieved, that is, how systems can be sustained over time to achieve that desired state (Bansal & Song, 2017). In this sense, a distinction could be made between different levels of action of each concept where sustainable development would relate to the macro level while corporate sustainability and CSR would relate to the micro-level, with the latter being further differentiated by the level at which CSR practices become effectively integrated with the organisation's corporate objectives (Ashrafi et al., 2018).

Therefore, although both CSR and sustainability share many characteristics such as their focus on the triple bottom line (Ashrafi et al., 2018; Montiel, 2008), as well as shared value creation approach (Bansal & Song, 2017), it should be noted that this distinction around levels of action implies decision-making by different types of actors in promoting or developing these kinds of responsible strategies. This aspect may explain why compliance with sustainable standards does not solely rely on initiatives by supranational institutions promoting responsible action or setting global targets but requires the active participation of companies at the micro level and alignment with other levels. In this way, it is worth focusing on the involvement of all stakeholders surrounding the same activity, that is, at both the microeconomic and macroeconomic levels, which involves the private and public spheres, and especially on how to establish linkages between them, which will make it possible to respond to the traditional gap between responsible business strategy and the sustainable goals to be achieved.

In this sense, the purpose of this book is based on applying a two-fold analysis of CSR and sustainability strategy, combining the public–private perspective of the different levels of stakeholders in charge of developing this type of practices in a multi-sectoral context, with the aim of providing useful conclusions to address the existing gap between action at company level and public policies that seek to promote sustainable development.

It is well known that multiple perspectives can serve as theoretical basis for corporate sustainability, such as stakeholder theory, resource-based theory, and institutional theory (Montiel & Delgado-Ceballos, 2014), among others. However, in this book, we highlight the importance of stakeholder theory (Freeman, 1984) and institutional theory (Jennings & Zandbergen, 1995) as key approaches for resolving the gap between the actions undertaken by companies and the global goals set.

On the one hand, stakeholder theory not only considers the needs of the different agents with which the firm relates, but also the interaction between them and the creation of value derived from these relationships (Freeman, 1984). Indeed, the very concept of the firm "is based on how [...] customers, suppliers, employees, financiers, [...] communities and managers interact and create value" (Freeman et al., 2017, p. 9). It is worth noting that there are new theoretical trends that have evolved towards the consideration of multi-stakeholder theory, which, unlike conventional stakeholder theory in which the manager was responsible for ensuring that the interests of the other groups were met, in this new, more advanced form, all stakeholders (corporate and non-corporate) are engaged, which allows interactions to be sustained over time and provides insight into whether multi-stakeholder governance initiatives foster new standards that generate social and environmental solutions to governance problems (Moog et al., 2015).

On the other hand, institutional or legitimacy theory is based on the notion of adaptation by companies to the paradigms or social norms of the environment that surrounds them in order to achieve certain levels of legitimacy (Jennings & Zandbergen, 1995; Meyer & Rowan, 1977). Thus, institutional perspective provides a context and not only that, but also the way in which companies carry out such practices since societies and the organisations that make up these depend on paradigms that to a certain extent guide and give meaning to their actions (Jennings & Zandbergen, 1995). In this sense, the presence of institutions that promote CSR encourages the development of CSR reporting (Khan et al., 2020).

Considering both theoretical perspectives, several authors (Lee, 2011; Vashchenko, 2017) defend the combination of stakeholder theory and institutional theory, defending the idea that institutional norms or paradigms should be reinforced by the demands of interest groups closer to the organisation, a line of research on which this book is based.

Indeed, recent approaches highlight the interlinkage between institutional pressure and multi-stakeholder perspective, due to the moderating effect of multi-stakeholder orientation on the relationship between institutional pressure and CSR (Tolmie et al., 2020), which corroborates the complementarity between the approaches to enhance responsible practices at different levels of action.

To fulfil the purpose of the book, it is structured in two main blocks, distinguishing between the private level of action (the action of companies in developing CSR) and the public level of activity (addressing stakeholders who act at a macroeconomic level to meet the desired levels of legitimacy). So far, existing academic research has mainly focused on one of the two perspectives (private or public) and this book will consider possible alternatives to find out how to combine public–private perspectives, showing examples applied to both spheres that will enable the formulation and implementation of CSR from a strategic perspective to fulfil the desired levels of sustainable development.

The first section contains chapters that analyse characteristics that affect companies when developing their CSR strategy, applying the analysis to various sectors. Initially, the stage of the life cycle to which the company belongs is analysed as a key characteristic to explain the type of CSR developed by the company (Chapter 2), as well as the role of certification and ethical behaviour in the proper development of these strategies, especially in controversial industries such as mining (Chapter 3). Chapter 4 analyses the role played by technological intensity in the level of financial performance, green innovation, and sustainable performance achieved by industrial companies. In addition to the characteristics linked to the company itself outlined in the first three chapters, the advantages of analysing how the location of companies itself could enhance CSR and sustainability strategies of companies located in specialised environments are also addressed (Chapter 5). In addition, the role of transport in the proper development of the circular economy cycle is also analysed (Chapter 6).

The second section focuses on the public initiatives that influence the development of CSR, that is, in the relationship between the public stakeholders' actions and its effects on the private stakeholders' development of CSR. In this sense, the implication of regulation or legislation and, specifically, the role of the media in promoting moral judgements and interpretations of questionable practices in sectors such as fashion is examined (Chapter 7). In addition, the role of public–private collaboration to achieve sustainable models is highlighted (Chapter 8) as well as the strength of certain agents such as governments when it comes to promoting sustainable behaviour patterns in the projects developed (Chapter 9). The strength of this type of public agent is also highlighted in the last chapter of the book, in this case praising their ability to create and impose specific laws for sectors such as tourism that allow changing the sustainable performance patterns of the companies that comprise it (Chapter 10).

As a summary, the book is enriched by the combination of theoretical and practical chapters, which allows to advance the research area from a holistic perspective, able to integrate theoretical contributions to the academic debates around the interconnection between CSR and sustainability and, at the same time, practical solutions for all types of sectors (primary, secondary, and tertiary). In this way, solutions are provided linking CSR and sustainability to the specific context in which they are developed, that is, to both the type of sector and agent that puts it into practice.

Consequently, this book will be of interest to internal and external stakeholders. Among the internal stakeholders, general managers, and specifically CSR and sustainability managers, regardless of their sector of activity, will be able to benefit from all the proposals set out in each of the chapters contained in the book, as they will provide useful advice on the factors or activities that should be addressed to improve the development of their internal CSR strategies as well as their relations with external stakeholders, which will increase the impact of their activity. In addition, it is also aimed at external stakeholders such as the state (city councils, government, among other typologies) as well as the local or regional community, who will find useful information in the chapters so that public policies or legislation have a greater level of involvement in companies, encouraging collaboration between both types of agents, and designing optimal models for the sustainable approach of both types of stakeholders.

References

Ashrafi, M., Adams, M., Walker, T. R., & Magnan, G. (2018). How corporate social responsibility can be integrated into corporate sustainability: A theoretical review of their relationships. *International Journal of Sustainable Development and World Ecology, 25*(8), 672–682.

Azcárate, T., Benayas, J., Nerilli, G., & Justel, A. (2019). *GUIA PARA UN TURISMO SOSTENIBLE. Retos del sector turístico ante la Agenda 2030.* REDS, Madrid.

Bansal, P., & Song, H. C. (2017). Similar but not the same: Differentiating corporate sustainability from corporate responsibility. *Academy of Management Annals, 11*(1), 105–149.

EM2030. (2022). *"Back to normal" is Not enough: the 2022 SDG Gender Index:* https://www.equalmeasures2030.org/wp-content/uploads/2022/03/SDG-index_report_FINAL_EN.pdf

Freeman, E. R., Dmytriyev, S., & Strand, R. G. (2017). Managing for Stakeholders in the Digital Age. In A. Rasche, M. Morsing, & J. Moon (Eds.), *Corporate Social Responsibility: Strategy, Communication, Governance* (pp. 110–135). Cambridge University Press.

Freeman, R. E. (1984). *Strategic Management: A Stakeholder Approach.* Cambridge University Press.

International Labor Organization [ILO]. (2022). *La COVID-19 y el mundo del trabajo: Estimaciones actualizadas y análisis* (Séptima edición): https://www.ilo.org/wcmsp5/groups/public/---dgreports/---dcomm/documents/briefingnote/wcms_767045.pdf

Jennings, P. D., & Zandbergen, P. A. (1995). Ecologically Sustainable Organizations: An Institutional Approach. *Academy of Management Review, 20*(4), 1015–1052.

Khan, M., Lockhart, J., & Bathurst, R. (2020). A Multi-level institutional perspective of corporate social responsibility reporting: A mixed-method study. *Journal of Cleaner Production, 265*, 121739.

Lankoski, L. (2016). Alternative conceptions of sustainability in a business context. *Journal of Cleaner Production, 139*, 847–857.

Lee, M. D. P. (2011). Configuration of external influences: The combined effects of institutions and stakeholders on corporate social responsibility strategies. *Journal of Business Ethics, 102*(2), 281–298.

Meyer, J. W., & Rowan, B. (1977). Institutionalized organizations: Formal structure as myth and ceremony. *American Journal of Sociology, 83*(2), 340–363.

Montiel, I. (2008). Corporate social responsibility and corporate sustainability: Separate pasts, common futures. *Organization and Environment, 21*(3), 245–269.

Montiel, I., & Delgado-Ceballos, J. (2014). Defining and measuring corporate sustainability: Are we there yet? *Organization and Environment, 27*(2), 113–139.

Moog, S., Spicer, A., & Böhm, S. (2015). The politics of multi-stakeholder initiatives: The crisis of the forest stewardship council. *Journal of Business Ethics, 128*(3), 469–493.

Rasche, A., Morsing, M., & Moon, J. (2017). The changing role of business in global society: CSR and beyond. In A. Rasche, M. Morsing, & J. Moon (Eds.), *Corporate social responsibility: Strategy, communication, governance* (pp. 1–28). Cambridge University Press.

Tolmie, C. R., Lehnert, K., & Zhao, H. (2020). Formal and informal institutional pressures on corporate social responsibility: A cross-country analysis. *Corporate Social Responsibility and Environmental Management, 27*(2), 786–802.

United Nations [UN]. (2022). *Ending poverty:* https://www.un.org/en/global-issues/ending-poverty. Retrieved 4 January 2024.

Van Marrewijk, M., & Werre, M. (2003). Multiple levels of corporate sustainability. *Journal of Business Ethics, 44*(2–3), 107–119.

Vashchenko, M. (2017). An external perspective on CSR: What matters and what does not? *Business Ethics, 26*(4), 396–412.

Companies as Agents of Change in the Development of CSR and the Achievement of Sustainability Goals: A Private Sector Perspective

The Systemic Contexts and Dynamic Trajectories of Corporate Social Responsibility in Chinese Automobile Industry

Yufei Wang and Lin Peng

1 Introduction

With the continuous promotion of CSR concept, the importance of CSR in enterprise strategy formulation has been recognized (Porter & Kramer, 2011). Through the fulfillment of CSR, enterprises can improve corporate reputation, accumulate the moral resources, increase the soft power, and thus bring more economic profits (Fombrun & Shanley, 1990). However, CSR is not static and will change based on changes in internal and external influencing factors. The extent and fervor of fulfilling CSR may vary across different stages of the life cycle. The sense of urgency to fulfill CSR varies among enterprises at different stages of the business

Y. Wang (✉)
Zhejiang Sci-Tech University, Hangzhou, China
e-mail: wyf121143@outlook.com

L. Peng
Training Academy for Executive Leadership, Ministry of Emergency Management, Beijing, China

E. Poveda-Pareja et al. (eds.), *The Strategic Paradigm of CSR and Sustainability*, Palgrave Studies in Governance, Leadership and Responsibility,
https://doi.org/10.1007/978-3-031-58889-1_2

life cycle. Fulfilling CSR is a dynamic process that drives transformations across the economy, society, and environment. To maximize profits, CSR should be continuously adapted throughout the life cycle to ensure effective alignment between the life cycle and CSR (Hasan & Habib, 2017). When enterprises aim to derive strategic value from CSR, it is crucial to recognize that CSR evolves throughout the enterprise life cycle (Udayasankar, 2008).

Based on enterprise life cycle theory, this article introduces the concept of dynamic trajectories (Verk et al., 2021). Dynamic trajectories can represent the changing paths of a specific corporate behavior under the combined action of multiple factors. Dynamic trajectories of CSR mean that in the process of implementing CSR initiatives, CSR may experience variation, selection, retention, and struggle under the joint influencing factors, similar to enterprise may experience birth, growth, decline, or even death along with life cycle (Midttun & Koefoed, 2005). The reasons for the formation of dynamic trajectories in CSR are diverse, including influencing factors at different levels.

Based on the different sources of influencing factors, this study selected political factors, social factors, and corporate factors to study their impact on CSR. Political factors represent the impact of institutional environment on CSR, including laws, policies, regulations, etc. (Osuji, 2011). CSR is usually not reflected in legal provisions, requiring companies to assume CSR through mandatory enforcement. The impact of institutional environment on CSR is mainly reflected in regulations (Buhmann, 2011). The central and local governments will call on enterprises to undertake CSR and give back to society through the issuance of documents. Social factors encompass other stakeholders besides governments and enterprises. In this article, public participation is mainly selected as a representative, reflecting the supervisory role of the public in CSR (Kim & Ferguson, 2018). For enterprises, the most important driving force for undertaking CSR lies in internal drive. The CSR friendly tendency within enterprises is usually manifested in the recognition of CSR concepts by senior managers, as well as the ethical atmosphere and culture of the enterprise (Ferrell et al., 2019; Székely & Knirsch, 2005).

Chinese automotive industry will be the subject of case studies to validate CSR dynamic trajectories. As a nation with a large automobile industry scale, China's automobile industry has faced strong CSR pressure in the past, such as environmental pressure. Thus, the promotion of the transformation and upgrading of the automobile industry by CSR is urgently needed. The Chinese government has realized the important role of CSR and has introduced some policies to encourage its development. Currently, environmental assessment and legal norms are the main policies of CSR in China. The main reason for choosing the automotive industry as the research object is that China's automotive industry has entered a relatively mature business stage after years of development. Both in terms of CSR awareness and CSR funding scale, it is superior to other industries.

Existing research has achieved rich publications in the influencing factors and outcome elements of CSR. However, there are still some shortcomings regarding the properties of CSR. Firstly, existing research considers CSR as a cross-sectional concept, and rarely combines CSR with time changes to consider the evolution of CSR behavior at different stages of enterprise development. Secondly, previous studies have validated the effectiveness of a single policy on CSR, but CSR is a complex concept which was influenced by various factors, such as economic, social, and organizational, and existing studies lack integration of influencing factors at different levels.

This paper supplements the existing literature on CSR in the following ways. First, we build a system dynamic evolutionary model of CSR from the perspective of dynamic evolution and examine the four stages of the variation, selection, retention, and struggle CSR. Second, compared with the previous literature that only considers the effect of a single policy, our research verifies the actual effects of the different implementation strengths of a single policy, the four of policy, and the policy mix on CSR. Notably, this paper also provides empirical evidence that may lay a foundation for the relating policy optimizations of the development of automobile industry.

The rest of the paper is arranged as follows. Section 2 provides a comprehensive literature review. It introduces three factors that affect CSR, namely political factors, social factors, and organizational factors.

In Sect. 3, we describe the research methods, model establishment process, and data sources in detail. Section 4 summarizes research conclusions and gives corresponding implications.

2 Literature Review

Policy Influencing Factors

Economic Policy Uncertainty

Economic policy uncertainty refers to the inability of enterprises to accurately predict policy changes in the country's economic regulation process (Gulen & Ion, 2016). Especially when the macroeconomic environment changes frequently and violently, countries often adjust their economic policies more actively than before to meet the needs of stable economic development, resulting in enterprises being unable to reasonably predict the direction of future economic policies (Rjiba et al., 2020). When enterprises are unable to reasonably predict the direction of future economic policies, they are unable to make targeted strategic decisions and need to adopt strategies different from usual to cope with uncertain risks in the external environment, in order to ensure the long-term survival and stable development (Zhao et al., 2021).

When economic policy uncertainty increases, whether enterprises fulfill CSR mainly considers two aspects. On the one hand, the increase in economic policy uncertainty is often accompanied by changes in the distribution of industry benefits, which are mainly reflected in the financing ability, profitability, growth ability, and debt repayment ability (Borghesi & Chang, 2020; Ongsakul et al., 2021; Rjiba et al., 2020). The changes in these financial indicators will increase the operational risk, leading to a decrease in the cash flow level of the enterprise. The vast majority of enterprises view CSR as a strategic and competitive embedded activity (Muriithi et al., 2022). By undertaking CSR, enterprises can release positive signals to stakeholders, gain their investment and attention in business operations, and provide more resource support in the subsequent innovation and transformation process (Yuan et al., 2022).

On the other hand, CSR may also become a means for enterprises to alleviate the uncertainty and contradiction of the external macro environment, in order to ensure their own business safety. In the context of constantly changing policy content and guidelines, the demands of stakeholders are stronger, and the financing constraints in the financing process are relatively higher (Vural-Yavas, 2021). Stakeholder theory and signal theory believe that CSR can release positive signals to multiple stakeholders to alleviate operational pressure, improve risk tolerance, and reduce business activity risks in dynamic and uncertain environments (Peng et al., 2023). By undertaking CSR, enterprises can achieve the following goals to alleviate external conflicts caused by increased economic policy uncertainty: (1) convey signals to stakeholders that the company is operating well. If a company can actively implement CSR, it indicates that it is in good operating condition and has additional time and energy to carry out social responsibility behaviors (Dao et al., 2020). When a company is willing to undertake CSR, employees may have more work enthusiasm, and shareholders will also have greater confidence in the company, bringing more cooperation opportunities to the company (Buhmann, 2011; Cezarino et al., 2022). (2) The difficulty and cost of obtaining bank loans for enterprises are reduced. The signal conveyed by CSR will bring more loan convenience to enterprises, increase loan limits, and lower loan interest rates (Iiyas et al., 2022). (3) Establish closer and friendly relationships with the local government. CSR can help enterprises create an image of serving and giving back to society, gain recognition from the government and the public, and thus obtain more reliable financing channels (Borghesi & Chang, 2020).

Political Connections

Fan et al. (2007) proposed that political connection is one of the main means of government intervention in enterprises, and enterprises with political connections are more susceptible to government intervention. No matter which stage of development an enterprise is in, it needs to rely on surrounding resources to meet its own survival and development needs. In the current social and institutional environment of China, the government has the right to allocate scarce resources such as land and credit (Cheng & Leung, 2016). It is likely that some enterprises will establish political connections with the government for their own needs, in order to gain positive connections with politics (Bliss & Gul, 2012).

The impact of political connections on corporate strategic decision-making typically manifests in two forms: the first is the influence of central or local government officials on CSR behavior. The second type is that senior managers of enterprises have a certain political background or work experience, and have close connections with the government, driving enterprises to assume CSR (Lopez et al., 2022). In terms of the impact of government officials on CSR, officials may combine corporate management with public welfare for their own promotion, generating political demands for CSR. Enterprises with political connections may maintain positive interactions with the government through social responsibility behaviors, and receive more government subsidies (Li et al., 2015). For enterprises without political connections, they may also fulfill CSR as much as possible to compensate for their lack of political connections, in order to gain the favor of the government and help themselves survive and develop better (Lin et al., 2015; Xu & Liu, 2020).

The political connection of executives is a bridge that establishes good communication between enterprises and the government, forming a two-way resource dependence through this relationship. Enterprises with political backgrounds can obtain key information through the personal social relationships of executives over other competitors, consolidating the positive relationship between the enterprise and the government (Gu et al., 2013). In addition, Confucianism holds a very important position in China's political culture, advocating for social fairness, security, and sustainable development, which overlaps with the concept of CSR. Executives with political affiliations, or those currently working in government agencies, are closer to Confucian political culture and exhibit a preference for CSR (Bashir & Yu, 2020; Xu & Liu, 2020).

Social Influencing Factors

Public Participation

Public participation in CSR refers to participating in decision-making and management activities related to corporate social interests through certain procedures or channels, and supervising CSR behaviors to meet the public's social preferences and interests (Lee et al., 2020). The emergence of CSR is often accompanied by certain conflicts and social issues, which are closely related to public daily life or work practices. Therefore, public participation on social issues is often more urgent, and this sense of urgency also strengthens public attention to CSR (Wan et al., 2022). The consequences of CSR behaviors can directly or indirectly cause damage to the public's rights and interests, leading to a gradual increase in public attention and guiding negative public opinion toward the enterprise (Tang-Lee, 2016). Therefore, social responsibility events can turn into social issues under the influence of factors such as public attention, public comments, media dissemination, and government intervention. In this process, public participation will have a significant impact on the consequences of CSR.

The impact of public participation on CSR first stems from the public's attention to social issues. When an individual's expectations for the enterprise or society are inconsistent with reality and may pose risks to personal interests, it will attract public attention and spread widely (Cho et al., 2017; Lee et al., 2020; Wan et al., 2022). The public's attention to CSR is influenced by various factors. Externally, media coverage, government intervention, and visibility of social events can trigger widespread public attention. From the perspective of the public itself, public relevance and individual oriented needs can also trigger public attention (Lee et al., 2020). As the public's understanding of CSR continues to deepen, they will also conduct judgments and discussions on social responsibility events (Hung-Baesecke et al., 2016). The implementation mechanism of this process mainly manifests in the following aspects: firstly, the public distinguishes CSR events based on the information they have. By discussing and disseminating social events, the public can expand their influence and attempt to influence others (Tang-Lee, 2016). Secondly, as the impact of CSR events gradually expands, the public begins to demonstrate a certain level of transparency and interactivity in information search, and gradually reaches a consensus (Reed et al., 2018). Finally, based on the recognition of established social responsibility events, the public will shift their focus to exploring solutions or expressing their attitudes after comprehensive consideration, that is, to conduct a final evaluation of social responsibility events (Cho et al., 2017).

Social Transformation

Social transformation is the transformation of the economic system, usually from the traditional planned economy system to the market economy system. This transformation process can change the perception of the public and enterprises in society (Tsui et al., 2004). Social transformation is often accompanied by richer resources that can enhance corporate competitiveness. But at the same time, social transformation also implies greater uncertainty and risks (Nee & Matthews, 1996). During the transformation period, the economic system undergoes rapid transformation, resulting in institutional and legal loopholes. The supervision of corporate dereliction of duty may also decrease, leading to public and corporate distrust of society.

CSR, which usually aligns with the governments' public value creation goals, can also attract more attention from the government toward enterprises. In the vast majority of developed countries, CSR is an effective market competition strategy, but in developing countries, CSR tends to be a strategic political contribution behavior (Sakarya et al., 2012). When the government is unable to provide sufficient funding for infrastructure and public services, it will seek additional financial assistance from enterprises (Maton, 2000). Therefore, in the transitional period of China's overall society, CSR is more manifested as rent-seeking behavior (Tsui et al., 2004). Therefore, in the period of social transformation, whether it is obtaining government policy information and preferential policies, or avoiding political risks under policy uncertainty, enterprises have a stronger motivation to fulfill CSR.

Organizational Influencing Factors

Responsible Leadership

Responsible leadership is a comprehensive concept that integrates theories from the fields of corporate social responsibility and leadership (Maak, 2007). The proposal of this concept responds to the expectations of the state and society for social activities in recent years. Maak and Pless (2006) defined responsible leadership as the ability to establish, cultivate, and maintain mutual trust relationships with stakeholders both inside and outside the organization. The purpose of responsible leadership is to achieve a shared business vision (Maak, 2007; Székely & Knirsch, 2005). Compared to other traditional forms of leadership, responsible leadership is an ethical leadership behavior that emphasizes the mutual influence between the leader and the led, and this influence is closely related to the corporate culture and corporate purpose (Waldman & Balven, 2014).

Responsible leadership is a moral norm that avoids risks through equal dialogue and democratic consultation with internal and external stakeholders, in order to establish trust relationships and play an important role in the construction of CSR (Voegtlin, 2016). Responsible leaders will first consider the potential impact their decisions may have on various stakeholders, and then include these affected stakeholders in the decision-making process, attempting to reach consensus with all parties to address corporate social responsibility issues (Maak & Pless, 2006). Social learning theory suggests that employees will seek their role models and imitate them in the enterprise, and the leaders are the most likely to become role models for employees (Maak et al., 2016). Leaders' recognition and encouragement of CSR can motivate employees to engage more in socially responsible behavior, and this role model can subtly influence subordinates (Voegtlin et al., 2012). Responsible leaders attach great importance to assuming social responsibility in their work and often guide employees to develop CSR behaviors in their daily work by establishing formal or informal social responsibility strategic decisions (Schinzel, 2018). Under the influence of responsible leadership, companies will implement a series of CSR practices such as charitable donations, green environmental protection, and community services (Voegtlin, 2016). When facing ethical dilemmas, companies will have more confidence and courage to solve and address the problems.

Business Ethics

Ethics refers to widely recognized social norms and behavioral norms that should be followed when dealing with mutual relationships. Unlike the mandatory nature of law, ethics is formed in human daily life and is a set behavioral norm with non-mandatory nature (Werhane & Freeman, 1999). Ethics can permeate various fields of social life, adjust social relationships between people, and treat all members of society equally (De Bakker et al., 2019). In a competitive market, the vast majority of production and business activities are also subject to ethical constraints. Although the organization itself does not have emotions and perceptions, there are members within the organization, which leads to a more profound impact of ethics on strategic decision-making and organizational behaviors (Joyner & Payne, 2002). In addition, the connotation and form of ethics are generally accepted and recognized by the public, with natural convenience. Nowadays, the business management activities of enterprises cannot do without the carrier of society (Cacioppe et al., 2008). Therefore, there is also a strong internal connection and correlation between management and ethics, and corporate behavior is naturally constrained by ethical factors.

In terms of CSR, ethics always plays an effective driving role. The foundation of business ethics is a sense of responsibility, which is the main manifestation of corporate values (Ferrell et al., 2019). The advanced concept of CSR is the soft competitiveness of a company, which can influence its future development direction through subtle influence (Cacioppe et al., 2008; Fatima & Elbanna, 2023). Starting from guiding enterprises to establish lofty corporate goals, business ethics endows them with a solemn sense of mission, driving them to continuously develop productivity, improve business scale and economic efficiency, solve social employment problems, and link their own development with the direction of national development (Singhapakdi et al., 1996; Valentine & Fleischman, 2008).

Moreover, the driving effect of business ethics on CSR is also reflected in its impact on employees. Business ethics play a positive role in improving the overall quality of employees, continuously optimizing personnel structure and resource allocation, creating an organizational ethical atmosphere, and widely mobilizing employees' enthusiasm and creativity (Fassin et al., 2011). The positive impact of business ethics can also be reflected in the business results of enterprises, such as improving labor productivity, increasing market value, and ultimately achieving a win–win situation between enterprise profits and employee career development. Business ethics, as a soft constraint on social behavior, points out the bottom line and moral boundaries for employees, who can form their own value judgment system through ethical norms (Joyner & Payne, 2002). The convergence of employees on social responsibility issues can lead enterprises to fulfill their CSR, improve their overall values and performance, and further gain social recognition (Singhapakdi et al., 1996). Managers who consciously abide by ethical norms can enhance their self-discipline, conduct market transactions within the framework of ethical norms.

The impact mechanism of political influencing factors, social influencing factors, and organizational influencing factors on CSR is shown in Fig. 1.

Dynamics of CSR

According to corporate lifecycle theory, enterprises may go through the process of launch, growth, shake-out, maturity, and decline (Habib & Hasan, 2019). Although the lifespan of different enterprises varies, the characteristics exhibited by each enterprise at different stages of its lifecycle have certain commonalities. Understanding these commonalities helps companies to clearly identify their lifecycle stages, adjust their strategic direction, and extend their lifespan as much as possible. Similar

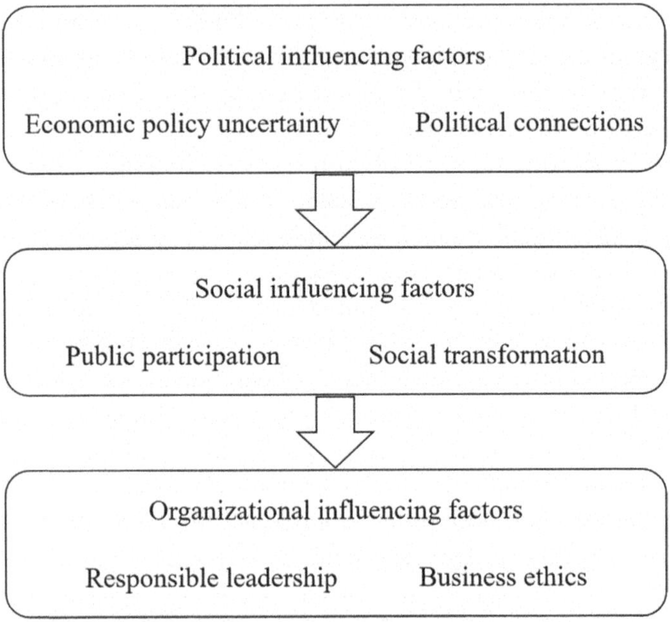

Fig. 1 Theoretical framework (*Source* Author's own research)

to the corporate life cycle, the attention and funding investment of enterprises in CSR will also constantly undergo dynamic changes (Hasan & Habib, 2017; Jiang et al., 2023). Under the joint influence of political, social, and organizational influencing factors, CSR also undergoes several processes of variation, selection, retention, and struggle.

From an evolutionary perspective, the variation of CSR typically occurs in the early stages. Afterward, there is the promotion of CSR, which enters the stage of selection and retention. Finally, part of CSR behaviors will enter the final stable state and be retained, while others will be eliminated in market competition. The variation stage reflects the process of CSR from scratch. At this stage, companies begin to realize the importance of taking on social responsibility, but there are still doubts and uncertainties about whether and how to fulfill CSR. The selection stage represents the process of widespread popularization of CSR. During this stage, enterprises begin to follow the social orientation and assume CSR, and the number of socially responsible behaviors rapidly increases.

However, companies at this stage have not made CSR a part of their future development goals and have not truly realized the importance of CSR. Retention stage refers to the process in which CSR shifts from pursuing quantity to pursuing quality. At this stage, companies that focus on the short-term benefits of CSR will gradually give up undertaking CSR, while companies that are truly willing to take the initiative to take on CSR will persist. The final struggle stage represents the outcome of the CSR evolution process. At this stage, due to the influence of political, social, and organizational influencing factors, many companies will give up CSR due to considerations of operating conditions (Fig. 2).

Based on the above analysis, this article proposes the following propositions:

Proposition 1: Political influencing factors can affect CSR behaviors and have different impacts at different stages.
Proposition 2: Social influencing factors can affect CSR behaviors and have different impacts at different stages.
Proposition 3: Organizational influencing factors can affect CSR behaviors and have different impacts at different stages.

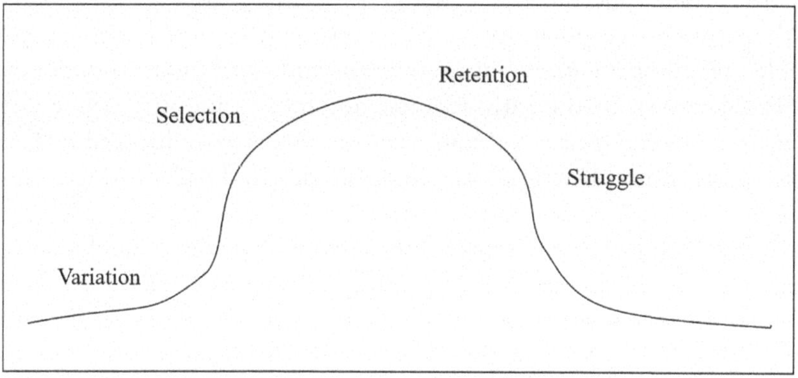

Fig. 2 Dynamic trajectories of CSR (*Source* Midttun and Koefoed [2005])

3 Methodology

Research Design

This article selects the Chinese automotive industry as the case study object. 25 interviews were conducted, each lasting 30–75 minutes. The entire interview process was recorded and converted into written materials. The interviewees were selected based on relevance of research question, which came from automotive companies, transportation departments, online taxi platforms, new energy vehicle companies, and consumers. In addition, this paper also selects some written materials as auxiliary data, including Report on the Work of the Government, policy documents, corporate social responsibility report, sustainable development report, etc.

The main reasons for choosing Chinese automotive industry as the research object are as follows. Firstly, the acceptance and recognition of CSR by Chinese enterprises are in a transitional period, and they are not just in the rapid development period, nor have they entered a mature period. Therefore, they are suitable for conducting dynamic change research. Secondly, the development of Chinese automotive industry is relatively stable, and the scale of automotive enterprises is generally large, with mature management models. This type of enterprise has a relatively stable operating situation and more funds and capabilities to undertake CSR. Moreover, in the early Chinese automotive industry, there were many foreign enterprises and joint ventures that were influenced by CSR culture and atmosphere in Europe and America, and had a stronger sense of CSR.

In addition, in order to enhance the credibility of the research conclusions, this article also selected some business cases as auxiliary materials. These business cases include FAW Volkswagen, SAIC Volkswagen, FAW Audi, Toyota, etc. We mainly collected official media reports, internal reports, and external media evaluations of the aforementioned companies as auxiliary analytical materials for research propositions.

Political Influencing Factors

Economic Policy Uncertainty

Economic Policy Uncertainty (EPU) is an indicator used to measure economic and policy uncertainty in major economies around the world. China's EPU refers to the news index, which selects large Chinese newspapers and filters articles related to economic policy uncertainty through search keywords such as 'unknown/unknown', 'economic/economy', 'policy', 'tax', 'spending', 'regulation', 'central bank', 'budget', and 'deficit'. After statistical and standardized processing, the results are obtained. Although it is only a news index, scholars still believe that this indicator is representative because it has a strong correlation with the EPU overall index.[1]

China's EPU index has shown several peaks since 2008. The first was from 2008 to 2009, when the impact of the subprime mortgage crisis on China gradually became prominent, and the government had to introduce several response measures and policies. However, the limited scope and intensity of these stimulating policies have led to the dual difficulties faced by the Chinese government in policy choices. The second wave occurred around 2012, on the one hand, due to a leadership reshuffle, and on the other hand, the European debt crisis reached its climax, with increased uncertainty in the external environment transmitted to the internal Chinese economy. The third wave occurred in 2015, when China's economic growth rate reached its lowest level in 25 years, and the volatility of the stock market also increased concerns about economic policy uncertainty. The most recent occurrence occurred after 2020, as China is experiencing the impact of COVID-19 and the economic situation is rapidly changing, leading to difficulties in government decision-making.

[1] The EPU overall index is a weighted composite of four sub-indices. Sub-indices include news index, tax expiration index, economic forecaster disagreement index, and federal/state and local government expenditure disagreement index.

Political Connections

In the Chinese automotive industry, the government will clearly regulate the emissions, emissions, energy efficiency, and other aspects of enterprises by issuing policies. However, in terms of CSR, it is difficult for the government to directly issue relevant policies requiring enterprises to fulfill their CSR. The impact of political connections on CSR is mainly reflected in the fact that the government can convey some social responsible friendly messages to enterprises, expressing a preference for enterprises voluntarily assuming CSR, and corporate executives actively implement CSR behaviors in order to establish a communication bridge with the government.

> Before issuing a policy, the government usually invites representatives from the local automotive industry to attend hearings and listen to the opinions of business representatives. Because government decision-makers sometimes cannot fully understand the needs and ideas of enterprises, it is necessary to communicate more with the government.
>
> Our company is a state-owned enterprise, and our leaders have close connections with the government, so the government has higher expectations for us in terms of CSR. But these are not mandatory, whether to do them or not depends on the enterprise itself...
>
> Policies can indeed impose significant constraints on us, but if it is CSR, I think the impact of policies is not significant. Our company's main motivation for CSR is voluntary, and it is the company's own desire to do it...

Therefore, this article believes that political influencing factors play the greatest role in the variation and struggle stages of CSR, mainly manifested in the relatively short period of time, through policy constraints and supervision, to motivate enterprises to assume CSR or to ensure the basic level of CSR.

Social Influencing Factors

Public Participation

During the variation stage of CSR, there are usually only two stakeholders: enterprise and government. When entering the selection stage, CSR behavior will involve more stakeholders, including government, shareholders, employees, suppliers, the public, third-party institutions, etc. Although public participation cannot directly affect CSR, the evaluation of CSR by the public can affect corporate reputation and thus affect their development. In the Chinese automotive industry, the impact of public participation is mainly manifested in the public's concern for the quality of ecological environment. Chinese automotive industry is one of the highly polluting industries, which inevitably generates some waste, wastewater, and metal waste, affecting the quality of life of surrounding residents.

And most of CSR behaviors are aimed at the public, and companies that consider more public interests often gain the favor of the public. The selection stage of CSR mainly exists in large scale, high market share, and high operating profit automotive enterprises. This type of automobile enterprise has sufficient resources and capital to give back to society, while large enterprises also bear more public expectations. At this stage, companies typically engage in a large number of CSR behaviors, covering employee health and safety, gender equality, assisting vulnerable groups and donations.

> After our company builds a new factory, we will invite public representatives or nearby residents to visit to ensure that the factory's emissions do not affect the public's quality of life, and listen to the public's opinions...
>
> ...Communication with the public is definitely only available in large automobile companies, and small automobile companies rarely consider these needs. They also lack the ability to consider these needs, and usually only some companies with a relatively complete sense of CSR will do so...
>
> Our company regularly fulfills its CSR. For example, in China, when encountering major disasters, the company donates money. Recently, due to the shortage of masks and protective clothing due to the impact of COVID-19 in China, I wouldn't be worried about the lack of masks.

Later, the company did help us solve the problem of masks, making employees very reassured.

Social Transformation

In terms of CSR, China's social transformation is manifested as the process of CSR consciousness from scratch to strength. As a highly polluting industry, Chinese automobile industry emits waste, exhaust gas, and wastewater into the surrounding natural environment every year. Before the social transformation, there was no clear policy on the emission levels of automobile enterprises. After the social transformation, especially after the Chinese government established the goal of "carbon peak and carbon neutrality", there is a clear definition of the amount of pollution that each production factory of the automobile enterprise can emit each year. Not only in terms of pollution and carbon footprint, the impact of social transformation is also reflected in the automotive production process. In response to the call of society for ecological environment protection, automobile companies producing fuel vehicles have begun to establish green factories. The significance of green factories is to reduce pollution emissions at all stages of production and assembly, while reducing the impact of industrial production on employee health.

> In the past, there was no awareness of CSR, and no one would have thought of doing such a thing. It was only in the past five or ten years that everyone began to realize the importance of CSR...Due to the irresponsible behavior of enterprises, the public has suffered a lot of harm. Previously, there were no clear regulations to protect the public's interests. Even if the public realized that their rights and interests were being harmed, they could not seek help... With the continuous development of society, we are now able to find some basis to protect the public and avoid the irresponsible behavior of enterprises...
>
> Our group has established green factories in both Qingdao and Foshan, which can achieve almost zero emissions and is a new production mode. When it was built, we also invited people from various industries to visit, and everyone felt very impressed...

Therefore, this article believes that the role of social influencing factors is mainly reflected in the selection stage of CSR. The improvement of social systems and the enhancement of social awareness are the main driving factors for substantive CSR behavior.

Organizational Influencing Factors

Responsible Leadership

Political influencing factors and social influencing factors belong to external influencing factors, while organizational influencing factors belong to internal influencing factors. External influencing factors can motivate enterprises to assume CSR, while internal influencing factors can enhance the foresight and voluntariness of enterprises in terms of CSR. Under the influence of organizational influencing factors, regardless of how the political environment and social development process change, enterprises can still realize the importance of assuming CSR and adopt a series of high-quality CSR behaviors. During the retention stage, companies have accumulated mature experience in CSR. Although it has passed the stage of rapid growth in terms of quantity, the retention stage has also filtered out many short-term CSR behaviors and some IRCSR behaviors. After going through all these processes, the remaining CSR behaviors are more representative of the company's CSR willingness.

CSR strategies usually come from leadership or top management team, and it is difficult for employees to participate in this process. Due to the large scale of the vast majority of Chinese automobile enterprises, they have a mature strategic system framework and a sound corporate system. All strategic decisions must go through a standard process from formulation to implementation, where managers propose the concept of assuming corporate social responsibility and functional departments are responsible for implementation.

> All decisions related to corporate social responsibility in a company come from senior management, and it is usually the executive team who decides how to assume CSR. As a large state-owned enterprise, managers of our

type also have to bear social responsibility in addition to economic benefits...Our company's CSR is not a policy requirement, nor is it actually due to social expectations. As a leading enterprise in the Chinese automotive industry, our managers believe that large enterprises should help more people in need while making money...

Our company is a wholly-owned subsidiary of a foreign enterprise. The leaders of the core departments in the company are all foreign representatives. Their management philosophy is also Western, so they will pay more attention to social responsibility. For example, they do a good job in ensuring employees' job security, living welfare, gender equality, workplace equality, etc.

Business Ethics

Like responsible leadership, business ethics also plays a role in the retention stage of CSR. Business ethics is the ethics of business operations. Not only enterprises, but also organizations related to business operations contain ethical issues. As long as a collection of people conducts business activities, there are always ethical issues in essence. A moral enterprise should value human nature, avoid conflicts and frictions with society, and actively adopt behaviors that are beneficial to society. The automotive industry is not only a highly polluting industry, but also a high-risk industry. Especially for employees working on production lines or factories, they may come into contact with a lot of chemicals and heavy machinery in their daily work, which may pose a threat to personal safety. Due to the inadequate legal system in ensuring employee safety in China, business ethics appears to be more effective in these areas.

My company is a large state-owned enterprise, and our company places special emphasis on employee welfare, employee health, workplace safety and peace, and so on...The scale of the company is also large, with a large number of employees, so the company should try its best to meet the needs of its employees, which not only include work needs, but also some life needs and psychological needs.

Therefore, this article believes that the role of organizational influencing factors is mainly reflected in the retention stage of CSR. After CSR enters a stable state, the internal driving factors of the enterprise have the greatest impact, while the external influencing factors generally have a relatively short effect. Only organizational influencing factors are the key to transforming CSR into corporate competitive advantage.

Dynamics of CSR

Chinese automotive industry's focus on CSR originated from some CSR crisis events. These CSR crisis events have brought great economic uncertainty to the business performance of automotive companies. In order to address this economic uncertainty, companies have begun to recognize the importance of CSR. In order to avoid the occurrence of CSR crisis, Chinese government attempted to improve CSR awareness through policy constraints. Automobile companies must comply with government regulations, which solves the problem of automobile companies being unwilling to invest too much prerequisite capital in CSR.

> If you ask when to start valuing CSR, there should be no clear point in time... However, the reputation crisis of automobile enterprises has clear events, such as the quality problems of GAC Motor and Changan Automobile before, as well as the integrity of the automobile trading platform. These events have seriously affected the production and sales of automobiles. It is also these events that have made all automotive companies realize the importance of reputation and CSR.

After the government issued relevant policies, the public and consumers also began to use CSR as a standard to measure automobile consumption. As one of the highly polluting industries, the location of automobile production factories will affect the living environment of surrounding residents in the automotive industry. For consumers, car emissions are one of the important factors affecting air quality, which affects everyone's health. These factors have led to an increasing focus on CSR in the entire social environment year by year.

> There was a period of severe smog in China, probably starting from 2010, which seriously affected people's health. There are many cases of lung disease due to air quality in Beijing. So from this moment on, people are very concerned about indicators such as automobile exhaust, wastewater, and pollutant emissions. It was also from this time that the entire automotive industry began to establish strict emission standards and gradually restrict the use of substandard vehicles...

Although after experiencing the above two stages, both the government, enterprises, and the public have developed CSR awareness, the CSR strategy has not yet formed a complete system within the automotive industry. There are no dedicated employees or departments within the company responsible for developing and executing CSR strategies. It was not until 2015 that more and more automotive companies began to incorporate CSR as part of their core strategy, attempting to integrate it into the entire lifecycle of automotive production.

> I majored in environmental protection in college and have been working in a Chinese automotive company since graduation. When I first graduated, work related to CSR/environmental related work was not valued within the company, and our work belonged to other functional departments, while also balancing some other job content. But now we have a dedicated ESG department and some employees. Although the number is not large, our work is specific and highly related to CSR...

In relation to proposition 1, we find that political influencing factors can affect CSR behaviors and their impact is mainly reflected in the variation stage. Among all the different types of influencing factors, political influencing factors have the widest scope and fastest implementation. In China, policies have the greatest impact on various industries, and significant changes and upgrades in the industry usually begin with policy changes. Especially for automotive companies, CSR cannot bring economic benefits in the variation stage, so only policy intervention is the most effective measure to promote CSR. Policy influencing factors can only define the bottom line of CSR and require automotive companies to comply with basic ethical standards. And at variation stage, the vast majority of Chinese automobile companies are only constrained

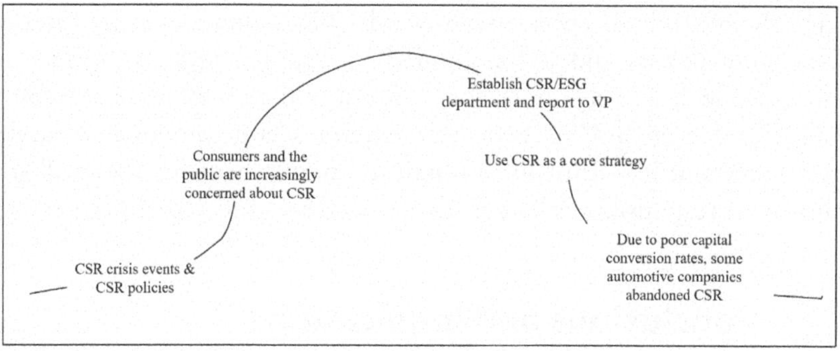

Fig. 3 Dynamics of CSR in Chinese automotive industry (*Source* Author's own research)

by policy enforcement and engage in superficial CSR activities, such as donating to disaster stricken areas, establishing Hope Primary Schools, and helping vulnerable groups (Fig. 3).

In relation to proposition 2, we find that social influencing factors can affect CSR behaviors and their impact is mainly reflected in the selection stage. The selection stage is the period when the CSR strategy and behavior of automotive companies are increasing at the fastest rate. At this stage, in addition to basic charitable behavior, automotive companies realize that CSR should be reflected in their products, or the concept of CSR should be linked to production. In the Chinese automotive market, the impact of technology on the competitive landscape is becoming increasingly small, and CSR has gradually become the main source of attention for consumers and the public. Especially for domestic cars in China, in order to compensate for the disadvantages of core technology, it is necessary to produce CSR friendly products to gain market recognition.

In relation to proposition 3, we find that organizational influencing factors can affect CSR behaviors and their impact is mainly reflected in the retention stage. In the retention stage, automotive companies have gradually formed a relatively complete CSR strategic framework. Some CSR behaviors that are incompatible with the characteristics of the enterprise will be eliminated, while CSR behaviors that are compatible with their own products and value chain will be retained. In addition, at this stage, the attitude of enterprises toward CSR is dominated by internal influencing factors and is less limited by external influencing factors. Enterprises will actively undertake CSR out of their own sense of responsibility, and even if CSR behaviors require a large amount of capital investment and it is difficult to obtain economic benefits, they will still implement responsible behavior from the ethical and moral perspective.

4 Conclusions and Implications

Research Conclusion

Political influencing factors have the greatest impact on the variation stages of CSR. Economic policy uncertainty and political connection can convey a signal to enterprises that the government is paying attention to CSR, driving companies to start thinking about whether to fulfill CSR. This impact is mainly reflected in variation stage. The effect of political factors is also dominant in the struggle stage of CSR. In the struggle stage, managers realize that institutions and laws cannot become the main means of constraining CSR. As the effectiveness of institutional constraints decreases, more and more companies will give up undertaking CSR.

Social influencing factors have the greatest impact on the selection stage of CSR. Compared to political factors, public participation and social transformation have a more significant impact on CSR. The public will expect enterprises to better give back to society by fulfilling CSR, thus generating a large number of CSR behaviors under the influence of social influencing factors. Through this way, enterprises will gain public trust and win better word-of-mouth.

The effect of organizational influencing factors is mainly reflected in the retention stage of CSR. The retention stage is the core stage in the evolution of CSR, during which high-quality CSR behaviors are preserved. The ultimate goal of CSR is to integrate the concept of CSR into the overall strategic framework of the enterprise, and to reflect CSR in daily business activities. And this type of CSR is usually spontaneous, which means that without any external intervention and under the influence of organizational factors, companies are more likely to voluntarily assume CSR.

In addition, there is an interaction between political, social, and organizational factors, which can affect CSR behavior. Political influencing factors can affect the overall social environment and trends. The shift of public attention to hot topics will also draw the attention of policymakers to formulate policies that are more in line with the maximization of overall social welfare. And this kind of interactive influence is also dynamic and will generate dynamic trajectories based on the lifecycle. In China, organizational decision-making is also influenced by the political and social environment. In order to meet consumer expectations for CSR as much as possible, organizations need to constantly grasp the changing trends in the political and social environment and make dynamic changes.

Contributions to Literature

Compared with previous research, the major contributions of this paper are as follows.

First, bring evolutionary theory to CSR research, enriching the boundary of theory. Evolutionary theory has been widely adopted in the study of corporate strategic management. Based on the theory of corporate life cycle, enterprises have dynamic growth rules and differentiated strategies in different growth stages. With the change of life cycle, CSR will also go through four different stages, we examine the role of evolutionary theory in explaining CSR, elaborating enterprises' sustainable development strategy.

Second, shift the focus of CSR research from static to dynamic. Previous research emphasized the importance of understanding how CSR evolves or changes over time and how firms respond to such dynamics. Our attempt is to address this issue by examining how firms' motivations for engaging in CSR and its effects have changed over time. CSR undergo four stages over life cycles, namely variation, selection, retention, and struggle.

Third, profiting from the specific practice of China's automobile industry, we comprehensively consider the impact of political factors, social factors, and organizational factors on CSR. The results exposed that the driving effects of political factors, social factors, and organizational factors on CSR are reflected in different stages of evolution. Although existing studies have demonstrated that these variables are related to CSR, they have paid little attention to which variable plays a dominant role in different stages of CSR.

However, this study still has certain limitations as there are numerous factors that influence enterprises in the implementation of CSR. In this research, we have only focused on the three dominant factors—political, social, and organizational factors—represented by economic policy uncertainty and political connections, public participation and social transformation, responsible leadership and business ethics, respectively. While previous research has indicated that regulation, standards and certification, and corporate governance structures are important factors in the implementation of CSR, their impact at different stages of CSR must be taken into consideration for future studies.

Managerial Implications

This article has certain enlightenment for enterprise managers and government regulatory departments. First, it helps enterprise managers realize that CSR has a life cycle. Enterprises at different stages face distinct external environments and internal challenges, resulting in varying CSR behaviors. During the variation stage of CSR, enterprises' behavior toward CSR exhibits a clear "disorder", often characterized by external actions with obvious "free-riding" characteristics. During the selection stage of CSR, to better adapt to dynamic external environments, enterprises' CSR behavior reflects more purposeful and long-term characteristics. During the retention stage of CSR, in order to stabilize the corporate brand image, standardized and organized CSR practices are implemented, primarily demonstrated through responsible stakeholder engagement. During the struggle stage of CSR, continuity and conservatism become defining characteristics.

Second, this article can assist enterprises in selecting a more effective CSR strategy'. It is crucial to recognize that the key drivers of CSR vary across different stages of the business life cycle. In order to gain a competitive edge in CSR, companies must adapt their management strategies accordingly. Enterprises should shorten the hesitation in the variation and selection stage of CSR, select responsible leaders, and actively create a good ethical atmosphere to win the initiative in selection stage of CSR. If the company persists in adhering to the original strategic direction during the struggle stage of CSR, it will become increasingly disconnected from reality. Therefore, enterprises must undertake reform and innovation in the approach to CSR at this stage.

Thirdly, closer collaboration between the government and enterprises can lead to mutually beneficial outcomes. The government can facilitate sustainable development for businesses by taking into account the entire life cycle of CSR and implementing tailored regulatory policies that correspond with each stage of CSR life cycle. In particular, when enterprises shift from retention to struggle, their endogenous motivation to fulfill CSR declines. The government would increase positive CSR policies to provide guidance and extend enterprises' retention lifeline.

Limitations and Future Research

There are still some limitations when analyzing Chinese automotive industry in this article. The automotive companies we have chosen are mainly large-scale Chinese automotive companies, which have a large market share, and the vast majority of these companies rely on fuel-powered vehicles to open up the Chinese market and occupy a leading position. However, in fact, these enterprises cannot fully represent the current Chinese automotive industry. Due to the support of the Chinese government for new energy vehicles, many local enterprises specializing in the production of new energy vehicles have begun to develop rapidly. The new energy vehicles produced by these emerging automotive companies are more popular among young consumers, causing a significant impact on traditional automotive companies. However, due to the relatively short establishment time of these emerging automotive companies (within 10 years), they have not yet fully reflected the CSR life cycle, so they have not been included in the research object. This leads to the research conclusion of this article being more suitable for traditional automotive companies with a longer establishment time and more business experience, which may be less suitable for emerging automotive companies. In future research, these relatively young new energy vehicle companies can be taken as research objects to explore the manifestations of CSR dynamic trajectories in different types of enterprises.

References

Bashir, U., & Yu, Y. (2020). Do confucianism and political connections affect stock price crash risk: Evidence from Chinese economy? *Applied Economics Letters, 27*(7), 569–575.

Bliss, M. A., & Gul, F. A. (2012). Political connection and leverage: Some Malaysian evidence. *Journal of Banking & Finance, 36*(8), 2344–2350.

Borghesi, R., & Chang, K. (2020). Economic policy uncertainty and firm value: The mediating role of intangible assets and R&D. *Applied Economics Letters, 27*(13), 1087–1090.

Buhmann, K. (2011). Integrating human rights in emerging regulation of Corporate Social Responsibility: The EU case. *International Journal of Law in Context, 7*(2), 139–179.

Cacioppe, R., Forster, N., & Fox, M. (2008). A survey of managers' perceptions of corporate ethics and social responsibility and actions that may affect companies' success. *Journal of Business Ethics, 82*, 681–700.

Cezarino, L. O., Liboni, L. B., Hunter, T., Pacheco, L. M., & Martins, F. P. (2022). Corporate social responsibility in emerging markets: Opportunities and challenges for sustainability integration. *Journal of Cleaner Production, 362*, 132224.

Cheng, L. T., & Leung, T. Y. (2016). Government protection, political connection and management turnover in China. *International Review of Economics & Finance, 45*, 160–176.

Cho, M., Furey, L. D., & Mohr, T. (2017). Communicating corporate social responsibility on social media: Strategies, stakeholders, and public engagement on corporate Facebook. *Business and Professional Communication Quarterly, 80*(1), 52–69.

Dao, V. T., Phung, M. T., & Cheng, H. (2020). The relationship between corporate social responsibility and corporate financial performance: A moderating effect of economic policy uncertainty. *International Journal of Financial Research, 11*(5), 304–318.

De Bakker, F. G., Rasche, A., & Ponte, S. (2019). Multi-stakeholder initiatives on sustainability: A cross-disciplinary review and research agenda for business ethics. *Business Ethics Quarterly, 29*(3), 343–383.

Fan, J. P., Wong, T. J., & Zhang, T. (2007). Politically connected CEOs, corporate governance, and Post-IPO performance of China's newly partially privatized firms. *Journal of Financial Economics, 84*(2), 330–357.

Fassin, Y., Van Rossem, A., & Buelens, M. (2011). Small-business owner-managers' perceptions of business ethics and CSR-related concepts. *Journal of Business Ethics, 98*, 425–453.

Fatima, T., & Elbanna, S. (2023). Corporate social responsibility (CSR) implementation: A review and a research agenda towards an integrative framework. *Journal of Business Ethics, 183*(1), 105–121.

Ferrell, O. C., Harrison, D. E., Ferrell, L., & Hair, J. F. (2019). Business ethics, corporate social responsibility, and brand attitudes: An exploratory study. *Journal of Business Research, 95*, 491–501.

Fombrun, C., & Shanley, M. (1990). What's in a name? Reputation building and corporate strategy. *Academy of Management Journal, 33*(2), 233–258.

Gu, H., Ryan, C., Bin, L., & Wei, G. (2013). Political connections, guanxi and adoption of CSR policies in the Chinese hotel industry: Is there a link? *Tourism Management, 34*, 231–235.

Gulen, H., & Ion, M. (2016). Policy uncertainty and corporate investment. *The Review of Financial Studies, 29*(3), 523–564.

Habib, A., & Hasan, M. M. (2019). Corporate life cycle research in accounting, finance and corporate governance: A survey, and directions for future research. *International Review of Financial Analysis, 61*, 188–201.

Hasan, M. M., & Habib, A. (2017). Corporate life cycle, organizational financial resources and corporate social responsibility. *Journal of Contemporary Accounting & Economics, 13*(1), 20–36.

Hung-Baesecke, C. J. F., Chen, Y. R. R., & Boyd, B. (2016). Corporate social responsibility, media source preference, trust, and public engagement: The informed public's perspective. *Public Relations Review, 42*(4), 591–599.

Jiang, X., Li, G., & Fan, X. (2023). Environmental protection fee-to-tax and corporate environmental social responsibility: A test based on corporate life cycle theory. *Sustainability, 15*(3), 2128.

Joyner, B. E., & Payne, D. (2002). Evolution and implementation: A study of values, business ethics and corporate social responsibility. *Journal of Business Ethics, 41*, 297–311.

Kim, S., & Ferguson, M. A. T. (2018). Dimensions of effective CSR communication based on public expectations. *Journal of Marketing Communications, 24*(6), 549–567.

Kramer, M. R., & Porter, M. (2011). *Creating shared value* (Vol. 17). FSG.

Lee, S. Y., Kim, Y., & Kim, Y. (2020). The co-creation of social value: What matters for public participation in corporate social responsibility campaigns. *Journal of Public Relations Research, 32*(5–6), 198–221.

Li, S., Song, X., & Wu, H. (2015). Political connection, ownership structure, and corporate philanthropy in China: A strategic-political perspective. *Journal of Business Ethics, 129*, 399–411.

Lin, K. J., Tan, J., Zhao, L., & Karim, K. (2015). In the name of charity: Political connections and strategic corporate social responsibility in a transition economy. *Journal of Corporate Finance, 32*, 327–346.

Lopez, B., Rangel, C., & Fernández, M. (2022). The impact of corporate social responsibility strategy on the management and governance axis for sustainable growth. *Journal of Business Research, 150*, 690–698.

Maak, T. (2007). Responsible leadership, stakeholder engagement, and the emergence of social capital. *Journal of Business Ethics, 74*, 329–343.

Maak, T., & Pless, N. M. (2006). Responsible leadership in a stakeholder society—A relational perspective. *Journal of Business Ethics, 66*, 99–115.

Maak, T., Pless, N. M., & Voegtlin, C. (2016). Business statesman or shareholder advocate? CEO responsible leadership styles and the micro-foundations of political CSR. *Journal of Management Studies, 53*(3), 463–493.

Maton, K. I. (2000). Making a difference: The social ecology of social transformation. *American Journal of Community Psychology, 28*(1), 25–57.

Midttun, A., & Koefoed, A. L. (2005). Green innovation in Nordic energy industry: Systemic contexts and dynamic trajectories. *Towards Environmental Innovation Systems*, 115–136.

Muriithi, S. G., Walters, B. A., McCumber, W. R., & Robles, L. R. (2022). Managerial entrenchment and corporate social responsibility engagement: The role of economic policy uncertainty. *Journal of Management and Governance, 26*, 621–640.

Nee, V., & Matthews, R. (1996). Market transition and societal transformation in reforming state socialism. *Annual Review of Sociology, 22*(1), 401–435.

Ongsakul, V., Jiraporn, P., & Treepongkaruna, S. (2021). Does managerial ownership influence corporate social responsibility (CSR)? The role of economic policy uncertainty. *Accounting & Finance, 61*(1), 763–779.
Osuji, O. (2011). Fluidity of regulation-CSR nexus: The multinational corporate corruption example. *Journal of Business Ethics, 103*(1), 31–57.
Peng, D., Colak, G., & Shen, J. (2023). Lean against the wind: The effect of policy uncertainty on a firm's corporate social responsibility strategy. *Journal of Corporate Finance, 79*, 102376.
Porter, M. E., & Kramer, M. R. (2011). Creating shared value. *Harvard Business Review, 89*(1/2), 62–77.
Rebs, T., Brandenburg, M., & Seuring, S. (2019). System dynamics modeling for sustainable supply chain management: A literature review and systems thinking approach. *Journal of Cleaner Production, 208*, 1265–1280.
Reed, M. S., Vella, S., Challies, E., De Vente, J., Frewer, L., Hohenwallner-Ries, D., Huber, T., Neumann, R. K., Oughton, E. A., del Ceno, J. S., & van Delden, H. (2018). A theory of participation: what makes stakeholder and public engagement in environmental management work? *Restoration Ecology, 26*, S7–S17.
Rjiba, H., Jahmane, A., & Abid, I. (2020). Corporate social responsibility and firm value: Guiding through economic policy uncertainty. *Finance Research Letters, 35*, 101553.
Sakarya, S., Bodur, M., Yildirim-Öktem, Ö., & Selekler-Göksen, N. (2012). Social alliances: Business and social enterprise collaboration for social transformation. *Journal of Business Research, 65*(12), 1710–1720.
Schinzel, U. (2018). Responsible leadership and corporate social responsibility (CSR) in Luxembourg. *International Journal of Organizational Analysis, 26*(3), 415–431.
Singhapakdi, A., Vitell, S. J., Rallapalli, K. C., & Kraft, K. L. (1996). The perceived role of ethics and social responsibility: A scale development. *Journal of Business Ethics, 15*, 1131–1140.
Székely, F., & Knirsch, M. (2005). Responsible leadership and corporate social responsibility: Metrics for sustainable performance. *European Management Journal, 23*(6), 628–647.
Tang-Lee, D. (2016). Corporate social responsibility (CSR) and public engagement for a Chinese state-backed mining project in Myanmar-Challenges and prospects. *Resources Policy, 47*, 28–37.

Tsui, A. S., Schoonhoven, C. B., Meyer, M. W., Lau, C. M., & Milkovich, G. T. (2004). Organization and management in the midst of societal transformation: The People's Republic of China. *Organization Science, 15*(2), 133–144.

Udayasankar, K. (2008). Corporate social responsibility and firm size. *Journal of Business Ethics, 83*(2), 167–175.

Valentine, S., & Fleischman, G. (2008). Professional ethical standards, corporate social responsibility, and the perceived role of ethics and social responsibility. *Journal of Business Ethics, 82*, 657–666.

Verk, N., Golob, U., & Podnar, K. (2021). A dynamic review of the emergence of corporate social responsibility communication. *Journal of Business Ethics, 168*, 491–515.

Voegtlin, C. (2016). What does it mean to be responsible? Addressing the missing responsibility dimension in ethical leadership research. *Leadership, 12*(5), 581–608.

Voegtlin, C., Patzer, M., & Scherer, A. G. (2012). Responsible leadership in global business: A new approach to leadership and its multi-level outcomes. *Journal of Business Ethics, 105*, 1–16.

Vural-Yavas, C. (2021). Economic policy uncertainty, stakeholder engagement, and environmental, social, and governance practices: The moderating effect of competition. *Corporate Social Responsibility and Environmental Management, 28*(1), 82–102.

Waldman, D. A., & Balven, R. M. (2014). Responsible leadership: Theoretical issues and research directions. *Academy of Management Perspectives, 28*(3), 224–234.

Wan, X., Zhang, Y., Mao, P., Li, H., Wang, R., Yi, X., & Zhao, X. (2022). How perceived corporate social responsibility and public knowledge affect public participation intention: Evidence from Chinese waste incineration power projects. *Engineering, Construction and Architectural Management, 29*(10), 4107–4131.

Werhane, P. H., & Freeman, R. E. (1999). Business ethics: The state of the art. *International Journal of Management Reviews, 1*(1), 1–16.

Xu, S., & Liu, D. (2020). Political connections and corporate social responsibility: Political incentives in China. *Business Ethics: A European Review, 29*(4), 664–693.

Yuan, T., Wu, J. G., Qin, N., & Xu, J. (2022). Being nice to stakeholders: The effect of economic policy uncertainty on corporate social responsibility. *Economic Modelling, 108*, 105737.

Zhao, T., Xiao, X., & Zhang, B. (2021). Economic policy uncertainty and corporate social responsibility performance: Evidence from China. *Sustainability Accounting, Management and Policy Journal, 12*(5), 1003–1026.

Corporate Social Responsibility Challenges in the Mining Industry and ISO 26000

Beatriz Garcia-Ortega, Daniel Catalá-Pérez, Blanca de-Miguel-Molina, and María de-Miguel-Molina

1 Introduction

Corporate Social Responsibility (CSR) has become a prominent issue in today's business world, with increasing expectations from stakeholders and society for companies to operate in a socially responsible manner. CEOs and boards are called upon to lead CSR initiatives and address significant challenges in its approach and implementation (Maignan &

B. Garcia-Ortega (✉) · D. Catalá-Pérez · B. de-Miguel-Molina · M. de-Miguel-Molina
Universitat Politècnica de València, Valencia, Spain
e-mail: beagaror@doctor.upv.es

D. Catalá-Pérez
e-mail: dacapre@ade.upv.es

B. de-Miguel-Molina
e-mail: bdemigu@omp.upv.es

M. de-Miguel-Molina
e-mail: mademi@omp.upv.es

E. Poveda-Pareja et al. (eds.), *The Strategic Paradigm of CSR and Sustainability*, Palgrave Studies in Governance, Leadership and Responsibility, https://doi.org/10.1007/978-3-031-58889-1_3

Ralston, 2002). In fact, one of their main challenges is balancing economic benefits with social and environmental concerns.

Industries such as mining, oil and gas, chemicals, paper products, petrochemical products, steel and other metals, rubber and plastic, electricity, and gas distribution are considered sensitive due to their activities involving a higher risk of negative impacts, which makes them susceptible to criticism in CSR matters. Among these, mining companies have a significant impact on social and environmental factors, resulting in controversies, opposition, conflicts, and rejection (Conde, 2017; O'Faircheallaigh, 2015; Jenkins & Yakovleva, 2006). Consequently, a CSR strategy is crucial for mining companies to obtain a social licence to operate (SLO) (Holley & Mitcham, 2016), which is a way to reduce resistance and opposition from local communities and other stakeholders to their establishment and activities (Campero & Barton, 2015; De-Miguel-Molina et al., 2019).

In light of the significant challenges faced by companies operating in the mining industry and other sensitive industries in terms of CSR, the ISO 26000:2010 standard (ISO, 2010) emerges as a useful framework to guide their CSR initiatives. This widely recognized international standard was established by the International Organization for Standardization on November 1, 2010, with the aim of identifying and defining the normative field of CSR. It incorporates insights and perspectives from a broad range of stakeholders, including businesses, government, NGOs, labour organizations, and other relevant parties, to provide guidelines for socially responsible operations.

The selection of ISO 26000 in our study, over other more specific standards, is grounded in its comprehensive nature, considered as an international consensus on CSR's definition, and its ability to address its wide spectrum of dimensions (Chakroun et al., 2020). As highlighted by Balzarova and Castka (2012), ISO 26000:2010 offers a unique approach to CSR, providing organizations with a framework to develop and implement their own CSR strategies and practices. Although not a certifiable standard, adherence to the principles outlined in the ISO 26000:2010 standard can improve a company's sustainability reporting, reputation, financial performance, and SLO. In addition, it can help organizations identify and manage social responsibility-related risks, such as reputational or legal risks.

The consideration of ISO 26000 in our study reflects its broad applicability, stakeholder inclusivity during its development, and its ability to guide companies across various industries towards socially responsible practices. Despite the existence of more specific standards such as the Global Reporting Initiative (GRI), Social Accountability International's SA8000 Social Responsibility Certification, or the United Nations Global Compact, ISO 26000 comprehensively addresses a diverse range of CSR issues, making it a pragmatic and all-encompassing choice for our research.

In all, CSR is a crucial issue for companies operating in mining and other sensitive industries, and the ISO 26000:2010 standard offers a valuable reference point for facing inherent problems in these industries. By implementing effective CSR strategies that address key aspects in these sectors, companies can improve their sustainability performance, reduce resistance and opposition from local communities and stakeholders, and ultimately contribute to a more sustainable future for all parties involved.

In this context, considering the CSR and sustainability challenges and specificities of sensitive industries such as the mining industry and recognizing the potential role of ISO 26000:2010 in helping companies address these challenges, we believe it is crucial to investigate existing research and consolidate findings to support companies and management in developing effective CSR strategies and to advance knowledge in this field.

Thus, in this chapter, a primary literature review examines the principles of social responsibility in the ISO 26000:2010 standard within the context of mining and other sensitive or controversial industries. The objective is to evaluate the interrelationships and significance of the collected principles and their implications.

Following this, a systematic literature review is conducted to identify papers dealing with ISO 26000:2010 in the mining industry. A text mining analysis is used to identify the theories, core subjects, and issues related to ISO 26000:2010 in these papers, including their frequency of occurrence and interconnections. Next, the findings are discussed, and the last section gathers the conclusions, limitations, and suggestions for future research.

To the best of our knowledge, this is the first systematic literature review conducted from the perspective of ISO 26000:2010 with a focus on the mining industry. Among other interesting findings, we identify how the literature emphasizes the significance of the principles outlined by ISO 26000:2010, their interdependence, and the central role of ethics underlying the other principles. Moreover, through text mining analysis of connections between theories, core subjects, and issues in the examined papers, three clusters are identified: business, reporting, and SLO. Each of them incorporates different theories and core subjects, but there is still ample room to consider further potential interrelations and connections either in terms of theories and core subjects as presented in ISO 26000:2010.

2 Principles of Social Responsibility in the Mining Industry

The standard ISO 26000:2010 states that, when approaching and practicing social responsibility, an organization should respect the seven principles outlined below:

1. Accountability
2. Transparency
3. Ethical behaviour
4. Respect for stakeholder interests
5. Respect for the rule of law
6. Respect for international norms of behaviour
7. Respect for human rights

Accountability and Transparency

When addressing the two first principles in the list, accountability and transparency appear closely linked. In fact, for experts in open government, accountability is a consequence of transparency (Criado et al.,

2018). In this sense, ISO 26000 states that "an organization should be accountable for its impacts on society, the economy and the environment" which implies "that an organization should accept appropriate scrutiny and also accept a duty to respond to this scrutiny" (ISO, 2010). But how can an organization be scrutinized? Well, being "transparent in its decisions and activities that impact on society and the environment" which means that this "organization should disclose in a clear, accurate and complete manner, and to a reasonable and sufficient degree, the policies, decisions and activities for which it is responsible, including their known and likely impacts on society and the environment" (ISO, 2010). In this regard, Sethi et al. (2017) argue that the voluntary nature of disclosing corporate social responsibility has resulted in inconsistencies and a lack of robust measures concerning the quality, objectivity, and accuracy of the reports.

The study from Ben Amar and Chakroun (2018), focused on French industrial companies (secondary sector companies), discusses indirectly the links between transparency and accountability, their importance in CSR initiatives, and their effects on earnings management. The authors mention the importance of transparent and reliable financial statements to meet stakeholder expectations and stake a company's reputation and, thus, they conclude that a company that undertakes to respect those principles (transparency and accountability) does not manage earnings and does provide credible information to its stakeholders.

In addition, transparency and accountability have also a positive impact on financial performance. The results of a later study from Chakroun et al. (2020) also focused on French industrial companies (secondary sector companies) evidence that companies that disclose more information and have better corporate governance tend to have higher financial performance. The authors also suggest that companies should adopt a voluntary approach to improve their transparency and accountability, which can lead to better financial performance and a competitive advantage.

In terms of transparency and accountability, reporting refers to the aforementioned process of disclosing information about a company's economic, environmental, and social performance to its stakeholders. In the specific case of the Peruvian mining sector, Cesar (2021) states that reporting can help companies to communicate their CSR practices and their impacts on the environment and society, which can help to build a positive reputation and earn their social licence to operate (SLO), understood as the consent given by the community to the mining activities (de-Miguel-Molina et al., 2019), a critical factor for mining companies to operate successfully. In his work, Cesar identifies different categories of CSR initiatives in the aforementioned sector and, related to accountability, emphasizes the importance of active participation by interested parties, including representation of the interested parties in decision-making committees, to show that mining companies are aware of the concerns of the interested parties and are trying to address them. Therefore, this work shows the relationship between these first two principles and the fourth principle, which calls for respect for stakeholders' interests.

Sustainability reporting is becoming increasingly important as investors and other stakeholders seek more information about a company's environmental, social, and governance (ESG) performance and its impact on long-term value creation. Mohammadi et al. (2018) analyse 98 firms from various industry sectors that are listed on the Tehran Stock Exchange, including both sensitive and non-sensitive industries. The study finds that sustainability reporting is still a relatively new phenomenon in Iran, with an average sustainability reporting score of only 12% for all listed firms, but firms operating in sensitive industries had a much higher level of sustainability reporting than other firms because they face risk of dealing with possible litigation and future environmental liabilities. The paper suggests that high levels of sustainability disclosure can be a powerful tool in raising stock market valuations and can be rewarded by shareholders. However, on the other hand, Mahjoub (2019) argues that in the case of more sensitive firms it is difficult for an interested party to differentiate between credible and opportunistic societal reporting.

Keeping in mind the importance of reporting, Ranängen et al. (2014) discuss the possible merits of ISO 26000 for CSR development in the mining industry in the developing world through the case of a mining and construction company located in the Zambian Copperbelt. These authors conclude that "despite the fact that ISO 26000 is a set of guidelines, rather than being certifiable, it can be used to evaluate and improve a company's CSR practice in a developing country, even if that company already can be considered a frontrunner" (Ranängen et al., 2014, p. 513). And, in addition, it can help the analysed company providing a framework for transparent and accountable reporting and for identifying and prioritizing the key issues related to CSR communication.

This key role of the ISO 26000 in terms of reporting in the sensitive industries sector has been also analysed by Mahjoub (2019) through an empirical study that examines the relationship between CSR reporting through ISO 26000 and information asymmetry in Saudi companies (the sample includes 89 companies belonging to 7 industries, among them, several cement companies). These authors conclude that there is a positive relationship between CSR reporting through ISO 26000 framework and transparency and accountability in the analysed companies. The study finds that companies that disclose more information about their CSR activities through ISO 26000 framework have lower levels of information asymmetry, which indicates higher transparency and accountability, and thus, are more likely to attract investors and improve their performance.

In all, companies should be accountable by providing transparent and reliable information as part of their social responsibility, also considering that it may bring added benefits to their performance, which may become even more evident in the case of mining and other extractive sectors, for example, concerning the obtention of a social licence to operate. However, studies such as Garcia-Ortega et al. (2020) show that stakeholders of mining companies question the objectivity, rigorousness, and credibility of their reporting. They appraise that mining companies tend to downplay their negative impacts and overestimate the benefits for stakeholders and the level of stakeholder involvement. In this regard, ISO 26000 seems to be an interesting framework to guide these companies to better realize and address these two principles within their CSR reporting.

Ethical Behaviour

Ethical behaviour is the third principle of social responsibility addressed by ISO 26000, and could be deemed as the overarching principle that interconnects and underpins the other principles. Indeed, according to Swanson (2008), the moral obligation that businesses have to society is stressed by corporate social responsibility.

The ethical behaviour principle refers to the notion that "an organization should behave ethically" (ISO, 2010). It calls for values of honesty, equity, and integrity, and implies "a concern for people, animals and the environment and a commitment to address the impact of its activities and decisions on stakeholders' interests" (ISO, 2010). Thus, the standard directly links ethical behaviour with the fourth identified principle of social responsibility.

Further evident connections exist between the principle of ethical behaviour and the other principles. According to ISO 26000, organizations should be accountable and transparent about the impact of their activities. Additionally, following the principle of ethical behaviour by an organization implies "recognizing and addressing situations where local laws and regulations either do not exist or conflict with ethical behaviour" (ISO, 2010). Lastly, "concern for people" within its definition implicitly encompasses "respect for human rights".

Studies such as Caron et al. (2016) corroborate several of these connections by including respect for the rights of local communities, ensuring the health and safety of workers, and minimizing the environmental impact of mining activities within the commitment to ethical behaviour. Other authors argue that organizations such as financial institutions should adopt ethical principles and best practices that prioritize the protection of cultural heritage and the interests of local communities and other stakeholders, as well as comply with international norms and standards in this area.

Furthermore, Hąbek and Lavios (2021) relate ethical behaviour with fair and transparent communication with suppliers, respect for human rights, and compliance with labour and environmental standards. Meanwhile, Mahjoub (2019) argues that the adoption of ISO 26000 by a company can enhance its ethical behaviour, such as the promotion of human rights and fair labour practices, and Panagiotakopoulos et al.

(2015) discuss the role of codes of conduct, ethical frameworks, and stakeholder engagement in promoting ethical behaviour.

According to Ranängen et al. (2014), sensitive industries such as mining are more likely to have a code of ethics because they must respond to a significantly increasing pressure from stakeholders and society, and they need to specially care for their social licence to operate (de-Miguel-Molina et al., 2019; Ranängen & Zobel, 2014). Bluszcz and Kijewska (2015) argue that sustainable development in the mining and metallurgy sector requires a commitment to ethical behaviour, including transparency, accountability, and responsible management practices.

Respect for Stakeholders' Interests

An illustration of the significance of considering the interests of the different stakeholders is evidenced in the elaboration of the ISO 26000 standard itself, since the standard was developed through a multi-stakeholder approach, incorporating insights and perspectives from a broad and diverse range of different groups of stakeholders (Balzarova & Castka, 2012; ISO, 2010).

When addressing transparency and accountability principles, we have identified them as key reputational factors for stakeholders. From a strategic point of view, stakeholder management is important because it helps companies to identify and understand the needs, expectations, and concerns of their stakeholders, including employees, customers, suppliers, communities, and shareholders. In this regard, Mahjoub (2019) in its study of Saudi Arabian listed companies stresses the role of ISO 26000 adoption to help promoting respect for stakeholders' interests by engaging with them in the company's decision-making processes and taking into account their concerns.

In the specific context of mining and other extractive companies, effective stakeholder management is particularly crucial compared to less sensitive industries, since it helps to identify and address the impacts of mining activities on local communities, workers, and the environment; to build trust and reduce conflicts; to contribute to sustainable development; to comply with legal and regulatory requirements; and to enhance their reputation and social licence to operate (Ranängen & Zobel, 2014), also linked to community involvement (de-Miguel-Molina et al., 2019).

In alignment with this perspective, Rangriz and Abyar (2015) assert that there exists a significant relationship between the social responsibility of gas and oil extractive companies and various factors, including community involvement. Consequently, companies in these industries should prioritize factors such as community engagement to enhance their overall social responsibility performance. The acknowledgement of this relationship underscores the importance of actively involving and managing stakeholders, especially within sensitive industries like mining, to achieve responsible and sustainable business practices.

Moreover, Chakroun et al. (2020) in their analysis of diverse French firms in diverse industries including mining suggest that companies that adopt ISO 26000 are more likely to engage in practices that align with stakeholder expectations, including those supporting social and environmental sustainability. Meanwhile, Rangriz and Abyar (2015) bet for strengthening the communication channels with stakeholders and become familiar with their expectations and needs in their social responsibility approach. Other studies specifically focused on the mining industry such as Bluszcz and Kijewska (2015), Caron et al. (2016) or García-Ortega et al. (2020) highlight the need for mining companies to engage in meaningful dialogue with stakeholders and consider their concerns in decision-making processes. In particular, Caron et al. (2016) emphasize the importance of respect for stakeholders' interests, such as local communities, governments, and non-governmental organizations (NGOs).

Furthermore, as previously exposed, Cesar (2021) explores the relation between CSR and SLO in the mining industry and confirms that the companies that cooperate with both the government and local communities end up in a better position to achieve SLO.

Respect for the Rule of Law and Respect for International Norms of Behaviour

ISO 26000 is intended among other purposes to encourage companies to comply with the laws and regulations related to social responsibility (Mohd Fuzi et al., 2017). According to Mahjoub (2019), the adoption of ISO 26000 helps companies comply with international norms of behaviour by aligning their CSR practices with globally accepted principles and standards. But its wider scope than other standards, makes it not to be very specific regarding which are those legal requirements (Panagiotakopoulos et al., 2015).

Primarily, governments have the legal power to protect landscapes in the event of mining impact, and they can also strengthen this protection by working hand in hand with financial institutions (Mason & Ying, 2020). They can even provide specific national standards that are compatible with ISO 26000 (Bluszcz & Kijewska, 2015).

Moreover, code-law countries—those countries that have a legal system based on codified written laws by legislative bodies—favour a broader stakeholder orientation of companies beyond shareholders and it shows a positive influence on comprehensive and more credible social responsibility disclosures (Sethi et al., 2017). Nonetheless, local legislation may be absent, not appropriate, or conflict with international norms of behaviour. According to ISO 26000 (2010), rather than becoming complicit and benefiting from it, organizations should manage such potential duality and seek to exert their influence over other relevant organizations and authorities to address and remedy such situation or conflict.

In addition, different studies highlight the importance of respecting international norms of behaviour, such as those set forth in the International Council on Mining and Metals (ICMM) Principles, and the United Nations' Global Compact which outline principles for responsible business practices, in order to assess and improve their sustainability performance (Bluszcz & Kijewska, 2015; Caron et al., 2016; Panagiotakopoulos et al., 2015). As an example, Ranängen and Zobel (2014) in their case study of a Swedish mining company addressed the compliance with national laws and regulations and international labour standards.

Respect for Human Rights

Respect for human rights has always been contentious issue in sensitive sectors such as mining and other extractive industries. For instance, in the context of electrical mobility, Hąbek and Lavios (2021) highlight "an increase in the so-called conflict minerals (tin, tantalum, tungsten, and gold) in the automotive industry and …their supply chains have a high risk of human rights violation, labour condition breaches, and unethical behaviour that could threaten the future of the communities involved". One of the main concerns is the level of safety for mineworkers because mining sector could be considered the most hazardous industrial sector (Ranängen et al., 2014).

ISO 26000 places a strong emphasis on human rights management and fair practices for establishing and maintaining legitimate relationships with stakeholders (Ben Amar & Chakroun, 2018). In this vein, Kholaif et al. (2022) found that ISO 26000 policies positively impact health and safety at work, whereas Mohammadi et al. (2018) consider human rights as one of the main core subjects in assessing corporate sustainability disclosure.

For Ranängen and Zobel (2014), the respect for human rights and fair operating practices are not fully covered by international standards in the mining sector, and it is essential to complement them with the company code of conduct. They confirm this need with the case study of a Swedish mining and metals company that applies successfully an analytical framework based on the ISO 26000. Even if the general opinion of the academia seems to be that established management systems can be used as a basis, they need to be supplemented because fair operating practices concern different ethical conducts. In the same line, Caron et al. (2016) suggest that mineral exploration companies should develop and implement a code of ethics because sometimes mutual agreements often reduce citizens' analysis. For Sethi et al. (2017), it could be an individual company code of conduct or an industry code of conduct (such as the International Council on Mining and Metals, ICMM, 2022).

3 Systematic Literature Review and Analysis

Methodology

We have performed a qualitative content analysis, based on the papers detected in searches in Web of Science (WoS) and Scopus databases. The literature on this topic is scarce and only 9 papers fit the keywords selected. This section is centred on the analysis of the nine papers detected in searches in Web of Science and Scopus databases. The queries and results obtained in the searches are the following:

a. *WoS* (All databases):
   - Query #1:
     "mining industries" (Topic) and "mining sector" (Topic) and "extractive sector" (Topic) and "extractive industries" (Topic) and "conflict sector" (Topic) and "conflict industries" (Topic) and "sensitive industries" (Topic)
   - Query #2:
     "ISO 26000" (Topic)
   - Results: (#1 AND #2) = **1** (Mohammadi et al., 2018)

b. Scopus:
   - Query #1:
     TITLE-ABS-KEY("mining industries") OR TITLE-ABS-KEY("mining sector") OR TITLE-ABS-KEY("extractive sector") OR TITLE-ABS-KEY("extractive industries") OR TITLE-ABS-KEY("conflict sector") OR TITLE-ABS-KEY("conflict industries") OR TITLE-ABS-KEY("sensitive industries")
   - Query #2:
     TITLE-ABS-KEY("ISO 26000")
   - Results: (#1 AND #2) = **7** (excluded 2)
   - c. Additional searches in queries #2 of both WoS and Scopus
   - Results: **4**
   - Results selected for the analysis: **9**

The complete papers in pdf format were analysed with the software QDAMiner 5 and WordStat 8, the former to create the variables, review the codes and obtain tables with results, while the latter was used to conduct a text mining analysis. Table 1 presents the papers analysed and the variables defined for the analysis (Table 2).

The analysis conducted with the data obtained is descriptive, extracting frequencies and cooccurrences of codes. The frequencies indicate the importance of codes defined through the two software. The

Table 1 Variables in the analysis

File	Core ISO	Country	Dependent variable	CSR impact
Amar_2018	Yes	France	Earnings_ management	Negative
Chakroun_2020	Yes	France	Financial_ performance	Depends_on_ core_subject
Mahjoub_2019	Yes	Saudi Arab	Core_subjects_ ISO_26000	No_Measured
Mohammadi_ 2018	Yes	Iran	Market_valuation	Depends_on_ sector
Ranangen_2014a	Yes	Zambia	None	No_Measured
Ranangen_ 2014b	Yes	Sweden	None	No_Measured
Rangriz_2015	Yes	Iran	None	No_Measured
Saenz_2021	Yes	Peru	None	No_Measured
Sethi_2017	Yes	Various	CSR_assurance	Positive

Source Author's own research

Table 2 Variables in the analysis (cont.)

File	Industry	Mining	Firm size	Num. firms
Ben_Amar_2018	Various	Analysed but no results by sector	Various	Various
Chakroun_2020	Various	Analysed but no results by sector	Various	Various
Mahjoub_2019	Various	Analysed but no results by sector	Various	Various
Mohammadi_ 2018	Various	Analysed but no results by sector	Various	Various
Ranangen_2014a	Mining	YES	Big	One
Ranangen_2014b	Mining	YES	Big	One
Rangriz_2015	Mining	YES	Big	One
Saenz_2021	Mining	YES	Various	Various
Sethi_2017	Various	YES	Big	Various

Source Author's own research

codes represent the theories detected in the nine papers and the core subjects and issues from ISO 26000. For all the codes, in the text mining two criteria were selected:

a. sentences composed by a minimum of three words, and

Table 3 Theories detected in the papers

Code	Cases	% Cases
5.2. Agency costs	2	22.2
5.3. Corporate culture	2	22.2
5.4. Stakeholder theory	4	44.4
5.5. Signalling theory	2	22.2
5.6. Image and reputation of companies	4	44.4
5.7. Agency theory	4	44.4
5.8. Competitive advantage	2	22.2
5.10. Resource dependence theory	1	11.1
5.11. Legitimacy theory	2	22.2
5.12. Life-cycle of products and services	2	22.2
5.15. Social Licence to Operate	2	22.2
5.16. Report assurance	1	11.1

Source Text mining with WordStat 8 and QDAMiner 5

b. the frequency by sentence should be ≥ 4.

Results

This section presents the results for the codes defined supported by theories and the core subjects in the ISO 26000.

Results for Theories

Table 3 shows the theories that were detected through the text mining for the nine papers.

Results for ISO 26000 Core Subjects

Table 4 presents the frequency of papers in which the core subjects and issues of social responsibility in the ISO 26000 standard appeared.

Table 4 Frequency of codes in the ISO 26000

Category	Code	Cases	% Cases
6.2. Organizational governance	6.2.1. Corporate governance	8	88.9
	6.2.2. Code of conduct or ethics	5	55.6
6.3. Human rights	6.3.1. Human rights_general	8	88.9
	6.3.10. Fundamental principles and rights at work	3	33.3
	6.3.3. Due diligence		
	6.3.4. Human rights risk situations		
	6.3.5. Avoidance of complicity		
	6.3.6. Resolving grievances		
	6.3.7. Discrimination and vulnerable groups	6	66.7
	6.3.8. Civil and political rights	2	22.2
	6.3.9. Economic, social, and cultural rights	3	33.3
6.4. Labour practices	6.4.1. Labour practices_ general	5	55.6
	6.4.3. Employment and employment relationships	6	66.7
	6.4.4. Conditions of work and social protection	4	44.4
	6.4.5. Social dialogue	2	22.2
	6.4.6. Health and safety at work	8	88.9
	6.4.7. Human development and training in the workplace	4	44.4
6.5. The environment	6.5.1. The environment_ general	8	88.9
	6.5.3. Prevention of pollution	2	22.2
	6.5.4. Sustainable resource use	6	66.7
	6.5.5. Climate change mitigation and adaptation	5	55.6

(continued)

Table 4 (continued)

Category	Code	Cases	% Cases
	6.5.6. Protection of the environment, biodiversity, and restoration of natural habitats	7	77.8
6.6. Fair operating practices	6.6.1. Fair operating practices_general	5	55.6
	6.6.3. Anti-corruption	4	44.4
	6.6.4. Responsible political involvement	1	11.1
	6.6.5. Fair competition	5	55.6
	6.6.6. Promoting social responsibility in the value chain		
	6.6.7. Respect for property rights	1	11.1
6.7. Consumer issues	6.7.1. Consumer issues_ general	5	55.6
	6.7.3. Fair marketing, factual, and unbiased information and fair contractual practices	3	33.3
	6.7.4. Protecting consumers' health and safety	1	11.1
	6.7.5. Sustainable consumption	2	22.2
	6.7.6. Consumer service, support, and complaint and dispute resolution	2	22.2
	6.7.7. Consumer data protection and privacy	3	33.3
	6.7.8. Access to essential services	2	22.2
	6.7.9. Education and awareness		
6.8. Community involvement and development	6.8.1. Community involvement and development_general	3	33.3
	6.8.3. Community involvement	9	100.0
	6.8.4. Education and culture	1	11.1
	6.8.5. Employment creation and skills development	4	44.4

(continued)

Table 4 (continued)

Category	Code	Cases	% Cases
	6.8.6. Technology development and access		
	6.8.7. Wealth and income creation	3	33.3
	6.8.8. Health		
	6.8.9. Social investment	4	44.4

Source Text mining with WordStat 8 and QDAMiner 5

Cooccurrence of Codes

Table 5 presents the cooccurrence of codes and Fig. 1 depicts the diagram of networks. Finally, Table 6 shows the clusters of codes, with three main categories: business, reporting, and SLO.

Discussion

Despite our systematic literature review yielding a limited number of studies within our scope of research, indicating a need for further investigation of ISO 26000 in relation to mining and other sensitive industries, our analysis revealed significant insights, underscoring the need for further research in this area. First and foremost, a wide variety of theories were considered in the collected papers. The stakeholder theory, company image and reputation, and agency theory were the most frequently addressed, followed by agency costs, corporate culture, signalling theory, legitimacy theory, product and service life-cycle, and SLO, among others. Our initial literature review highlights the importance of companies in sensitive or controversial industries seeking a SLO, although it is not one of the most prominent theories addressed in these papers. This underscores the need for further research to fully explore the potential implications and practical applications of the SLO approach.

Regarding the core subjects and issues of social responsibility, the analysed works collectively cover the vast majority of topics. However,

Table 5 Cooccurrence of codes

	5.10. Resource dependence theory	5.11. Legitimacy theory	5.12. Life-cycle of products and services	5.15. Social Licence to Operate	5.16. Report assurance	5.2. Agency costs	5.3. Corporate culture	5.4. Stakeholder theory	5.5. Signaling theory	5.6. Image and reputation of companies	5.7. Agency theory	5.8. Competitive advantage
5.10. Resource dependence theory	1	1	0	0	0	1	0	0	1	0	1	0
5.11. Legitimacy theory	1	2	0	0	0	1	0	1	1	0	2	0
5.12. Life-cycle of products and services	0	0	2	1	0	0	0	0	0	1	0	0
5.15. Social Licence to Operate	0	0	1	2	1	0	0	0	0	1	0	1
5.16. Report assurance	0	0	0	1	1	0	0	0	0	0	0	1
5.2. Agency costs	1	1	0	0	0	2	1	1	2	1	2	0
5.3. Corporate culture	0	0	0	0	0	1	2	2	1	2	2	1
5.4. Stakeholder theory	0	1	0	0	0	1	2	4	1	2	3	1
5.5. Signaling theory	1	1	0	0	0	2	1	1	2	1	2	0
5.6. Image and reputation of companies	0	0	1	1	0	1	2	2	1	4	2	1
5.7. Agency theory	1	2	0	0	0	2	2	3	2	2	4	1
5.8. Competitive advantage	0	0	0	1	1	0	1	1	0	1	1	2
6.2.1. Corporate governance	1	2	1	1	1	2	2	4	2	3	4	2
6.2.2. Code of conduct or ethics	0	0	0	1	1	1	2	3	1	3	2	2
6.3.1. Human rights_general	1	2	1	1	1	2	2	4	2	3	4	2
6.3.10. Fundamental principles and rights at work	0	1	0	0	0	0	0	2	0	1	1	0
6.3.7. Discrimination and vulnerable groups	0	0	2	2	1	0	1	2	0	3	1	2
6.3.8. Civil and political rights	0	0	0	1	1	0	1	1	0	1	1	2
6.3.9. Economic, social and cultural rights	0	0	1	0	0	0	1	1	0	2	1	1
6.4.1. Labour practices_general	1	2	0	0	0	2	1	3	2	2	3	0
6.4.3. Employment and employment relationships	1	1	0	1	1	2	2	3	2	3	3	2
6.4.4. Conditions of work and social protection	0	1	0	0	0	1	1	3	1	2	2	0
6.4.5. Social dialogue	0	0	0	1	1	0	0	1	0	0	0	1
6.4.6. Health and safety at work	1	2	1	1	1	2	2	4	2	3	4	2
6.4.7. Human development and training in the workplace	0	1	1	0	0	0	0	2	0	1	1	0
6.5.1. The environment_general	1	2	1	1	1	2	2	4	2	3	4	2
6.5.3. Prevention of pollution	0	0	1	0	0	0	0	1	0	0	0	0
6.5.4. Sustainable resource use	0	1	1	2	1	0	1	3	0	3	2	2
6.5.5. Climate change mitigation and adaptation	0	1	1	2	1	0	1	3	0	2	2	2
6.5.6. Protection of the environment, biodiversity, and restoration of natural habitats	1	2	2	1	0	1	1	3	1	3	3	1
6.6.1. Fair operating practices_general	1	2	0	0	0	2	2	4	2	2	4	1
6.6.3. Anti-corruption	0	1	0	1	1	0	0	2	0	1	1	1
6.6.4. Responsible political involvement	0	0	0	0	0	0	0	1	0	0	0	0
6.6.5. Fair competition	0	0	1	0	0	1	2	3	1	3	2	1
6.6.7. Respect for property rights	0	0	0	0	0	0	0	1	0	0	0	0
6.7.1. Consumer issues_general	1	2	0	0	0	2	2	4	2	2	4	1
6.7.3. Fair marketing, factual and unbiased information, and fair contractual practices	1	2	0	0	0	2	1	2	2	1	3	0
6.7.4. Protecting consumers' health and safety	0	0	0	0	0	0	0	0	0	1	0	0
6.7.5. Sustainable consumption	0	1	0	0	0	0	0	2	0	0	1	0

(continued)

Table 5 (continued)

	5.10. Resource dependence theory	5.11. Legitimacy theory	5.12. Life-cycle of products and services	5.15. Social Licence to Operate	5.16. Report assurance	5.2. Agency costs	5.3. Corporate culture	5.4. Stakeholder theory	5.5. Signaling theory	5.6. Image and reputation of companies	5.7. Agency theory	5.8. Competitive advantage
6.7.6. Consumer service, support, and complaint and dispute resolution	0	1	1	0	0	0	0	1	0	0	1	0
6.7.7. Consumer data protection and privacy	0	1	1	0	0	0	0	2	0	0	1	0
6.7.8. Access to essential services	0	0	0	0	0	0	0	1	0	1	0	0
6.8.1. Community involvement and development_general	0	1	0	0	0	0	0	2	0	1	1	0
6.8.3. Community involvement	1	2	2	2	1	2	2	4	2	4	4	2
6.8.4. Education and culture	0	0	0	0	0	0	0	1	0	0	0	0
6.8.5. Employment creation and skills development	0	0	2	1	0	0	0	1	0	2	0	0
6.8.7. Wealth and income creation	0	0	1	1	1	0	0	1	0	0	0	1
6.8.9. Social investment	0	0	2	1	0	0	0	1	0	2	0	0

Source Text mining with WordStat 8 and QDAMiner 5

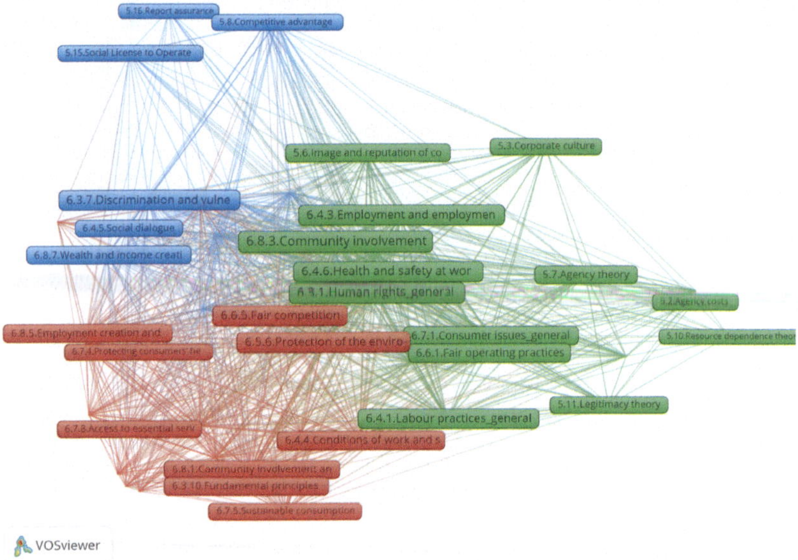

Fig. 1 Network of keywords in the nine papers (*Source* Author's own research)

Table 6 Clusters of codes

Cluster 1. Business: Respect for the rule of law & Respect for international norms of behaviour	Cluster 2. Reporting: Accountability & Transparency	Cluster 3. SLO: Ethical behaviour & Respect for stakeholder interests & Respect for human rights
5.12. Life-cycle of products and services	5.10. Resource dependence theory	5.15. Social Licence to Operate
6.3.10. Fundamental principles and rights at work	5.11. Legitimacy theory	5.16. Report assurance
6.3.9. Economic, social and cultural rights	5.2. Agency costs	5.8. Competitive advantage
6.4.4. Conditions of work and social protection	5.3. Corporate culture	6.2.2. Code of conduct or ethics
6.4.7. Human development and training in the workplace	5.4. Stakeholder theory	6.3.7. Discrimination and vulnerable groups
6.5.3. Prevention of pollution	5.5. Signaling theory	6.3.8. Civil and political rights
6.5.6. Protection of the environment, biodiversity, and restoration of natural habitats	5.6. Image and reputation of companies	6.4.5. Social dialogue
6.6.4. Responsible political involvement	5.7. Agency theory	6.5.4. Sustainable resource use
6.6.5. Fair competition	6.2.1. Corporate governance	6.5.5. Climate change mitigation and adaptation
6.6.7. Respect for property rights	6.3.1. Human rights_ general	6.6.3. Anti-corruption
6.7.4. Protecting consumers' health and safety	6.4.1. Labour practices_ general	6.8.7. Wealth and income creation
6.7.5. Sustainable consumption	6.4.3. Employment and employment relationships	
6.7.6. Consumer service, support, and complaint and dispute resolution	6.4.6. Health and safety at work	
6.7.7. Consumer data protection and privacy	6.5.1. The environment_ general	

(continued)

Table 6 (continued)

Cluster 1. Business: Respect for the rule of law & Respect for international norms of behaviour	Cluster 2. Reporting: Accountability & Transparency	Cluster 3. SLO: Ethical behaviour & Respect for stakeholder interests & Respect for human rights
6.7.8. Access to essential services	6.6.1. Fair operating practices_general	
6.8.1. Community involvement and development_general	6.7.1. Consumer issues_ general	
6.8.4. Education and culture	6.7.3. Fair marketing, factual and unbiased information, and fair contractual practices	
6.8.5. Employment creation and skills development	6.8.3. Community involvement	
6.8.9. Social investment		

Source Text mining with WordStat 8 and QDAMiner 5; Clusters with VOSviewer

community involvement is the only code that appears in all the examined papers, indicating its importance and prominence. The other frequently addressed topics include corporate governance, human rights (in a general sense), health and safety at work, and the environment (in a general sense). On the other hand, several topics such as due diligence, human rights risk situations, avoidance of complicity or resolving grievances related to human rights, promoting social responsibility in the value chain, consumer education and awareness, and health and technology development and access for the community are not addressed at all. Some of these topics, such as due diligence on human rights or community health, are of special interest within mining and other similar controversial industries and should be considered in future research.

In addition, a significant number of connections were found between theories and core subjects and issues of social responsibility. Through the analysis of these connections, three main clusters were identified: Business, Reporting, and SLO. The intricate relationship among these clusters signifies the complexity of integrating social responsibility principles within the mining industry.

Starting with the Business cluster, which includes as main components the respect for the rule of law and respect for international norms of behaviour, the dominance of the life-cycle theory indicates a focus on sustainable practices throughout the entire lifespan of products and services. This emphasis extends to critical issues such as fair competition, respect for property rights, sustainable consumption, consumer service support, and effective complaint and dispute resolution. The life-cycle theory underscores the industry's commitment to ethical and responsible business practices.

Moving to the Reporting cluster, which gathers accountability and transparency, and where theories like legitimacy, stakeholder, signalling, and company image and reputation play a crucial role, a more nuanced understanding is required. These theories not only guide CSR reporting practices but also influence corporate behaviour. For instance, the legitimacy theory emphasizes the need for organizations to align their actions with societal expectations, reflecting a deeper connection between corporate behaviour and social responsibility reporting. Furthermore, core subjects like corporate governance, employment relationships, workplace health and safety, and community involvement are intricately linked to these reporting theories, emphasizing their practical implications in the mining and other sensitive industries.

Finally, concerning the third cluster, namely SLO, and gathering aspects such as ethical behaviour, respect for stakeholder interests, and respect for human rights, the core subjects and issues associated with social responsibility demand closer scrutiny. The presence of ethical considerations, discrimination prevention, civil and political rights, social dialogue, sustainable resource use, climate change mitigation and adaptation, anti-corruption efforts, and wealth and income creation underscores the comprehensive scope of social responsibility within the mining and other sensitive industries. Interestingly, theories such as legitimacy theory or signalling theory which has been directly related to CSR reporting theories applied to SLO (de-Miguel-Molina et al., 2019) are indeed included in the second cluster only and not in the third one despite their clear relationship. This evidences a significant gap in the literature addressing ISO 26000:2010 within these industries, with the need for a more explicit exploration of their role in bridging these conceptual domains.

Overall, the identified clusters are not appearing as isolated entities but as interconnected components of a broader framework that delineates the multifaceted nature of social responsibility in these industries. To gain a deeper understanding of how theoretical concepts translate into real-world practices, a closer examination of the relationships among these clusters is needed through further studies addressing such connections. This exploration will help bridge existing gaps in the literature and improve the theoretical foundation guiding CSR practices in sensitive industries such as the mining sector.

4 Conclusions, Future Research, and Limitations

In this chapter, we conducted a first literature review to examine how relevant works in the subject address the principles of social responsibility in the mining and other sensitive industries as outlined in the standard ISO 26000. Through our analysis, we assessed how these principles articulate and relate to each other in the literature and unveiled some of their connections. Among the most relevant findings of this section is the importance that ISO 26000 places on accountability and transparency and how the literature reflects their close relationship. Moreover, we found that accountability and transparency can effectively address stakeholder expectations, a crucial principle of corporate social responsibility that has a direct impact on a company's reputation and financial performance, as well as its ability to obtain a SLO. Overall, the literature reflects that standards such as ISO 26000 can facilitate companies to improve their sustainability reporting with the aforementioned positive consequences.

Another important outcome is the pivotal role of ethical behaviour as the backbone of the remaining principles, particularly within controversial industries subjected to heightened scrutiny and that must pay special attention to obtaining a SLO. Furthermore, connections are evidenced between the adoption of the ISO 26000 standard as a reference framework and the adoption of practices that align with stakeholder expectations, both in terms of social and environmental sustainability. In this task, the importance of dialogue between companies and their stakeholders is emphasized, and how this alignment can contribute to obtaining a SLO. Likewise, the importance of respecting the rule of law and international norms of behaviour is highlighted, as well as the usefulness of ISO 26000 in filling possible gaps in local legislation, while also acknowledging its limitations in this mission due to the breadth of its scope. To conclude with the principles of social responsibility in the aforementioned industries, the literature highlights the importance that ISO 26000 places on human rights and the positive effect of its application in relation to human rights management and fair practices. It also questions whether these principles are guaranteed by international law. Once again, the ethical approach and behaviour of these companies and their managers are of relevance.

In the second part of our analysis, we conducted a systematic literature review to identify papers that deal with ISO 26000 in the mining and other extractive and conflict-sensitive industries. We found a total of nine relevant papers. Through a text mining analysis of the selected papers, we identified their approach in terms of the theories considered and the core subjects and issues related to ISO 26000. We established their frequency of appearance and their connections and interrelations. In this context, it is not surprising to observe the prevalence of the stakeholder theory in this field. As we have seen, the identification and understanding of the needs, expectations, and concerns of different stakeholders represent a crucial element in defining the strategy, including obtaining a SLO, which is essential for firms operating in these industries.

As another relevant outcome, the analysis of these connections led to identification of three main clusters, namely business, reporting, and SLO, along with their corresponding most relevant theories and core subjects and issues within each of them. This outcome provides a foundation for further exploration of potential approaches to social responsibility within these industries, within the framework of the ISO 26000.

Moreover, the range of aspects covered by the analysed papers is quite comprehensive in terms of theories and core subjects and issues of social responsibility and their connection. However, some interesting topics of increasing interest, such as some of the ones related to human rights, or education and awareness on consumer issues, along with community health, appear to be underexplored and are identified as interesting areas for future research. The same applies when assessing the theories within each cluster.

In addition, as for managerial implications, our focus on CSR strategic aspects within the framework of ISO26000 can help managers of private companies in these industries to gain awareness and to further understand and leverage the potential benefits from its application in order to better address the significant challenges ahead.

As for the main limitations of this research, despite the valuable insights obtained, the limited works identified and analysed constraint generalizability and validity of the findings, also indicating an early stage in CSR research in mining and other sensitive industries within the framework of ISO 26000:2010, and highlighting a crucial opportunity for further investigation. Future studies can delve deeper into the identified underexplored topics and understanding of potential interconnections to strengthen and enrich the present findings and inform responsible practices within these industries.

Furthermore, future research could expand this methodology by incorporating specific frameworks with a further focus on aspects related to environmental impacts, relations, and contributions to local communities or improvement of working conditions, which are particularly relevant in industries such as mining.

Lastly, the approach outlined in this paper holds the potential to serve as a template for evaluating other industries with a similar perspective, enabling comparative analyses. This endeavour might contribute to crafting a flexible and comprehensive assessment tool adaptable to various industries, promoting a nuanced comprehension of CSR principles and practices across sectors.

References

Balzarova, M. A., & Castka, P. (2012). Stakeholders' influence and contribution to social standards development: The case of multiple stakeholder approach to ISO 26000 development. *Journal of Business Ethics, 111*, 265–279.

Ben Amar, A., & Chakroun, S. (2018). Do dimensions of corporate social responsibility affect earnings management? Evidence from France. *Journal of Financial Reporting and Accounting, 16*(2), 348–370.

Bluszcz, A., & Kijewska, A. (2015). Challenges of sustainable development in the mining and metallurgy sector in Poland. *Metalurgija, 54*(2), 441–444.

Campero, C., & Barton, J. R. (2015). 'You have to be with God and the Devil': Linking Bolivia's extractive industries and local development through social licences. *Bulletin of Latin American Research, 34*(2), 167–183.

Caron, J., Durand, S., & Asselin, H. (2016). Principles and criteria of sustainable development for the mineral exploration industry. *Journal of Cleaner Production, 119*, 215–222.

Cesar, S. (2021). Corporate social responsibility fit helps to earn the social license to operate in the mining industry. *Resources Policy, 74*, 101814.

Chakroun, S., Salhi, B., Ben Amar, A., & Jarboui, A. (2020). The impact of ISO 26000 social responsibility standard adoption on firm financial performance: Evidence from France. *Management Research Review, 43*(5), 545–571.

Conde, M. (2017). Resistance to mining. A review. *Ecological Economics, 132*, 80–90.

Criado, J. I., Ruvalcaba-Gómez, E. A., & Valenzuela-Mendoza, R. (2018). Revisiting the open government phenomenon. A meta-analysis of the international literature. *JeDEM—EJournal of EDemocracy and Open Government, 10*, 50–81.

de-Miguel-Molina, B., Chirivella-González, V., & García-Ortega, B. (2019). CEO letters: Social license to operate and community involvement in the mining industry. *Business Ethics: A European Review, 28*(1), 36–55.

García-Ortega, B., De-Miguel-Molina, B., & Chirivella González, V. (2020). Responsabilidad social corporativa en la minería de Latinoamérica: un modelo multiactor. *América Latina Hoy, 86*, 23–40.

Holley, E. A., & Mitcham, C. (2016). The pebble mine dialogue: A case study in public engagement and the social license to operate. *Resources Policy, 47*, 18–27.

Hąbek, P., & Lavios, J. J. (2021). Striving for enterprise sustainability through supplier development process. *Energies, 14*(19), 6256.

ICMM. (2022). *Mining principles: Performance expectations.* International Council on Mining and Metals.

ISO. (2010). *ISO 26000:2010 Guidance on social responsibility.* International Organization for Standardization.

Jenkins, H., & Yakovleva, N. (2006). Corporate social responsibility in the mining industry: Exploring trends in social and environmental disclosure. *Journal of Cleaner Production, 14*(3–4), 271–284.

Kholaif, M. M. N. H. K., Ming, X., Moosa, A., & David, K. G. (2022). The ISO 26000's labor environmental issues during COVID-19: Does corporate social responsibility help? Evidence from the Egyptian small and medium enterprises. *Environmental Science and Pollution Research International, 29*(12), 17117–17131.

Mahjoub, L. B. (2019). Disclosure about corporate social responsibility through ISO 26000 implementation made by Saudi listed companies. *Cogent Business & Management, 6*(1), 1609188.

Maignan, I., & Ralston, D. A. (2002). Corporate social responsibility in Europe and the US: Insights from businesses' self-presentations. *Journal of International Business Studies, 33*, 497–514.

Mason, A. R., & Ying, M. (2020). Evaluating standards for private-sector financial institutions and the management of cultural heritage. *Advances in Archaeological Practice, 8*(1), 1–14.

Mohammadi, M. A. D., Mardani, A., Ali Khan, M. N. A., & Streimikiene, D. (2018). Corporate sustainability disclosure and market valuation in a Middle Eastern Nation: Evidence from listed firms on the Tehran Stock Exchange: Sensitive industries versus non-sensitive industries. *Economic Research-Ekonomska Istraživanja, 31*(1), 1488–1511.

Mohd Fuzi, N., Habidin, N. F., Hibadullah, S. N., & Ong, S. Y. Y. (2017). CSR practices, ISO 26000 and performance among Malaysian automotive suppliers. *Social Responsibility Journal, 13*(1), 203–220.

O'Faircheallaigh, C. (2015). Social equity and large mining projects: Voluntary industry initiatives, public regulation and community development agreements. *Journal of Business Ethics, 132*, 91–103.

Panagiotakopoulos, P., Espinosa, A., & Walker, J. (2015). Integrated sustainability management for organizations. *Kybernetes, 44*(6/7), 984–1004.

Rangriz, H., & Abyar, M. R. (2015). Identification and prioritization of the factors impacting the social responsibility of the extractive oil and gas industries. *Asian Social Science, 11*(2), 111.

Ranängen, H., & Zobel, T. (2014). Exploring the path from management systems to stakeholder management in the Swedish mining industry. *Journal of Cleaner Production, 84*, 128–141.

Ranängen, H., Zobel, T., & Bergström, A. (2014). The merits of ISO 26000 for CSR development in the mining industry: A case study in the Zambian Copperbelt. *Social Responsibility Journal, 10*(3), 500–515.

Sethi, S. P., Martell, T. F., & Demir, M. (2017). Enhancing the role and effectiveness of corporate social responsibility (CSR) reports: The missing element of content verification and integrity assurance. *Journal of Business Ethics, 144*, 59–82.

Swanson, D. L. (2008). 227 top managers as drivers for corporate social responsibility. In A. Crane, D. Matten, A. McWilliams, J. Moon, & D. S. Siegel (Eds.), *The Oxford handbook of corporate social responsibility*. Oxford University Press.

Sectorial Technological Intensity as a Differentiating Factor for Green Innovation and Economic and Sustainable Performance in Industrial Companies of the Valencian Community

Jeanneth Marcela Valdivieso-Uvidia, Manuel Expósito-Langa, and José Antonio Belso-Martínez

1 Introduction

Sustainability is a constant challenge that drives significant changes in both consumers and businesses (Carpenter & Feroz, 2001; Kiron et al., 2017; Neumann, 2021; Zeng et al., 2022). The 2030 Agenda (EU) and the Sustainable Development Goals (UN) place emphasis on the need for companies to adopt a sustainable approach to economic development. Against this backdrop, and the intensification of changes in recent years, companies are vying to balance their economic, environmental,

J. M. Valdivieso-Uvidia (✉) · M. Expósito-Langa
Universitat Politècnica de València, Valencia, Spain
e-mail: marvaluv@epsa.upv.es

M. Expósito-Langa
e-mail: maexlan@doe.upv.es

J. A. Belso-Martínez
Miguel Hernández University, Elche, Spain
e-mail: jbelso@umh.es

E. Poveda-Pareja et al. (eds.), *The Strategic Paradigm of CSR and Sustainability*, Palgrave Studies in Governance, Leadership and Responsibility,
https://doi.org/10.1007/978-3-031-58889-1_4

and social interests (Cai et al., 2017; Mbanyele et al., 2022; Vallet-Bellmunt et al., 2022), which implies a strategic shift in the short term. Thus, despite the difficulties involved in being sustainable and profitable in economic terms, an increasing number of companies contribute to this new paradigm, which is highly appreciated by stakeholders (Andersson et al., 2023).

On the other hand, in the current economic context, technology is a crucial element in fostering the growth and competitiveness of companies; indeed, it is one of the microorganisms that drive innovation (Zhao et al., 2021). Extensive research has been conducted in literature regarding the impact of technology on continuous innovation and its effects on the economic performance of industries (Bag et al., 2020; Hatzichronoglou, 1997; Zawislak et al., 2018) However, the socio-environmental aspects surrounding technology have received limited attention. This is primarily attributed to the historical focus that has prioritized the technical aspects of technological advancements, without conducting a thorough exploration of their extensive social and environmental consequences (Parrilli et al., 2023; Peiró-Signes et al., 2011).

Initially, the Organization for Economic Co-operation and Development (OECD, 2003) identified industries that are more technology-intensive, focusing solely on investment figures in research, development, and innovation (R&D&I). Subsequently, additional factors, such as the relationship between invested capital and the human factor, as well as the level of knowledge transferred to the final product, have been integrated into the analysis (OECD, 2003; Zawislak et al., 2018). This transformative shift in our approach, aligned with the principles expounded in "The strategic paradigm of CSR and sustainability: A public-private approach," has paved the way for a substantially more comprehensive comprehension of the socio-environmental implications of technology. However, recognizing the evolving landscape, further research is imperative to delve deeper into the broader socio-environmental impact of technology, particularly within the intricate contexts of businesses and industries.

Therefore, we will focus our analysis on two main aspects:

- Firstly, we will examine green innovation as a driver of sustainable performance. Companies place significant priority on promoting green innovation by developing environmentally friendly products and production models (Chen et al., 2006; Díez-Vial et al., 2023; Lee et al., 2018) to achieve sustainable advantages.
- Secondly, we will adopt a sectoral approach to understand the variations in company performance based on the technological intensity within their respective sectors.

To achieve this, a multisectoral empirical study was conducted in 189 industrial companies in the Valencian Community, Spain. The companies were classified according to the technological intensity of the sector to which they adhered, utilizing the classification provided by the OECD. The quantitative analysis of the database provides evidence of the existing sectoral discrepancies in the development of green innovations, as well as the economic and sustainable performance of the companies.

The results attained illustrate the significance of the sector factor under technological intensity, which, from a strategic management perspective, reinforces the complementary relationship between green innovation and technological intensity in the economic and sustainable performance of industrial companies. Furthermore, the chapter adopts a strategic management perspective, elucidating the complementary relationship between green innovation and technological intensity in shaping overall company performance. These findings offer valuable insights for a more contemporary conceptualization of business performance outcomes in the broader context of CSR and sustainability.

This paper is structured as follows: In Sect. 2, the theoretical background of this research and the research questions are presented. Section 3 describes the setting of the empirical study. In Sect. 4, the results are presented, and the theoretical implications that can lead to future investigations are studied, and finally, conclusions are summarized.

2 Theoretical Framework and Research Questions

Economic and sustainable performance in business has catalyzed a compelling debate in recent scientific literature, highlighting the limitations of solely technical approaches that neglect socio-environmental aspects (Belso-Martínez et al., 2020; Carberry et al., 2019; González-Masip et al., 2019; Moneva-Abadía et al., 2019; Moyano Fuentes et al., 2019; Liu et al., 2020; Van Wijk et al., 2019).

Sustainability

Sustainability refers to the capacity to maintain or improve certain processes or states over time (Criado-Gomis et al., 2018). Sustainability drives actions to address societal imbalances (Moulaert & Nussbaumer, 2005; Mumford, 2002; Westley & Antadze, 2010), usually through programs and products that propagate these changes in the social system (Westley & Antadze, 2010). Sustainability mitigates the social shortcomings of the traditional capitalist model by innovating novel procedures to effectively integrate interest into the market and the productive system. From a business perspective, sustainability induces actions that simultaneously generate economic and social value through innovation (Howaldt & Kopp, 2012).

Sustainable Performance

Sustainable performance refers to achieving a balance between economic, social, and environmental aspects through actions involving all stakeholders, without compromising the needs of future generations (Khan & Quaddus, 2015). Moving toward a genuinely sustainable model involves integrating financial and socio-environmental aspects to transcend the one-dimensional focus solely on economic realms (Díez-Vial et al., 2023; Guo et al., 2020; Schneider, 2015).

Green Innovation

Contributing to sustainability is the goal of green innovation, which emerges as a strategy to contribute to enhance well-being and reduce the environmental impact of the global production chain (Chang, 2011; Chen et al., 2006; Chiou et al., 2011; Eiadat et al., 2008). From a business perspective, green innovation is a crucial component in supporting the transition to a green economy, enabling companies to address the conflicting needs of various stakeholders (De Marchi & Grandinetti, 2013; Díez-Vial et al., 2023).

Currently, the constant increase in pressure from stakeholders compels companies to innovate through more eco-friendly practices and products as the only way to survive in changing markets and comply with increasingly strict regulations (Becker, 2023; Horbach, 2008; Porter & Van Der Linde, 1995; Weng et al., 2015). In this context, green innovation involves the development of environmentally friendly products and production models (Chen et al., 2006; Díez-Vial et al., 2023; Lee et al., 2018).

The extent of green innovation ranges from the "greening" of product design to production models that encompass energy-saving; pollution management; and waste recycling (Chen, 2008; Lee et al., 2018; Oduro et al., 2022). Green innovation goes beyond the traditional concept of innovation (Thompson, 1965; Zeng et al., 2022) and involves exploring more in-depth innovative ideas, business models, and technological advancements that provide not only economic benefits, but also socio-environmental advantages.

Green innovation is therefore a determinant of sustainable performance in both companies and key sectors, standing alongside technological development (Becker, 2023; Mulgan et al., 2007; Nicholls et al., 2015; Vallet-Bellmunt et al., 2022). Therefore, being sustainable transforms a company into a true agent of change (Ambec et al., 2013; Andersson et al., 2023).

Sectoral Technology Intensity (STI)

The concept of sectorial technological intensity has emerged, which involves the specific level of technology within a sector, measured by the relationship between R&D expenditures and value-added, as well as the technology-knowledge embedded in products (Abdal et al., 2016; Botey Fullat et al., 2018). Sectoral Technology Intensity characterizes how technologically advanced and technology-oriented a specific sector of the economy is (Sinha et al., 2022; Yao et al., 2023).

The OECD Secretariat (2003) has made considerable progress in studying the technological development of industries and harmonizing the classification of technological intensity at an international level (Hatzichronoglou, 1997). Industries are categorized into four groups based on their degree of technological intensity: high technology, medium–high technology, medium–low technology, and low technology.

Technological intensification requires a certain level of innovation and several authors (Frantzen, 2000; Godin, 2004; Yao et al., 2021) associate this with a company's ability to benefit from new knowledge, expand their markets, use available resources, expand productively and enhance their dynamism to improve business performance in various aspects (Hatzichronoglou, 1997).

Based on these arguments, we formulated the research questions as follows:

> ***Research Question 1***: *Does the financial performance of companies differ based on the technological intensity of the sector to which they belong?*
> ***Research Question 2***: *Does the level of green innovation development in companies differ based on the technological intensity of their sector?*
> ***Research Question 3***: *Does the sustainable performance of companies differ based on the technological intensity of the sector to which they belong?*

3 Methodology

Research Context: Traditional Industrial Sectors of the Valencian Community

The research context is focused on the region of the Valencian Community in Spain, which, according to the Valencian Institute of Economic Studies (IVIE, 2021) represents 10.6% of the population, 9.3% of GDP, and 8.1% of the total R&D expenditure in the country. In the industrial landscape of Spain, the Valencian Community stands out significantly, contributing 11.4% to the national total, second only to Catalonia, which contributes 25.1%. This prominence is noted against the backdrop of other industrial regions such as Navarre, La Rioja, and the Basque Country, where the weight of the manufacturing industry exceeds 20% of the regional GDP, compared to the 12.3% Spanish average (Ibáñez & Álvarez, 2022). Thus, the Valencian Community firmly positions itself as a pivotal player in Spain's industrial sector.

According to data from the European Commission, Spain invested approximately 1.24% of its GDP in R&D in 2020 and ranks among the leading European economies in terms of technological intensity, based on the relationship between industrial automation and manufacturing value-added, trailing only Germany, the Czech Republic, Slovakia, Slovenia, and Italy.

The empirical study was based on a sample of companies belonging to different productive sectors. To collect data, a cross-sectional electronic questionnaire was developed between November 2020 and January 2021. Surveys were applied to a variety of profiles, with significant representation from General Managers, R&D, and Technology Directors, and Production and Operations Staff. This allowed us to gain a comprehensive perspective from different areas of the organization concerning the topics of interest in the research.

The questionnaire was constructed based on the relevant literature (Chang, 2011; Chen et al., 2006; Chiou et al., 2011; Eiadat et al., 2008; Oduro et al., 2022) and pre-tested on a pilot sample of ten companies. Feedback from the pilot study allowed for improvements to be implemented, resulting in the definitive version of the questionnaire. The database obtained was cleaned and completed with the secondary information source SABI (Sistema Ibérico de Análisis de Balances). A valid sample of 189 companies was obtained for the study.

The obtained sample is composed of companies according to their size as follows: 15.9% have fewer than ten employees, 63.5% have between 11 and 49 employees, and 20.6% have more than fifty employees. Regarding revenue, 48.1% have a turnover of less than three million euros, 22.8% between 3 and 6 million euros, and finally, 29.1% have a turnover exceeding six million euros.

It is important to note that this study is a multisectoral analysis, which includes companies from traditional industries in the Valencian economy, such as furniture, construction, metal, ceramics, textiles, food, plastics, toys, machinery, and footwear.

Furthermore, given the OECD's esteemed credibility, academics frequently employ its classification of technological intensity across industrial sectors when seeking detailed insights into the global technological framework (Sinha et al., 2022; Yao et al., 2023). In this study, we have utilized this classification to delve into the strategic innovative behavior of companies within various industrial sectors in the Valencian Community. Consequently, manufacturing industries have been categorized into four distinct levels of technological intensity: high, medium–high, medium–low, and low.

Variables

Financial Performance

To assess the financial performance of the companies, the financial statements for the last three years prior to the study, corresponding to 2021, 2020, and 2019, were used by calculating the average value. These statements provide information on the profitability and operating efficiency of the company over the past three years, allowing an assessment of its financial health, whether it is generating profits or losses, and indirectly identify its ability to effectively manage resources and meet financial obligations (Bayaraa, 2017).

Green Innovation

For this variable, we considered a set of five items adapted to our context based on various previous studies (Barforoush et al., 2021; Cai & Zhou, 2014; Chen et al., 2006; Eiadat et al., 2008; Lee et al., 2018; Oduro et al., 2022). These items were measured on a 5-point Likert scale (Table 1). An exploratory factor analysis was conducted to assess the validity of the Green Innovation item scale, resulting in a Cronbach's Alpha of 0.815 and a significant result for the Bartlett's Test of Sphericity (Chi-square = 316.116; df = 10; sig. = 0.000). The Kaiser–Meyer–Olkin (KMO) measure was greater than 0.6 (KMO = 0.790). Finally, a one-factor solution with varimax rotation was obtained, explaining 57.958% of the total variance.

Sustainable Performance

To measure sustainable performance, the study relied on previous scientific research (Afeltra et al., 2023; Díez-Vial et al., 2023; Khan & Quaddus, 2015; Kraus et al., 2018), which considers indicators that are distinct from traditional financial performance metrics. Four items were considered for this variable (Table 1), measured on a 5-point Likert scale and subsequently subjected to an exploratory factor analysis establishing the validity of the construct scale. The results showed a Cronbach's Alpha of 0.853 and the Bartlett's Test of Sphericity was statistically significant (Chi-square = 325.318; df = 6; sig. = 0.000). The Kaiser–Meyer–Olkin (KMO) measure exceeded 0.6 (KMO = 0.800), making it appropriate to proceed with the factor analysis (Coakes & Steed, 2001). A one-factor solution with varimax rotation was obtained, explaining 69.712% of the total variance.

Sectoral Technology Intensity (STI)

Attempts to establish statistical methodologies for measuring the technological intensity of a sector often referred to as the OECD (2017, 2003)

Table 1 Variables analyzed for the research questions

Research question	Variable	Description (items)
Q1	Financial Performance	1. Average of the last 3 years of results of the year (years 2021, 2020, 2019 in Thousand EUR)
Q2	Green innovation	1. The company considers the environmental impact when developing products and processes 2. The company seeks efficiency in the consumption of energy, water, and other resources 3. The company takes actions to reduce waste 4. The company has measures in place for pollution prevention 5. The company follows the guidelines of the environmental management systems
Q3	Sustainable performance	1. The company takes measures to promote gender equality, the integration of minorities, and/or hiring of people with disabilities 2. The company promotes the development of employees' skills through actions such as training, awards, and/or career plans 3. The company communicates the importance of social and environmental responsibility to its employees 4. Employees participate in the decision-making process of the company
Q1-Q2-Q3	Sectoral technology intensity	1. Technological intensity of industry, according to the OECD classification, 2017

Note Questionnaire items, applied to the sample and adapted from the scientific literature
Source Own elaboration

and its classification of industries based on their technological intensity. This classification relies on three indicators that, to varying degrees, reflect aspects of technology production and technology use. These indicators include R&D expenditures as a proportion of value-added, R&D

expenditures as a proportion of production, and R&D expenditures plus technology-related expenditures incorporated in intermediate and capital goods. At the global level, manufacturing industries are differentiated into four categories: high, medium–high, medium–low, and low technological intensity (Table 2). Following these guidelines, the sample of companies has been classified into three groups: 1 indicates companies belonging to sectors with low technological intensity (61.9% of the sample), 2 indicates companies belonging to sectors with medium–low technological intensity (23.8% of the sample), and 3 indicates companies belonging to sectors with medium–high technological intensity (14.3% of the sample).

Table 2 Manufacturing industries classified according to their technological intensity

STI level	Industries
High-technology	Aerospace and space construction
	Office machinery and computer equipment
	Electronics and communications
	Pharmaceutical industry
Medium—high technology	Scientific instruments
	Motor vehicles
	Chemicals
	Electrical machinery
	Non-electrical machinery
	Transport equipment
Medium—low technology	Plastic and rubber products
	Non-ferrous metals
	Non-metallic mineral products
	Petroleum refining
	Ferrous metals
	Shipbuilding
	Other manufacturing products
	Fabricated metal products
Low-technology	Paper and cardboard printing
	Food, beverages, and tobacco
	Textile and clothing
	Wood and furniture

Note Classification updated by industrial sectors according to the OECD (2017)
Source Own elaboration from OECD (2017)

Analysis Techniques

To address the three research questions raised in this study, we will compare the main variables of the study (financial performance, green innovation, and sustainable performance) by the level of technological intensity of the sector in the sample companies. Since the groups of companies are not homogenous and the assumptions for conducting an ANOVA test cannot be met, we will perform non-parametric tests on the data (Coakes & Steed, 2001; George & Mallery, 2003).

The Kruskal and Wallis test was performed to determine if there are significant differences between the sectors based on technological intensity (Kruskal & Wallis, 1952). This test compares three or more samples and indicates whether the distribution of at least one of them is different from the others. Once the test has been performed, if differences are found, a post-hoc exercise will be conducted to complete the study and identify the differences between the groups.

4 Results and Discussion

This section compiles the results obtained from the application of the analysis techniques. As illustrated in Table 3, the financial performance shows statistically significant differences between low STI and medium–high STI. Results indicated, based on a positive relationship between R&D expenditure and income benefiting the company, that sectors intensifying their technological level are more profitable in economic terms (Segarra-Ciprés et al., 2012; Tunzelmann & Acha, 2005). They participate in more demanding markets, rapidly conquer international markets and utilize available resources more productively, leading to enhanced financial outcomes.

With this information we answer research question 1: Yes, the financial performance of firms varies according to the technological intensity of the sector to which they belong. This is evidenced by statistically significant differences in financial performance between low and medium–high technology-intensive sectors, with higher financial performance in more technology-intensive sectors.

Table 3 Kruskal–Wallis test statistics for study variables

STI[b]			[a]Mean rank			Pairwise comparison[bc]		
		X^2	*Low*	*Medium–Low*	*Medium–High*	*Low/Medium–Low*	*Low/Medium–High*	*Medium–Low/Medium–High*
Variables	Financial performance	28.086**	78.61	118.09	127.56	−39.482** (9.596)	−48.949** (11.679)	−9.467 (13.317)
	Green innovation	20.552**	83.36	101.06	135.35	−17.697 (9.593)	−51.993** (11.676)	−34.296* (13.313)
	Sustainable performance	12.684*	87.90	93.17	128.81	−5.265 (9.464)	−40.913** (11.519)	−35.648* (13.134)

Note: $N = 189$. Significance at level 0.05 (*); Significance at level 0.01 (**). [a]Kruskal–Wallis test; [b]Grouping variable: Technological Intensity of the Sector (ITS); [c]Higher values indicate the difference between groups and lower values represent the standard error

Source Own elaboration

Furthermore, a statistically significant difference is observed, through pairwise comparison, for the variable "green innovation" between the scores of companies from low STI and medium–high STI sectors. Similar to the previous variable, this allows us to affirm that the level of green innovation does indeed differ based on the technological intensity of the sector to which the companies belong. Thus, companies belonging to medium–high STI sectors are more innovative in terms of socio-environmental practices, suggesting that their industrial activities have a lower environmental impact, and this answers research question 2. They are more efficient in energy, water, and resource consumption, implement effective waste reduction and pollution control measures, and have successful environmental management policies or systems. These findings support the notion from previous studies that technology-intensive companies are more innovative (Belso-Martínez et al., 2020; Hatzichronoglou, 1997; Markwald, 2004; Santamaría et al., 2009).

Finally, examining the level of STI and conducting pairwise comparisons using the Dunn procedure (Pohlert, 2014), statistically significant differences are revealed for the variable "sustainable performance". The average score obtained for sustainable performance among medium–high STI sectors is significantly different from the other sectors. These results suggest that companies belonging to medium–high STI sectors tend to be more sustainable than those in low and medium–low STI sectors, this answers research question 3.

A preliminary reflection leads us to consider the presence of relational factors; companies in more technology-intensive sectors establish higher levels of technical and strategic cooperation within their value chain, generating greater dynamism that promotes both economic and sustainable performance through a contagion effect (Belso-Martinez et al., 2020; Expósito-Langa et al., 2015). However, in sectors with higher STI, there is a rapid obsolescence of available knowledge, which facilitates quick adaptation to growth and the emergence of new business models, where sustainability becomes a fundamental axis.

In addition to this, the results in Table 3 suggest that, in sectors with low technology intensity, companies may have less incentive to invest in green innovation and may focus more on short-term financial objectives. This can have a negative impact on the sustainable performance of the company and its reputation in the market. In summary, the technological intensity of the sector does have an impact on economic profitability, levels of green innovation, and sustainability. In sectors with high technology intensity, innovation and sustainability are crucial to staying competitive and improving long-term financial performance.

5 Conclusions and Implications

Technology plays a significant role in the development of the industry, and at the corporate level, it has become a topic of great interest. This study examined the importance of technological intensity in traditional industrial sectors regarding the level of financial performance, green innovation, and sustainable performance achieved by companies in the Valencian Community. The findings suggest that companies with higher ITS are more financially profitable, leading to increased investment in green innovation and, consequently, greater sustainability. Companies with strong financial performance can invest in short-term innovation, which, in turn, can improve their long-term performance.

While the industrial structure of the sample mainly comprises low and medium–low technology sectors, the growth level of the industry in the Valencian Community over the last decade has been characterized by significant potential for business innovation, which has shaped successful relational practices (Belso-Martinez et al., 2019); crucial in the development of green innovations directly related to the implementation of innovative environmental solutions to reduce the environmental impact of business operations. Green innovation, therefore, can enhance the sustainable performance of companies by reducing their environmental footprint, improving their energy efficiency, and lowering their long-term operational costs, thereby enhancing their financial performance.

Studying the level of technological intensity in relation to current variables that drive companies to invest in sustainable research and development is beneficial, as it strengthens their great growth potential through the creation of new products and processes in harmony with the environment, while also creating employment opportunities for a large number of people. A strong sustainable performance can enhance the company's image, increase customer satisfaction, and foster customer loyalty. Moreover, this can have a positive impact on the company's financial performance by boosting its revenue and improving its position in the current market.

From a business strategic perspective, the technological intensity of the sector is directly related to financial performance, since it enables companies to invest in green innovation, which may incur high short-term costs (Droste et al., 2016), leading to improved sustainable performance. A consistent sustainable performance can enhance the company's image and increase customer satisfaction, thereby positively impacting the financial performance of the company. Hence, these three variables are interconnected and mutually influence each other in creating long-term value for the company.

The theoretical contribution of the study is significant, highlighting the co-supportive behavior of green innovation and technological intensity in the financial and sustainable performance of companies. This offers a novel conceptualization of business outcomes, emphasizing that higher technological intensity in traditional industries correlates with better financial results, more investment in green innovation, and enhanced sustainable performance. This insight is particularly relevant for the Valencian Community's industries, known for their diverse technological intensities and potential for innovation.

Practically, the study underscores the strategic importance of technological intensity for businesses aiming to invest in sustainable development. It suggests that companies with strong financial performance are better positioned to invest in green innovation, leading to long-term benefits like reduced environmental impact, improved energy efficiency, and increased market competitiveness. This creates a positive cycle where financial health enables sustainable practices, which in turn can further improve financial performance.

However, this approach has limitations, as the R&D intensity may be biased in this sectorial view. The research in each sector is attributed to the main activity of the companies involved. Consequently, the technological intensity of several industries may be overestimated, while others may be underestimated. For example, industries such as textiles, footwear, plastics, or toys have intensified their investment in R&D in the specific case of the Valencian Community in recent years (Belso-Martinez et al., 2019; Botey Fullat et al., 2018; De Marchi, 2012; Vallet-Bellmunt et al., 2022).

Moreover, the lack of longitudinal data may limit the ability to address trends over time. Additionally, the absence of a separate analysis by company size and sector also represents a limitation in the research.

The limitations identified in this study and the conclusions drawn, as well as the new lines of research identified, will be addressed in subsequent studies. This will allow for a deeper exploration and a more comprehensive understanding of the investigated topics and their implications in the context of sustainability and innovation in businesses.

References

Abdal, A., Torres-Freire, C. E., & Callil, V. (2016). Rethinking sectoral typologies: A classification of activity according to knowledge and technological intensity. *RAI Revista de Administração e Inovação, 13*(4), 232–241.

Afeltra, G., Alerasoul, S. A., & Strozzi, F. (2023). The evolution of sustainable innovation: From the past to the future. *European Journal of Innovation Management, 26*(2), 386–421.

Ambec, S., Cohen, M. A., Elgie, S., & Lanoie, P. (2013). The porter hypothesis at 20: Can environmental regulation enhance innovation and competitiveness. *Review of Environmental Economics and Policy, 7*(1), 2–22.

Andersson, S., Svensson, G., Otero-Neira, C., Laurell, H., Lindgren, J., & Karlsson, N. P. E. (2023). Sustainable development considerations in supply chains: Firms' relationships with stakeholders in their business sustainability practices—A triangular comparison. *Business Strategy and the Environment, 32*(4), 1885–1899.

Bag, S., Gupta, S., & Luo, Z. (2020). Examining the role of logistics 4.0 enabled dynamic capabilities on firm performance. *International Journal of Logistics Management, 31*(3), 607–628.

Barforoush, N., Etebarian, A., Naghsh, A., & Shahin, A. (2021). Green innovation a strategic resource to attain competitive advantage. *International Journal of Innovation Science, 13*(5), 645–663.

Bayaraa, B. (2017). Financial performance determinants of organizations: The case of Mongolian companies. *Journal of Competitiveness, 9*(3), 22–33.

Becker, B. (2023). Green innovation strategies, innovation success, and firm performance—Evidence from a panel of Spanish Firms. *Sustainability, 15*(2), 1656.

Belso-Martinez, J. A., López-Sánchez, M. J., Diez-Vial, I. & Molina-Capel, P. (2019). *Innovación social y responsabilidad social corporativa en el calzado español.* Grupo M&G Difusión.

Belso-Martínez, J. A., Tomás-Miquel, J. V., Expósito-Langa, M., & Mateu-García, R. (2020). Delving into the technical textile phenomenon: Networking strategies and innovation in mature clusters. *The Journal of the Textile Institute, 111*(2), 260–272.

Botey Fullat, M., Arias Martín, P., & Alarcón Lorenzo, S. (2018). El proceso de innovación según la intensidad tecnológica de la industria manufacturera española. *Economía Industrial, 407*, 107–121.

Cai, W. G., & Zhou, X. L. (2014). On the drivers of eco-innovation: Empirical evidence from China. *Journal of Cleaner Production, 79*, 239–248.

Cai, Y., Lu, Y., Stegman, A., & Newth, D. (2017). Simulating emissions intensity targets with energy economic models: Algorithm and application. *Annals of Operations Research, 255*(1–2), 141–155.

Carberry, E. J., Bharati, P., Levy, D. L., & Chaudhury, A. (2019). Social movements as catalysts for corporate social innovation: Environmental activism and the adoption of green information systems. *Business & Society, 58*(5), 1083–1127.

Carpenter, V. L., & Feroz, E. H. (2001). Institutional theory and accounting rule choice: An analysis of four US state governments decisions to adopt generally accepted accounting principles. *Accounting Organizations and Society, 26*, 565–596.

Chang, C. H. (2011). The influence of corporate environmental ethics on competitive advantage: The mediation role of green innovation. *Journal of Business Ethics, 104*(3), 361–370.

Chen, Y. S., Lai, S. B., & Wen, C. T. (2006). The influence of green innovation performance on corporate advantage in Taiwan. *Journal of Business Ethics, 67*(4), 331–339.

Chen, Y. S. (2008). The driver of green innovation and green image-green core competence. *Journal of Business Ethics, 81*(3), 531–543.

Chiou, T. Y., Chan, H. K., Lettice, F., & Chung, S. H. (2011). The influence of greening the suppliers and green innovation on environmental performance and competitive advantage in Taiwan. *Transportation Research Part E: Logistics and Transportation Review, 47*(6), 822–836.

Coakes, S., & Steed, L. (2001). *SPSS analysis without Anguish. Version 10.0*. Wiley.

Criado-Gomis, A., Iniesta-Bonillo, M., & Cervera-Taulet, A. (2018). Sustainable entrepreneurial orientation within an intrapreneurial context: Effects on business performance. *International Entrepreneurship and Management Journal, 14*(2), 295–308.

De Marchi, V. (2012). Environmental innovation and R&D cooperation: Empirical evidence from Spanish manufacturing firms. *Research Policy, 41*(3), 614–623.

De Marchi, V., & Grandinetti, R. (2013). Knowledge strategies for environmental innovations: The case of Italian manufacturing firms. *Journal of Knowledge Management, 17*(4), 569–582.

Díez-Vial, I., Belso-Martínez, J. A., & Martín-de-Castro, G. (2023). Extending green innovations across clusters: HOW can Firms Benefit most? *International Regional Science Review, 46*(2), 149–178.

Droste, N., Hansjürgens, B., Kuikman, P., Otter, N., Antikainen, R., Leskinen, P., Pitkänen, K., Saikku, L., Loiseau, E., & Thomsen, M. (2016). Steering innovations towards a green economy: Understanding government intervention. *Journal of Cleaner Production, 135*, 426–434.

Eiadat, Y., Kelly, A., Roche, F., & Eyadat, H. (2008). Green and competitive? An empirical test of the mediating role of environmental innovation strategy. *Journal of World Business, 43*(2), 131–145.

Expósito-Langa, M., Tomás-Miquel, J. V., & Molina-Morales, F. X. (2015). Innovation in clusters: Exploration capacity, networking intensity and external resources. *Journal of Organizational Change Management, 28*(1), 26–42.

Frantzen, D. (2000). Innovation, international technological diffusion and the changing influence of R and D on productivity. *Cambridge Journal of Economics, 24*(2), 193–210.

George, D., & Mallery, P. (2003). *SPSS for windows step by step: A simple guide and reference11.0 update*. Allyn & Bacon.

Godin, B. (2004). The obsession for competitiveness and its impact on statistics: The construction of high-technology indicators. *Research Policy, 33*(8), 1217–1229.

González-Masip, J., Martín-de-Castro, G., & Hernández, A. (2019). Inter-organisational knowledge spillovers: Attracting talent in science and technology parks and corporate social responsibility practices. *Journal of Knowledge Management, 23*(5), 975–997.
Guo, Y., Wang, L., & Yang, Q. (2020). Do corporate environmental ethics influence firms' green practice? The mediating role of green innovation and the moderating role of personal ties. *Journal of Cleaner Production, 266*, 122054.
Hatzichronoglou, T. (1997). *Revision of the high-technology sector and product classification.* OECD Publishing.
Horbach, J. (2008). Determinants of environmental innovation-new evidence from German panel data sources. *Research Policy, 37*(1), 163–173.
Howaldt, J., & Kopp, R. (2012). Shaping social innovation by social research. In H.-W. Franz, J. Hochgerner, & J. Howaldt (Eds.), *Challenge social innovation* (pp. 43–55). Springer.
Ibáñez, J., & Álvarez, P. (2022). *Industria Manufacturera: Informe Sectorial 2022.* CaixaBank Research. https://www.caixabankresearch.com/sites/default/files/content/file/2022/04/20/91184/is-industria-2022-cast_web.pdf
IVIE. (2021). *Economía Circular en la región Comunitat Valenciana, España 2020 REDUCES-rethinking sustainable development in European regions by using circular economy business models.* https://innoecotur.webs.upv.es/wp-content/uploads/2022/06/GVA-UPV-IVE-Estado-del-arte-E.C.-en-la-CV.pdf
Kraus, S., Burtscher, J., Vallaster, C., & Angerer, M. (2018). Sustainable entrepreneurship orientation: A reflection on status-quo research on factors facilitating responsible managerial practices. *Sustainability, 10*(2), 444.
Khan, E. A., & Quaddus, M. (2015). Development and validation of a scale for measuring sustainability factors of informal microenterprises—A qualitative and quantitative approach. *Entrepreneurship Research Journal, 5*(4), 347–372.
Kiron, D., Unruh, G., Reeves, M., Kruschwitz, N., Rubel, H., & ZumFelde, A. M. (2017). Corporate sustainability at a crossroads. *MIT Sloan Management Review, 58*(4).
Kruskal, W. H., & Wallis, W. A. (1952). Use of ranks in one-criterion variance analysis. *Journal of the American Statistical Association, 47*(260), 583–621.
Lee, J. W., Kim, Y. M., & Kim, Y. E. (2018). Antecedents of adopting corporate environmental responsibility and green practices. *Journal of Business Ethics, 148*(2), 397–409.

Liu, A. Z., Liu, A. X., Wang, R., & Xu, S. X. (2020). Too much of a good thing? The boomerang effect of firms' investments on corporate social responsibility during product recalls. *Journal of Management Studies, 57*(8), 1437–1472.

Markwald, R. (2004). Intensidade tecnologica e dinamismo das exportações brasileiras. *Revista Brasileira de Comércio Exterior, 79*(2), 3–11.

Mbanyele, W., Huang, H., Li, Y., Muchenje, L. T., & Wang, F. (2022). Corporate social responsibility and green innovation: Evidence from mandatory CSR disclosure laws. *Economics Letters, 212*, 110322.

Moneva-Abadía, J. M., Gallardo-Vázquez, D., & Sánchez-Hernández, M. I. (2019). Corporate social responsibility as a strategic opportunity for small firms during economic crises. *Journal of Small Business Management, 57*(52), 172–199.

Moulaert, F., & Nussbaumer, J. (2005). Defining the social economy and its governance at the neighbourhood level: A methodological reflection. *Urban Studies, 42*(11), 2071–2088.

Moyano Fuentes, J., Jiménez Delgado, J. J., & Rodríguez Martínez, A. (2019). Territorial agglomerations and corporate social responsibility: The role of science and technology parks. *International Journal of Entrepreneurship and Innovation Management, 23*(2), 180–203.

Mulgan, G., Tucker, S., Ali, R., & Sanders, B. (2007). *Social innovation: What it is, why it matters, how it can be accelerated*. University of Oxford, Young Foundation.

Mumford, M. D. (2002). Social innovation: Ten cases from Benjamin Franklin. *Creativity Research Journal, 14*(2), 253–266.

Neumann, T. (2021). The impact of entrepreneurship on economic, social and environmental welfare and its determinants: A systematic review. *Management Review Quarterly, 71*(3), 553–584.

Nicholls, A., Simon, J., & Gabriel, M. (2015). *Introduction: Dimensions of social innovation.* New Frontiers in Social Innovation Research. Palgrave Macmillan.

Oduro, S., Maccario, G., & De Nisco, A. (2022). Green innovation: A multidomain systematic review. *European Journal of Innovation Management, 25*(2), 567–591.

OECD [Organisation for Economic Co-operation and Development]. (2003). *Science, technology and industry scoreboard. Spain.* https://stip.oecd.org/stats/SB-StatTrends.html?i=C_INDEX&v=3&t=2002,2003&s=OECD,ESP

OECD [Organisation for Economic Co-operation and Development]. (2017). *Indicadores de la OCDE de Ciencia, Tecnología e Industria 2017—La Transformación Digital: España*. https://www.oecd.org/spain/sti-scoreboard-2017-spain-spanish.pdf.

Parrilli, M. D., Balavac-Orlić, M., & Radicic, D. (2023). Environmental innovation across SMEs in Europe. *Technovation, 119*, 102541.

Peiró-Signes, Á., Segarra-Oña, M. del V., Miret-Pastor, L., & Verma, R. (2011). Eco-innovation attitude and industry's technological level-an important key for promoting efficient vertical policies. *Environmental Engineering and Management Journal, 10*(12), 1893–1901.

Pohlert, T. (2014). The pairwise multiple comparison of mean ranks package (PMCMR). *R Package, 27*.

Porter, M. E., & Van der Linde, C. (1995). Toward a new conception of the environment-competitiveness relationship. *Journal of Economic Perspectives, 9*(4), 97–118.

Segarra-Ciprés, M., Bou-Llusar, C., & Roca-Puig, V. (2012). Exploring and exploiting external knowledge: The effect of sector and firm technological intensity. *Innovation, 14*(2), 203–217.

Santamaría, L., Nieto, M. J., & Barge-Gil, A. (2009). Beyond formal R&D: Taking advantage of other sources of innovation in low- and medium-technology industries. *Research Policy, 38*(3), 507–517.

Schneider, A. (2015). Reflexivity in sustainability accounting and management: Transcending the economic focus of corporate sustainability. *Journal of Business Ethics, 127*(39), 525–536.

Sinha, A. K., Mishra, A. K., Manogna, R. L., & Prabhudesai, R. (2022). Examining the determinants of small firms' performance in India. *International Journal of Productivity and Performance Management, 71*(6), 2496–2533.

Thompson, V. (1965). Bureaucracy and innovation. *Administrative Science Quarterly, 5*, 1–20.

Tunzelmann, N., & Acha, V. (2005). Innovation in 'low-tech' industries. *In The Oxford Handbook of Innovation* (pp. 407–432). Oxford University Press.

Van Wijk, J., Zietsma, C., Dorado, S., de Bakker, F. G. A., & Martí, I. (2019). Social innovation: Integrating micro, meso, and macro level insights from institutional theory. *Business & Society, 58*(5), 887–918.

Vallet-Bellmunt, T., Fuertes-Fuertes, I., & Flor, M. L. (2022). Reporting sustainable development goal 12 in the Spanish food retail industry. An analysis based on Global Reporting Initiative performance indicators. *Corporate Social Responsibility and Environmental Management, 30*(2), 695–707.

Weng, H. H. R., Chen, J. S., & Chen, P. C. (2015). Effects of green innovation on environmental and corporate performance: A stakeholder perspective. *Sustainability, 7*(5), 4997–5026.

Westley, F., & Antadze, N. (2010). Making a Difference: Strategies for Scaling Social Innovation for Greater Impact. *The Innovation Journal: The Public Sector Innovation Journal, 15*(2), 2–20.

Yao, S., Song, Y., Yu, Y., & Guo, B. (2021). A study of group decision-making for green technology adoption in micro and small enterprises. *Journal of Business and Industrial Marketing, 36*(1), 86–96.

Yao, Y., Ling, Y., & Xu, Y. (2023). Technology-oriented M&A, market reaction and innovation output. *Nankai Business Review International, 14*(3), 400–424.

Zawislak, P. A., Fracasso, E. M., & Tello-Gamarra, J. (2018). Technological intensity and innovation capability in industrial firms. *Innovation & Management Review, 15*(2), 189–207.

Zeng, J., Pagàn-Castaño, E., & Ribeiro-Navarrete, S. (2022). Merits of intercity innovation cooperation of environment-friendly patents for environmental regulation efficiency. *Technological Forecasting and Social Change, 180*, 121404.

Zhao, N., Liu, X., Pan, C., & Wang, C. (2021). The performance of green innovation: From an efficiency perspective. *Socio-Economic Planning Sciences, 78*, 101062.

Agglomeration Environments to Enhance CSR Strategies: A Tourism District Approach Towards Sustainability

Esther Poveda-Pareja, Bartolomé Marco-Lajara, Mercedes Úbeda-García, Encarnación Manresa-Marhuenda, and Luis Antonio Millán-Tudela

1 Introduction

CSR and its impact on society remain overlooked in the literature. Indeed, it has traditionally been studied from the business-case approach (Barnett et al., 2020; Hafenbrädl & Waeger, 2017; Margolis & Walsh, 2003), where the search for economic outcomes prevails as one of the most analysed issues. This chapter establishes the foundations of a new theoretical framework that will help tourism SMEs overcome their main barriers when they try to develop CSR strategies and sheds light on the effects that CSR activities exert on the societies where they are developed. To contribute to the CSR societal approach, we combine two traditionally studied perspectives that have been analysed from different perspectives within management area, namely the CSR

E. Poveda-Pareja (✉) · B. Marco-Lajara · M. Úbeda-García ·
E. Manresa-Marhuenda · L. A. Millán-Tudela
University of Alicante, San Vicente del Raspeig, Spain
e-mail: esther.poveda@ua.es

E. Poveda-Pareja et al. (eds.), *The Strategic Paradigm of CSR and Sustainability*, Palgrave Studies in Governance, Leadership and Responsibility,
https://doi.org/10.1007/978-3-031-58889-1_5

approach and a specific location decision, concretely, the agglomeration approach through the Industrial District (ID) theory in order to understand CSR's effects on local societies. Both research lines place a great deal of importance to the context and the location characteristics. The choice of context for the analysis of CSR has been proposed as a key factor from both the sector point of view (Kong et al., 2020) and the location point of view (Ding et al., 2019). The ID theory considers that location in a geographical area is the essence of the concept, which means that focusing on a specific sector and concrete regions would be advisable (Becattini, 1990; Marshall, 1930). This chapter reflects on the growing importance of society in the field of tourism due to the real and potential impact of the sector at the global level. The sector could be considered one of the most responsible for environmental and societal damage, and at the same time one that has great potential to reduce such damage. Furthermore, since it is a very dynamic and complex sector, it is important to analyse its specific characteristics in order to develop efficient CSR strategies (Hatipoglu et al., 2019). To reach our objectives, the chapter is divided into 2 sections. The first section discusses the theoretical foundations of CSR and its evolution towards a focus on social impact. It also covers the main limitations traditionally faced by tourism SMEs when developing these strategies. After underlining the drawbacks of the traditional approach to CSR and stressing the need to move it towards a societal approach, we introduce the second section, which is focused on an explanation of how location, specifically TDs, is proposed as an optimal solution to the limitations presented in the first section and how it can be used to strengthen the impact of CSR on local communities.

2 Literature Review

CSR for Society—A Change of Focus

The Foundations of CSR

Since the emergence of CSR, which at the academic level dates back to the mid-twentieth century, the literature has developed in different directions, from the more sceptical vision towards social practices in the field of management (Friedman, 1970), to those that defend its effectiveness in improving the economic results of an organisation (Chrisman & Carroll, 1984). Many researchers, both contemporary with the pioneering visions of CSR Bowen (1953), and subsequently, have worked on definitions of the phenomenon, leading to a large amount of ambiguity around the concept (Bansal & Song, 2017). This ambiguity comes not only from the wide range of definitions of CSR, but also from the numerous lines of research that have sprung from it, making a single definition unviable (Okoye, 2009). Thus, authors such as Frynas and Yamahaki (2016) state that CSR can be studied from an inter-organisational approach, for which they recommend the Resource Based View and the Agency Theory, while they also suggest the possibility of a more external approach through the Stakeholder Theory (ST) and the Institutional Theory (IT). In this chapter we take an external approach, analysing theories based on the relationships between firms and the society around them. From this perspective, CSR can be the result of social relations and norms, in which external actors play a key role in transmitting to companies generally accepted values and ideas about the responsibilities that companies must assume when seeking social legitimacy.

The ST emerged from dissatisfaction with the then current ideology that revolved around a single interest group (shareholders). Freeman (1984) defended the need to consider the demands and needs of all the firm's interest groups (employees, customers, suppliers, society in general, government, among others). In a later study, Freeman et al. (2017) stress the need, in the new digital era, to include new interest groups in the classic model, once again demonstrating the utility of the approach as a way for firms to create value while interacting responsibly with the characteristic society of each time period.

The IT refers to the collection of values, paradigms, or social norms that influence firms in certain sectors to achieve the required legitimacy (Jennings & Zandbergen, 1995). The two theories have been jointly analysed. Lee (2011) demonstrated that a firm's relationship with society depends both on interest groups and on the institutional context. Along similar lines, Tolmie et al. (2020) proposed that the consideration of interest groups by firms could have positive or negative effects on the institutional pressure—CSR development relationship, reflecting the complementariness between the two theories.

Although it is true that the above theories have enabled links between business and society, from the academic point of view they are largely focused on explaining the influence of interest groups or the institutional context on the firm, in order that firms develop their CSR actions or strategies (Famiyeh et al., 2020).

Additionally, we can briefly mention the reasons why firms have decided to adopt CSR, with the aim of understanding the *raison d'etre* of these practices. Firm size has a positive relationship with CSR (Baumann-Pauly et al., 2013; Brammer & Millington, 2006). This effect is especially relevant for SMEs (Santos, 2011), in line with authors that consider that SMEs can be exponents of sustainability (Ţigu et al., 2016; Apospori, 2018). The age of the firm also positively influences CSR (Çera et al., 2020). Another well-studied factor is the influence of the characteristics of the management team on CSR, due to the presence of women (Claver-Cortés et al., 2021), sustainability orientation (Figueroa-Domecq et al., 2022), or the existence of committees responsible for social and environmental issues (Godos-Díez et al., 2018). Some authors consider that a firm's orientation towards CSR is determined by the existence of a formal strategic plan and the development of a humane culture (Kalyar et al., 2013) or through the levels of transparency, justice, ethical culture, and organisational engagement (Mory et al., 2016, 2017). Additionally, another influencing factor could be the individual knowledge and level of involvement around CSR on the part of managers (Aguinis & Glavas, 2012; Dobbs & Staden, 2016).

Both the perspective from which the ST and the IT have been studied and the classic perspective of CSR denote the need to incorporate new visions to resolve the inverse relationship, that is, how CSR affects society in general, abandoning the traditional perspective focused on internal aspects of the organisation. This will be developed in the following section.

CSR and Its Impact on Society

There is a clear call from academia about the need to focus CSR studies on their impact on the society in which they are developed (Gaither et al., 2018; Kotler & Lee, 2006), due to the lack of these type of studies (Naeem & Welford, 2009; Rowe et al., 2014). To some extent, we can even consider it paradoxical that although many researchers recognise the need to respect society and include societal impact in their definitions of CSR, they have only focused their analyses on the relationship between CSR and economic results or firm reputation (Juliasari et al., 2019; Park et al., 2014). Reviewing the work of Margolis and Walsh (2003), we see that firms, apart from seeking profit, has for centuries had additional responsibilities, leading to a paradigm shift that encompasses the conflict of interest between economic and social goals.

This chapter is based on CSR definitions that include its impact on society in general or, more precisely, on certain communities. We are in line with Yashchyshyna et al. (2020), considering CSR as the way in which firms, through individual actions, can contribute to a more global strategy of sustainable development, combining the search for profits with concern for the social and environmental effects of their activities and stressing CSR as an influencing tool for the community.

Along these lines, Brueckner and Mamun (2010) propose abandoning the capitalist view of CSR in order to adopt a more legitimate stance that prioritises CSR in the company's strategic objectives and protects the social interests that the economic perspective does not include. To this end, the authors refer to Porter and Kramer (2006), whose theory of shared value links the long-term goals of a company with the aim of community well-being. In this vein, Juliasari et al. (2019) recognise the moral responsibility of companies towards their local communities, because their activities have consequences on society, both positive and negative.

From this social approach, we analyse a series of studies that have empirical evidence on the phenomenon in general and, more precisely, on the context of tourism. The impact of CSR on local communities, through increased employment, educational or socioeconomic improvements (Kumari et al., 2017), the health and physical condition of certain social groups and their communities (Riggin et al., 2019), or even happiness levels (Chia et al., 2020) have been highlighted. Other researchers develop systematic frameworks to measure the effects on society (Idemudia & Osayande, 2018), or evaluate direct and indirect relationships between CSR and community well-being (Rela et al., 2020), showing the benefits that strategic CSR can create for the communities (Fordham et al., 2018).

Indeed, there are CSR models based on logical sequences of effects that lead to long-term effects on communities and ecosystems (Barnett et al., 2020). In this sense, it is important to reconsider the roots of corporate governance, reorienting the perspective of CSR analysis towards the study of its impacts on society, which would encourage companies to effectively put their promises into practice. In this sense, Wood (2010) explicitly recommends:

> Refocusing on stakeholders and society and crossing the disciplinary barriers in the name of CSP (corporate social performance) may be just what is needed to invigorate and sustain CSP scholarship and to discover the results that will be truly meaningful to corporate managers and their many stakeholders. (p. 76)

But, as we have been able to show through our review, CSR does not fit all contexts equally; thus, it is advisable to focus on how to promote its impact through the tourism activity. In this sense, Walmsley and Partington (2014), consider that labour costs help generate wealth and should not be seen as costs to be minimised. This would allow attention to be placed on the impact of tourism on society, in this case, by improving the labour conditions for tourism employees.

Other authors focus on testing how certain tourism CSR programmes improve quality of life and well-being in their local communities. Rakhmanissazly et al. (2018) show that the implementation of the "Green Belt Lubuk Kertang" programme, which promoted ecotourism in three regions of Indonesia, will reduce deforestation and improve local social and environmental conditions while Hatipoglu et al. (2019) design a model which, through an analysis of the unresolved social problems of a community, determines the type of tourism best adapted to the locally available culture and resources, and how to contribute to sustainable development through the help provided by SMEs.

Chilufya et al. (2019), on their side, introduce a new component, the role of the tourists as CSR promoters at destinations, defending the novel concept of Tourist Social Responsibility. This concept refers to tourists' demands that hotels become more involved with their local communities, contributing directly to local development. On their side, Rahmawati et al. (2019) believe that CSR in tourist destinations encourages the adaptation capacity of local communities and that this capacity will help increase community resilience levels, strengthening their climate change problem solving skills.

Additionally, Uduji et al. (2019) analyse the impact of a CSR programme (General Memorandum of Understandings) carried out by Multinational Oil Companies in collaboration with clusters of various communities of the Niger Delta in Nigeria. The programme was carried out in an area in which cultural tourism is one of the main economic pillars. The authors demonstrate that the implication promoted by the programme among the young rural population in terms of artisan craftwork (the main economic foundation of cultural tourism), would be low, which implies a limited capacity on the part of the local government of each community to reach the desired levels of equality and cultural change. As a result, they propose that a Cluster Development Board oversee carrying out the integration of the young rural population in artisanal activities, supporting the promotion of indigenous knowledge in these areas.

So, the way forward is clear: society, society, and society. Having a clear focus on society will help companies make the most of their CSR strategies. The key is to achieve this change of focus through an evolving thought process: (1) we need to know the main barriers for CSR in tourism; (2) we need to carry out that change of focus through a societal approach that helps companies, not only overcome their difficulties when developing CSR, but also achieve higher impacts initially on their respective communities and finally on society as a whole.

Barriers for CSR in Tourism SMEs

Now that we have addressed the change of focus to a social impact approach, we would like to offer a brief overview of the most studied traditional limitations, barriers, or constraints that SMEs face when they try to develop CSR, to establish a logical motive that explains why this change is needed. The objective of this chapter is to focus on the solutions rather than on the issues, so this section will briefly summarise these factors in the tourism sector. The traditional business-case focus has led to CSR programmes that are not only socially ineffective but are often not put into practice, as firms are incapable of solving certain limitations. To solve this problem, we have made a review of the literature to highlight the main barriers to CSR faced by tourism firms (Table 1).

Two of the problems faced by firms when implementing CSR are first, the above-mentioned barriers and second, the gap between what firms promise and what they actually do (Font et al., 2012). In the case of SMEs, a prevailing type of firm in tourism, they will face the largest amount of difficulties when implementing CSR (Manente et al., 2015). In this sense, little is known on how to promote CSR in SMEs (Murillo & Lozano, 2009), making it more important to clarify objectives, create synergies, and organise firms' efforts on society as a whole.

Table 1 Main limitations of tourism SMEs to develop CSR at the individual level

Main CSR barriers for SMEs	Authors
Lack of time	Kusyk and Lozano (2007)
Efforts needed to assess and implement it	Bohdanowicz (2005)
High investments and operational costs required	Bramwell and Alletorp (2001) and McNamara and Gibson (2008)
Lack of awareness and knowledge of sustainability and what CSR is and implies for tourism (among managers)	Sheldon and Park (2011), Garay and Font (2012), Sampaio et al. (2012), Font et al. (2016)
Lack of skills and competences about CSR	Manente et al. (2015)
Lack of momentum from stakeholders	Garay et al. (2018)
Lack of trust (for the expected results from those practices)	Garay et al. (2018)
Lack of resources	Coles et al. (2013)
Technical barriers, top management, and organisational barriers	Bohdanowicz et al. (2011)
Expense barriers	Frey and George (2010)
Infrastructure, age, and type of property	Wells et al. (2016)
Operational timeframe	Mair and Jago (2010)
Fear of bureaucracy	Apospori et al. (2012)
Difficulty to associate informal CSR actions with formal CSR efforts	Apospori et al. (2012)
Objective (related to the specific character of the hotel industry) and subjective barriers (barriers faced by hotels' stakeholders)	Bugdol et al. (2019)

Source Own elaboration

A Contextual Approach as an Enhancer of CSR Society Perspective

Location Approach

The choice of a context for the current study comes from both the sector approach (Kong et al., 2020) and the location approach (Ding et al., 2019). Authors such as Dey et al. (2018) have already shown the importance of firm location as a strong predictor of environmental management and CSR practices within SMEs. Following this same line,

Claver-Cortés et al. (2021) highlighted the importance of conducting a more in-depth examination of the role played by location in the development of CSR.

The previous section has highlighted how the tourism sector, through its CSR actions, can have a positive impact on societies as long as companies opt for a societal approach and abandon their traditional exclusive focus on economic results. However, companies in the sector face several barriers (detailed above) that may prevent them from fulfilling this approach. In this respect, the analysis of the barriers faced by SMEs in developing CSR has revealed a lack of studies on how factors or drivers linked to certain contexts can increase the development and real implementation of CSR. To this end, we turn to theoretical research lines that may explain the influence of location on CSR. Apart from the IT approach, which we discussed earlier, we should look at General Systems Theory (GST), which has become known as a "Skeleton of Science", acting as a general theoretical framework shared among various disciplines (Boulding, 1956). Boulding (1956) shows that the relationship between an individual (of any type but emphasising corporations or firms) and its environment conditions its behaviour, due to the relationships generated in the location between the individual and other elements. This will affect, among other theories, Management Science and will generate a move away from traditional models focused on the maximisation of profits towards more integral models in which communication, among other factors, plays an essential role. Along this line, Bueno (2010) considers that "organisations are social systems composed of variables of different types whose relationships are very complex" and points out that a lack of control over knowledge management would lead to failure of the organisational system.

The GST approach has also been adopted to achieve sustainable objectives. One example is Geels (2004), who proposes an analysis of the differences between various types of innovation systems and the evolution of sectorial innovation systems towards sociotechnical systems. While the sectorial innovation system approach is centred on knowledge development and pays less attention to social impacts and transformations, the sociotechnical system approach is based on achieving social functions, abandoning the exclusive focus on innovations in favour of including their functionality. Guo et al. (2018) attempt to explain the existence of dependent relationships between certain agents to reach green growth objectives, and to this end they adopt the GST approach (considering interactions between economy, population, resources, environment, and policies for the green growth of a given region).

Following this approach, Redding (2020) concludes that social progress can be achieved through competitive production in areas such as IDs, employing the complex adaptive systems approach. The relationship between the GST and the industrial district theory was previously analysed by other authors (Asheim et al., 2011; Cooke, 2008). We agree with Asheim et al. (2011), who consider Marshall (1930; Marshall & Marshall, 1879) as the essential antecedent of innovation systems. Asheim et al. (2011) highlight the growing interest in social innovation systems and make a distinction between regional and national innovation systems, promoting a debate on social, institutional, and economic processes at the regional level. They stress that national innovation systems arise to explain the economic performance and competitiveness of nations, whereas the regional innovation approach emerges later to indicate that geographical proximity plays an essential role in the generation of positive externalities related to knowledge and innovation.

Within this line, it is important to the common and distinct aspects of regional innovation systems and IDs (Asheim et al., 2011), highlighting that both perspectives analyse social and economic cooperative relationships between public and private actors. In terms of differences, while a cluster is linked to a concrete region, this does not necessarily occur with networks. Furthermore, we can conclude that regional innovation systems have a broader vision than clusters or IDs, which partially explain the suitability of adopting a district/cluster approach in the tourism context to increase the real impacts on local communities, given the contextual dependence of CSR. Among all the agents that form an ID, the institutions that provide technical support and information (technology centres, research institutes, universities, business associations, and inter-business organisations) should be highlighted, whose role is fundamental in the generation and transmission of knowledge to companies (Marco-Lajara et al., 2019).

Accordingly, we will briefly cover this concept below, as well as the positive externalities that may be generated in an ID context to later direct it towards the study of the social impact of tourism districts.

Tourism Districts as Agents of the Societal Approach

In this study we start from Becattini's (1990) original definition of ID defining it as a "socio-territorial entity which is characterized by the active presence of both a community of people and a population of firms in one naturally and historically bounded area where a permanent network of relationships between its agents takes place and where firms achieve improved aggregate performances due to the district effect". In this chapter, we broaden this definition to include the tourism context, highlighting the vision of Marco-Lajara et al. (2016), who consider the TD as "areas where tourism firms concentrate geographically around resources demanded by tourists, becoming important agglomerations of firms and institutions where knowledge externalities are generated".

To achieve the interconnection between CSR and the societal approach through the agglomeration lens, we highlight the vision of Santos (2014) as one of the most relevant given that the author stresses the need to consider a broader conception of CSR, through the combined actions of different actors (among which she names civil society, firms, and local authorities), as well as the creation of CSR networks that provide greater levels of sustainability. To develop this idea, the author begins with the concept of the CSR cluster (Zadek, 2004) and territorial SR (Argiolas et al., 2009), which allow her to conclude that CSR gains importance in a context of coordinated stakeholder networks, which we can directly relate with the concept of the TD. Several studies have found motives that favour the integration of tourism into ID theory (Marco-Lajara et al., 2019). Thus, Petric and Mrnjavac (2003) state that the tourism sector would benefit from advantages derived from an ID approach, and Bello and Kamanga (2020) consider that the different forms of sustainable tourism depend on the social and environmental context in which they are developed. Stoddart et al. (2020) demonstrate that sustainable tourism can be increased through the creation of tourism networks, with all these visions forming a breeding ground that perfectly fits the characteristics of a TD.

Along with the above perspectives, we have developed a summary of the main positive externalities that can be created in TDs, whose consecution would not only lead SMEs to overcome the barriers to CSR, but also to increase the effects on local communities. We base this on Bell's (2005) approach, classifying the effects identified in the literature that are generated in these environments into two groups: direct and indirect (see Table 2).

All the effects highlighted in Table 2 can have positive effects on local communities and thus contribute to the goal of achieving greater social impact through firms' CSR practices, even though these factors have traditionally been analysed from a competitive or economic paradigm.

TDs as Enhancers of CSR in Tourism Companies

Besides being able to extrapolate the effects of Table 2, traditionally analysed under an economic or competitive paradigm, to the creation of value for local societies and communities, in this section we highlight the literature that has specifically examined how a TD can promote such responsible actions.

Some of the more advanced visions in the societal perspective suggest the approach proposed in this chapter, that is, establishing a relationship between TDs and their effects on sustainable destinations or communities. The ability to enhance to a greater or lesser extent the positive or negative impacts of tourism may depend on the way in which local actors organise and interact with each other to jointly achieve the development of a region (Cunha & Cunha, 2005). Murillo and Lozano (2009) analyse how networks between intermediate organisations and companies can promote CSR in tourism SMEs. At the same time, DeBoer et al. (2017) find that the greater the number of competing companies that adopt CSR practices, the greater the predisposition to adopt environmental practices.

More recent studies continue to defend the localisation approach for sustainable practices in tourism (Bello & Kamanga, 2020; Ferrer-Roca

Table 2 Positive externalities generated in TD environments which help increasing the impact of CSR on local communities

	Analysing authors
Direct effects	
1. Agglomeration economies	Suppliers attaining efficient scale (Scott, 1992)
2. Direct observation of competitors	(Harrison et al., 1996; Rogers, 1995)
3. Isomorphism or mimetic attitude	– Firms that observe may try to mimic others in order to generate innovation (March, 1994) – Organisations inside a cluster tend to model themselves on other organisations (develop processes of isomorphism) due to the knowledge and information available that facilitate homogeneity (Tan, 2006) – Within a cluster, there is a collective identity among the actors of the "Who are we?" type that explains its way of understanding the industry and how it forms relationships within and outside the cluster, as well as how it reacts to environmental changes (Staber & Sautter, 2011)
4. Aspects related to the creation or exploitation of knowledge	– Exploit collective knowledge (Marshall, 1930; Paniccia, 1998). Knowledge Spillovers (Becattini, 1990) – Exchange and generation of specific technical knowledge (Marco-Lajara et al., 2016, 2018)

(continued)

Table 2 (continued)

	Analysing authors
5. Innovation	– Higher levels of innovation (Harrison, 1994) or generation of radical innovation through bridging and bonding capital effects inside cultural tourism clusters (Martínez-Pérez et al., 2019) – Higher levels of innovation due to the relationships with core agents (tacit and valuable knowledge) and peripheral agents (overcome initial knowledge barriers) (Elche et al., 2018) or due to trust relationships (Fernando & Long, 2012)
6. Network-based effects	Increase of social interaction (Harrison, 1992)
7. Access to resources	– Better access to information than other firms (Bianchi & Bellini, 1991; Pouder & St. John, 1996) – Possibility to exploit common resources (Marco-Lajara et al., 2017)
8. Existence of support systems	Institutions and rules (Becattini, 1990; Testa et al., 2012)
9. Internationalization	Increase the level of internationalization and attraction of foreign investment (Marco-Lajara et al., 2017)
10. Risk reduction	Possibility of sharing risks with other firms in their operations (Camisón et al., 2020)
11. Financial conditions	Access better marketing financial conditions (Camisón et al., 2020)
12. Control of opportunistic practices	Integrated lines of production and services (organized around the tourism product they constitute) that create close control over opportunism among partners (Crotts & Turner, 1999)

(continued)

Table 2 (continued)

	Analysing authors
13. Prestige and reputation	The cooperative atmosphere reduces inappropriate information (Elche et al., 2018)
Indirect effects	
1. Type of network in the district	– Managerial networks: Expose managers to a tacit flow of knowledge and useful information (Bell, 2005) – Institutional network: Opportunities to hear industry news (Bell, 2005)

Source Own elaboration

et al., 2021; Maté-Sanchez-Val & Teruel-Gutierrez, 2022). Thus, Bello and Kamanga (2020) state that the different forms of sustainable tourism depend on the social and environmental context where they are developed, while Stoddart et al. (2020) demonstrate that sustainable tourism could be increased through the creation of tourism networks. On the other hand, Moshe (2021) has shown that networks (ego-networks) are essential for tourism microenterprises to be able to face barriers such as lack of resources or skills. Moreover, Maté-Sanchez-Val and Teruel-Gutierrez (2022) highlight the role of geographical location in areas with a high concentration of green hotels as a driving factor for greater development of sustainable practices in hotels since they have close examples that can serve as a reference for successful practice.

Thus, Russo and Segre (2009) introduced the concept of Creative Tourism Districts, which would generate creative knowledge and embed it into the local community and its relational system. This would be difficult to copy by other companies and would help create an environment of quality, innovation, and flexibility as a new vision of sustainable tourism.

Petric and Mrnjavac (2003), on their side, defend the concept of sustainable development in an area through what they call locally embedded destinations, while Grimstad (2011) explains how institutional contexts in different TDs could favour or hinder the sustainability of a district. Finally, Kabanova and Vetrova (2017) hold that TDs help,

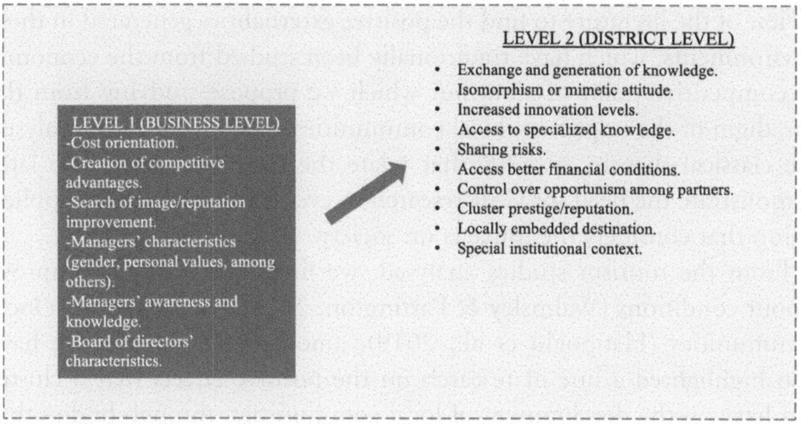

Fig. 1 Multilevel theoretical model (*Source* Own elaboration)

among other effects, to improve the quality of life of local communities by producing: (a) increased employment; (b) better conditions to solve social problems; (c) better image for the area; (d) development of more advanced business structures; (e) improved innovation levels.

Consequently, we have made an initial attempt at a theoretical multilevel approach, responding to the proposals of Frynas and Yamahaki (2016) around the inclusion of multilevel methodologies to study CSR that provide richer knowledge than studies based on a single level and explain how TDs can help companies overcome the barriers to CSR, and more importantly, increase the impact on local communities (see Fig. 1).

3 Discussion and Conclusions

In the present chapter we have made a theoretical contribution to the existing literature on CSR from the societal approach in the field of management. More precisely, we have developed a multilevel model which combines two theories that have traditionally been studied separately (CSR and ID) in tourism. To this end, we have taken the concept of the TD, which was developed and justified by pioneering authors in the field (Marco-Lajara et al., 2016), and we have made an exhaustive review of the literature to find the positive externalities generated in these environments, which have traditionally been studied from the economic or competitive point of view, but which we propose studying from the paradigm of the impact on local communities. Initially we have analysed the classical theories of CSR that relate the firm with society to later demonstrate the need for CSR research to evolve towards a more applied vision that considers the impacts on society.

From the tourism studies analysed, we find that CSR can improve labour conditions (Walmsley & Partington, 2014) or conditions in local communities (Hatipoglu et al., 2019), among other effects. We have also highlighted a line of research on the positive effects that a cluster can have on the development of local communities, through bodies that coordinate CSR actions (Uduji et al., 2019). This final contribution is of special relevance to our analysis, as is Moshe (2021), who recently indicated the essential role of networks to help tourism SMEs overcome the barriers to CSR. The authors above highlight the specific barriers found in the tourism sector, which can be alleviated through a TD approach. As an example, the problem of lack of knowledge or skills of CSR issues could be solved by the positive externalities generated in the TD, such as direct observation of competitors, isomorphism, and the creation of joint exploitation of knowledge. Consequently, we have focused our analysis on the elaboration of a complete list of factors that help firms effectively develop their CSR strategies, as long as they know how to properly exploit the advantages of being located in a TD, which will increase their impact on their local communities.

From this chapter, we can derive future lines of research such as the application of the theoretical model to an empirical study to test its effectiveness as well as the generalisation of the conclusions. The development of the model has allowed us to see that many studies under the societal approach have focused on the effect on small communities in developing countries. We propose to expand the field of study to include TD communities in developed countries which, despite achieving the desired level of competition, lack effective ways to achieve the social impacts demanded by today's society.

References

Aguinis, H., & Glavas, A. (2012). What we know and don't know about corporate social responsibility: A review and research agenda. *Journal of Management, 38*(4), 932–968.

Apospori, E. (2018). Regional CSR policies and SMEs' CSR actions: Mind the gap-the case of the tourism SMEs in Crete. *Sustainability, 10*(7), 2197.

Apospori, E., Zografos, K. G., & Magrizos, S. (2012). SME corporate social responsibility and competitiveness: A literature review. *International Journal of Technology Management, 58*(1–2), 10–31.

Argiolas, G., Cabras, S., Dessi, C., & Floris, M. (2009). Building innovative models of territorial governance. *Journal of Place Management and Development, 2*(3), 178–210.

Asheim, B. T., Smith, H. L., & Oughton, C. (2011). Regional innovation systems: Theory, empirics and policy. *Regional Studies, 45*(7), 875–891.

Bansal, P., & Song, H. C. (2017). Similar but not the same: Differentiating corporate sustainability from corporate responsibility. *Academy of Management Annals, 11*(1), 105–149.

Barnett, M. L., Henriques, I., & Husted, B. W. (2020). Beyond good intentions: Designing CSR initiatives for greater social impact. *Journal of Management, 46*(6), 937–964.

Baumann-Pauly, D., Wickert, C., Spence, L. J., & Scherer, A. G. (2013). Organizing corporate social responsibility in small and large firms: Size matters. *Journal of Business Ethics, 115*, 693–705.

Becattini, G. (1990). The Marshallian industrial district as a socio-economic notion. In F. Pyke, G. Becattini, & W. Sengenberger (Eds.), *Industrial districts and inter-firm cooperation in Italy* (pp. 37–51). International Institute for Labor Studies.

Bell, G. G. (2005). Clusters, networks, and firm innovativeness. *Strategic Management Journal, 26*(3), 287–295.

Bello, F. G., & Kamanga, G. (2020). Drivers and barriers of corporate social responsibility in the tourism industry: The case of Malawi. *Development Southern Africa, 37*(2), 181–196.

Bianchi, P., & Bellini, N. (1991). Public policies for local networks of innovators. *Research Policy, 20*(5), 487–497.

Bohdanowicz, P. (2005). European Hotelier's environmental attitudes: Greening the business. *Cornell Hotel and Restaurant Administration Quarterly, 46*(2), 188–204.

Bohdanowicz, P., Zientara, P., & Novotna, E. (2011). International hotel chains and environmental protection: An analysis of Hilton's we care! programme (Europe 2006–2008). *Journal of Sustainable Tourism, 19*(7), 797–816.

Boulding, K. E. (1956). General systems theory—The skeleton of science. *Management Science, 2*(3), 197–208.

Bowen, H. R. (1953). *Social responsibilities of the businessman.* Harper & Row.

Brammer, S., & Millington, A. (2006). Firm size, organizational visibility and corporate philanthropy: An empirical analysis. *Business Ethics: A European Review, 15*(1), 6–18.

Bramwell, B., & Alletorp, L. (2001). Attitudes in the Danish tourism industry to the roles of business and government in sustainable tourism. *International Journal of Tourism Research, 3*(2), 91–103.

Brueckner, M., & Mamun, M. A. (2010). Living downwind from corporate social responsibility: A community perspective on corporate practice. *Business Ethics: A European Review, 19*(4), 326–348.

Bueno, E. C. (2010). El gobierno del conocimiento organizativo: Un análisis interdisciplinar y una realidad multidisciplinar de naturaleza compleja. *Encuentros Multidisciplinares, 14*(36), 18–27.

Bugdol, M., Puciato, D., & Borys, T. (2019). Development of tourism-barriers to shaping and recommendations for further research. *Problemy Ekorozwoju-Problems of Sustainable Development, 14*(2), 157–170.

Camisón, C., Forés, B., Boronat-Navarro, M., & Puig-Denia, A. (2020). The effect of hotel chain affiliation on economic performance: The moderating role of tourist districts. *International Journal of Hospitality Management, 87*, 102493.

Çera, G., Belas, J., Marousek, J., & Çera, E. (2020). Do size and age of small and medium-sized enterprises matter in corporate social responsibility? *Economics and Sociology, 13*(2), 86–99.

Chia, A., Kern, M. L., & Neville, B. A. (2020). CSR for happiness: Corporate determinants of societal happiness as social responsibility. *Business Ethics: A European Review, 29*(3), 422–437.

Chilufya, A., Hughes, E., & Scheyvens, R. (2019). Tourists and community development: Corporate social responsibility or tourist social responsibility? *Journal of Sustainable Tourism, 27*(10), 1513–1529.

Chrisman, J. J., & Carroll, A. B. (1984). SMR forum: Corporate responsibility-reconciling economic and social goals. *Sloan Management Review, 25*(2), 59–65.

Claver-Cortés, E., Marco-Lajara, B., & Poveda-Pareja, E. (2021). CSR in the spotlight: Location and gender as drivers of its development. In G. Martín-de Castro & J. González-Masip (Eds.), *Knowledge Management for corporate social responsibility* (pp. 185–206). IGI Global.

Coles, T., Fenclova, E., & Dinan, C. (2013). Tourism and corporate social responsibility: A critical review and research agenda. *Tourism Management Perspectives, 6*, 122–141.

Cooke, P. (2008). Regional innovation systems: Origin of the species. *International Journal of Technological Learning, Innovation and Development, 1*(3), 393–409.

Crotts, J. C., & Turner, G. B. (1999). Determinants of intra-firm trust in buyer-seller relationships in the international travel trade. *International Journal of Contemporary Hospitality Management, 11*(2/3), 116–123.

Cunha, S. K. D., & Cunha, J. C. D. (2005). Tourism cluster competitiveness and sustainability: Proposal for a systemic model to measure the impact of tourism on local development. *BAR-Brazilian Administration Review, 2*(2), 47–62.

DeBoer, J., Panwar, R., & Rivera, J. (2017). Toward a place-based understanding of business sustainability: The role of green competitors and green locales in firms' voluntary environmental engagement. *Business Strategy and the Environment, 26*(7), 940–955.

Dey, P. K., Petridis, N. E., Petridis, K., Malesios, C., Nixon, J. D., & Ghosh, S. K. (2018). Environmental management and corporate social responsibility practices of small and medium sized enterprises. *Journal of Cleaner Production, 195*, 687–702.

Ding, D. K., Ferreira, C., & Wongchoti, U. (2019). The geography of CSR. *International Review of Economics & Finance, 59*, 265–288.

Dobbs, S., & Van Staden, C. (2016). Motivations for corporate social and environmental reporting: New Zealand evidence. *Sustainability Accounting, Management and Policy Journal, 7*(3), 449–472.

Elche, D., García-Villaverde, P. M., & Martínez-Pérez, Á. (2018). Inter-organizational relationships with core and peripheral partners in heritage tourism clusters: Divergent effects on innovation. *International Journal of Contemporary Hospitality Management, 30*(6), 2438–2457.

Famiyeh, S., Asante-Darko, D., Kwarteng, A., Gameti, D. K., & Asah, S. A. (2020). Corporate social responsibility initiatives and its impact on social license: Some empirical perspectives. *Social Responsibility Journal, 16*(3), 431–447.

Fernando, I., & Long, W. (2012). New conceptual model on cluster competitiveness: A new paradigm for tourism? *International Journal of Business and Management, 7*(9), 75–84.

Ferrer-Roca, N., Weston, R., Guia, J., Mihalic, T., Blasco, D., Prats, L., Lawler, M., & Jarratt, D. (2021). Back to the future: Challenges of European tourism of tomorrow. *Journal of Tourism Futures, 7*(2), 184–191.

Figueroa-Domecq, C., Kimbu, A., de Jong, A., & Williams, A. M. (2022). Sustainability through the tourism entrepreneurship journey: A gender perspective. *Journal of Sustainable Tourism, 30*(7), 1562–1585.

Font, X., Garay, L., & Jones, S. (2016). A social cognitive theory of sustainability empathy. *Annals of Tourism Research, 58*, 65–80.

Font, X., Walmsley, A., Cogotti, S., McCombes, L., & Häusler, N. (2012). Corporate social responsibility: The disclosure–performance gap. *Tourism Management, 33*(6), 1544–1553.

Fordham, A. E., Robinson, G. M., & Van Leeuwen, J. (2018). Developing community based models of corporate social responsibility. *The Extractive Industries and Society, 5*(1), 131–143.

Freeman, E. (1984). *Strategic management: A stakeholder approach.* Cambridge University Press.

Freeman, E. R., Dmytriyev, S., & Strand, R. G. (2017). Managing for stakeholders in the digital age. In A. Rasche, M. Mette, & J. Moon (Eds.), *Corporate social responsibility: Strategy, communication, governance* (pp. 110–135). Cambridge University Press.

Frey, N., & George, R. (2010). Responsible tourism management: The missing link between business owners' attitudes and behavior in the Cape Town tourism industry. *Tourism Management, 31*(5), 621–628.

Friedman, M. (1970). The social responsibility of business in to increase its profits. *The New York Times.* https://www.nytimes.com/1970/09/13/archives/a-friedman-doctrine-the-social-responsibility-of-business-is-to.html

Frynas, J. G., & Yamahaki, C. (2016). Corporate social responsibility: Review and roadmap of theoretical perspectives. *Business Ethics: A European Review, 25*(3), 258–285.

Gaither, B. M., Austin, L., & Schulz, M. (2018). Delineating CSR and social change: Querying corporations as actors for social good. *Public Relations Inquiry, 7*(1), 45–61.

Garay, L., & Font, X. (2012). Doing good to do well? Corporate social responsibility reasons, practices and impacts in small and medium accommodation enterprises. *International Journal of Hospitality Management, 31*(2), 329–337.

Garay, L., Gomis, J. M., & González, F. (2018). El valor de la sostenibilidad como factor de diferenciación en los procesos de intermediación turística: un análisis para el caso de las pymes catalanas. *Cuadernos De Turismo, 41*, 219–248.

Geels, F. W. (2004). From sectoral systems of innovation to socio-technical systems: Insights about dynamics and change from sociology and institutional theory. *Research Policy, 33*(6–7), 897–920.

Godos-Díez, J. L., Cabeza-García, L., Alonso-Martínez, D., & Fernández-Gago, R. (2018). Factors influencing board of directors' decision-making process as determinants of CSR engagement. *Review of Managerial Science, 12*, 229–253.

Grimstad, S. (2011). Developing a framework for examining business-driven sustainability initiatives with relevance to wine tourism clusters. *International Journal of Wine Business Research, 23*(1), 62–82.

Guo, L. L., Qu, Y., Wu, C. Y., & Wang, X. L. (2018). Identifying a pathway towards green growth of Chinese industrial regions based on a system dynamics approach. *Resources, Conservation and Recycling, 128*, 143–154.

Hafenbrädl, S., & Waeger, D. (2017). Ideology and the micro-foundations of CSR: Why executives believe in the business case for CSR and how this affects their CSR engagements. *Academy of Management Journal, 60*(4), 1582–1606.

Harrison, B. (1992). Industrial districts: Old wine in new bottles? *Regional Studies, 26*(5), 469–483.

Harrison, B. (1994). *Lean and mean: The changing landscape of corporate power in the age of flexibility*. Basic Books.

Harrison, B., Kelley, M. R., & Gant, J. (1996). Innovative firm behavior and local milieu: Exploring the intersection of agglomeration, firm effects, and technological change. *Economic Geography, 72*(3), 233–258.

Hatipoglu, B., Ertuna, B., & Salman, D. (2019). Corporate social responsibility in tourism as a tool for sustainable development: An evaluation from a community perspective. *International Journal of Contemporary Hospitality Management, 31*(6), 2358–2375.

Idemudia, U., & Osayande, N. (2018). Assessing the effect of corporate social responsibility on community development in the Niger Delta: A corporate perspective. *Community Development Journal, 53*(1), 155–172.

Jennings, P. D., & Zandbergen, P. A. (1995). Ecologically sustainable organizations: An institutional approach. *Academy of Management Review, 20*(4), 1015–1052.

Juliasari, D., Daniar, R. W., Muniarti, W., Setyobakti, M., & Solihin, M. R. (2019). Community response to corporate social action and impact on company performance. *Journal of Advanced Research in Dynamical and Control Systems, 11*(12), 1–8.

Kabanova, E. E., & Vetrova, E. A. (2017). Cluster approach as tourism development factor. *Journal of Environmental Management and Tourism, 8*(24), 1599–1606.

Kalyar, M. N., Rafi, N., & Kalyar, A. N. (2013). Factors affecting corporate social responsibility: An empirical study. *Systems Research and Behavioural Science, 30*(4), 495–505.

Kong, Y., Antwi-Adjei, A., & Bawuah, J. (2020). A systematic review of the business case for corporate social responsibility and firm performance. *Corporate Social Responsibility and Environmental Management, 27*(2), 444–454.

Kotler, P., & Lee, N. (2006). *Corporate social responsibility—Doing the most good for your company and your cause*. Wiley.

Kumari, S., Sehrawat, A., & Sharma, T. (2017). Corporate social responsibility practices and their impact on the community: A case study of Ambuja Cement Ltd. *Indian Journal of Management, 10*(1), 54–66.

Kusyk, S. M., & Lozano, J. M. (2007). SME social performance: A four-cell typology of key drivers and barriers on social issues and their implications for stakeholder theory. *Corporate Governance, 7*(4), 502–515.

Lee, M. D. P. (2011). Configuration of external influences: The combined effects of institutions and stakeholders on corporate social responsibility strategies. *Journal of Business Ethics, 102*, 281–298.

Mair, J., & Jago, L. (2010). The development of a conceptual model of greening in the business events tourism sector. *Journal of Sustainable Tourism, 18*(1), 77–94.

Manente, M., Minghetti, V., & Mingotto, E. (2015). Corporate social responsibility in the tourism industry: How to improve CSR through reporting systems. In H. Pechlaner & E. Smeral (Eds.), *Tourism and Leisure* (pp. 307–322). Springer Gabler.

March, J. G. (1994). *A primer on decision making: How decisions happen*. Free Press.

Marco-Lajara, B., Claver-Cortés, E., Úbeda-García, M., & Zaragoza-Sáez, P. (2016). Hotel performance and agglomeration of tourist districts. *Regional Studies, 50*(6), 1016–1035.

Marco-Lajara, B., Claver-Cortés, E., Úbeda-García, M., García-Lillo, F., & Zaragoza-Sáez, P. C. (2019). The role of internal knowledge generation and external knowledge acquisition in tourist districts. *Journal of Business Research, 101*, 767–776.

Marco-Lajara, B., Zaragoza-Sáez, P., Claver-Cortés, B., & Úbeda-García, M. (2018). Hotel performance and knowledge sources in Spanish tourism districts. *Current Issues in Tourism, 21*(17), 1988–2013.

Marco-Lajara, B., Zaragoza-Saez, P., Claver-Cortés, E., Úbeda-García, M., & García-Lillo, F. (2017). Tourist districts and internationalization of hotel firms. *Tourism Management, 61*, 451–464.

Margolis, J. D., & Walsh, J. P. (2003). Misery loves companies: Rethinking social initiatives by business. *Administrative Science Quarterly, 48*(2), 268–305.

Marshall, A. (1930). *Principles of economics* (8th ed.). Macmillan.

Marshall, A., & Marshall, M. (1879). *The economics of industry*. Macmillan.

Martínez-Pérez, Á., Elche, D., García-Villaverde, P. M., & Parra-Requena, G. (2019). Cultural tourism clusters: Social capital, relations with institutions, and radical innovation. *Journal of Travel Research, 58*(5), 793–807.

Maté-Sanchez-Val, M., & Teruel-Gutierrez, R. (2022). Evaluating the effects of hotel location on the adoption of green management strategies and hotel performance. *Journal of Sustainable Tourism, 38*(8), 2029–2052.

McNamara, K. E., & Gibson, C. (2008). Environmental sustainability in practice? A macro-scale profile of tourist accommodation facilities in Australia's coastal zone. *Journal of Sustainable Tourism, 16*(1), 85–100.

Mory, L., Wirtz, B. W., & Göttel, V. (2016). Corporate social responsibility strategies and their impact on employees' commitment. *Journal of Strategy and Management, 9*(2), 172–201.

Mory, L., Wirtz, B. W., & Göttel, V. (2017). Corporate social responsibility: The organizational view. *Journal of Management & Governance, 21*, 145–179.

Moshe, Y. J. (2021). Alters & functions: Exploring the ego-networks of tourism micro-firms. *Tourism Recreation Research, 46*(3), 319–332.

Murillo, D., & Lozano, J. M. (2009). Pushing forward SME CSR through a network: An account from the Catalan model. *Business Ethics: A European Review, 18*(1), 7–20.

Naeem, M. A., & Welford, R. (2009). A comparative study of corporate social responsibility in Bangladesh and Pakistan. *Corporate Social Responsibility and Environmental Management, 16*(2), 108–122.

Okoye, A. (2009). Theorizing corporate social responsibility as an essentially contested concept: Is a definition necessary? *Journal of Business Ethics, 89*, 613–627.

Paniccia, I. (1998). One, a hundred, thousands of industrial districts: Organizational variety in local networks of small and medium-sized enterprises. *Organization Studies, 19*(4), 667–699.
Park, J., Lee, H., & Kim, C. (2014). Corporate social responsibilities, consumer trust and corporate reputation: South Korean consumers' perspectives. *Journal of Business Research, 67*(3), 295–302.
Petric, L., & Mrnjavac, Ž. (2003). Tourist destination as a locally embedded system—Analogy between theoretical models of tourist destination and industrial district. *Tourism, an International Interdisciplinary Journal, 51*(4), 375–383.
Porter, M., & Kramer, M. (2006). Strategy and society. The link between competitive advantage and corporate social responsibility. *Harvard Business Review, 84*, 78–92.
Pouder, R., & St. John, C. H. (1996). Hot spots and blind spots: Geographical clusters of firms and innovation. *Academy of Management Review, 21*(4), 1192–1225.
Rahmawati, P. I., Jiang, M., & DeLacy, T. (2019). Framework for stakeholder collaboration in harnessing corporate social responsibility implementation in tourist destination to build community adaptive capacity to climate change. *Corporate Social Responsibility and Environmental Management, 26*(6), 1261–1271.
Rakhmanissazly, A., Permatasari, A. I., & Peranginangin, E. C. (2018). Edcotourism; A coastal management program to improve social economics. In *IOP conference series: Earth and environmental science, 116*(1). IOP Publishing.
Redding, G. (2020). Competitive productivity and the challenge of metastasis under rising societal complexity. *Cross Cultural & Strategic Management, 28*(1), 19–31.
Rela, I. Z., Ramli, Z., Rusdan, M., Mappasomba, M., & Nikoyan, A. (2020). Conceptual model of corporate social responsibility impact on community well-being. *Entrepreneurship and Sustainability Issues, 8*(2), 311–323.
Riggin, B., Danylchuk, K., Gill, D., & Petrella, R. (2019). Social impact of a corporate social responsibility initiative. *Sport, Business and Management: An International Journal, 9*(4), 344–362.
Rogers, E. M. (1995). *Diffusion of innovations* (4th ed.). New York.
Rowe, A. L., Nowak, M., Quaddus, M., & Naude, M. (2014). Stakeholder engagement and sustainable corporate community investment. *Business Strategy and the Environment, 23*(7), 461–474.

Russo, A. P., & Segre, G. (2009). Destination models and property regimes: An exploration. *Annals of Tourism Research, 36*(4), 587–606.
Sampaio, A. R., Thomas, R., & Font, X. (2012). Why are some engaged and not others? Explaining environmental engagement among small firms in tourism. *International Journal of Tourism Research, 14*(3), 235–249.
Santos, M. (2011). CSR in SMEs: Strategies, practices, motivations and obstacles. *Social Responsibility Journal, 7*(3), 490–508.
Santos, M. J. (2014). Theoretical contributions towards rethinking corporate social responsibility. *The Journal of the Iberoamerican Academy of Management, 12*(3), 288–307.
Scott, A. J. (1992). The role of large producers in industrial districts: A case study of high technology systems houses in Southern California. *Regional Studies, 26*(3), 265–275.
Sheldon, P. J., & Park, S. Y. (2011). An exploratory study of corporate social responsibility in the US travel industry. *Journal of Travel Research, 50*(4), 392–407.
Staber, U., & Sautter, B. (2011). Who are we, and do we need to change? Cluster identity and life cycle. *Regional Studies, 45*(10), 1349–1361.
Stoddart, M., Catano, G., Ramos, H., Vodden, K., Lowery, B., & Butters, L. (2020). Collaboration gaps and regional tourism networks in rural coastal communities. *Journal of Sustainable Tourism, 28*(4), 625–645.
Tan, J. (2006). Growth of industry clusters and innovation: Lessons from Beijing Zhongguancun Science Park. *Journal of Business Venturing, 21*(6), 827–850.
Testa, F., Battaglia, M., & Bianchi, L. (2012). The diffusion of CSR initiatives among SMEs in industrial clusters: Some findings from Italian experiences. *International Journal of Technology Management, 58*(1/2), 152–170.
Ţigu, G., Popescu, D., & Hornoiu, R. I. (2016). Corporate social responsibility—A European approach through the tourism SME's perspectives. *Amfiteatru Economic Journal, 18*(10), 742–756.
Tolmie, C. R., Lehnert, K., & Zhao, H. (2020). Formal and informal institutional pressures on corporate social responsibility: A cross-country analysis. *Corporate Social Responsibility and Environmental Management, 27*(2), 786–802.
Uduji, J. I., Okolo-Obasi, E. N., & Asongu, S. A. (2019). Does CSR contribute to the development of rural young people in cultural tourism of sub-Saharan Africa? Evidence from the Niger Delta in Nigeria. *Journal of Tourism and Cultural Change, 17*(6), 725–757.

Walmsley, A., & Partington, S. (2014). A stakeholder approach to working conditions in the tourism and hospitality sector. *Theory and Practice in Hospitality and Tourism Research, 77*(2), 142–143.

Wells, V. K., Smith, D. G., Taheri, B., Manika, D., & McCowlen, C. (2016). An exploration of CSR development in heritage tourism. *Annals of Tourism Research, 58*, 1–17.

Wood, D. J. (2010). Measuring corporate social performance: A review. *International Journal of Management Reviews, 12*(1), 50–84.

Yashchyshyna, I. V., Svider, O. P., Kushnir, O. K., & Konovalova, M. V. (2020). Corporate social responsibility of the enterprise: Shortcomings and social effects for Ukrainian society. *Scientific Bulletin of National Mining University, 1*, 152–157.

Zadek, S. (2004). The path to corporate responsibility. *Harvard Business Review, 82*(12), 125–132.

Sustainable Tourism: Toward a Circular Economy with Transportation as a Key Factor

Yolanda Trujillo-Adriá, María Belén Silva-Cárdenas, Marival Segarra-Oña, and Ángel Peiró-Signes

1 Introduction

The tourism sector generates environmental impacts and can generate tremendous pressure on local resources; besides land use, it necessitates intensive use of water resources, energy, and food, the high generation of waste along with the difficulty of its management in tourist areas due to less separation by users, as well as the continuous growth of nature-associated inland tourism, as well as congestion on roads, noise and air pollution including CO_2 emissions (Florido et al., 2019; Government of Spain, 2020; Kai, 2020). These negative externalities can be tackled by transitioning from the traditional linear economic model into more sustainable practices, pointing out the Circular Economy and Eco-innovation as potential solutions.

Y. Trujillo-Adriá (✉) · M. B. Silva-Cárdenas · M. Segarra-Oña · Á. Peiró-Signes
Universitat Politècnica de València, Valencia, Spain
e-mail: yotruad@etsid.upv.es

E. Poveda-Pareja et al. (eds.), *The Strategic Paradigm of CSR and Sustainability*, Palgrave Studies in Governance, Leadership and Responsibility,
https://doi.org/10.1007/978-3-031-58889-1_6

The circular economy in Spain has been studied as a fundamental basis for the country's economic development (Morató et al., 2017). In the Valencian region, it is especially important and essential in the tourism sector (Conselleria agriculture m. a., 2015); given its relevance in the community, it is critical to the tourism sector (Conselleria agriculture m. a., 2015), its significance to the Valencian economy. In this way, it is interesting to study the incidence of transport in tourism and, more specifically, in the life cycle of the circular economy (Conselleria d'Agricultura D. R., 2018). Tourism cannot be understood without transportation, not only of people, but also of goods. Both are related in different ways based on the approach that is provided. Tourists use other means of transport (car, train, plane, bus, boat, etc.), and there will always be a transfer aspect that directly impacts the tourism sector.

Another perspective is transporting raw materials, mainly food, to catering establishments. The framework is more complex since the relationship with the tourism sector must be studied in conjunction with logistics (UNO, 2021). The transport of goods and the final waste management will necessarily be the object of study in any circular economy model (European Commission, 2018). In this way, we can place the transport sector as a fundamental axis of the study of the circular economy, as it is among those that exert the most significant impact and environmental footprint while being, in turn, one of the least studied in terms of circular economy and that deserves a particular perspective of study that allows it to be associated and related to the life cycle and circular economy models for tourism (Sorin & Einarsson, 2020).

2 Purpose

To help companies in the Valencian tourism sector, especially hotel and restaurant companies, a project called "Innoecotur" has been designed in which the central Valencian universities participate. This work is the result of the first phases of the project.

This work aims to provide a perspective on the importance of the transport sector in tourism that can assist hotel and catering companies in transitioning to a circular business model. Specifically, it aims to identify the primary transport flows that can influence the implementable circular practices across customers' various touchpoints with accommodation and catering services.

3 State of the Art

The circular economy is the system that replaces the "end of life" concept of the existing linear model, promoting the reduction, reuse, recycling, and recovery of materials (Kirchherr et al., 2017).

The Ellen MacArthur Foundation, one of the great contributors to the definition and promotion of the current concept of Circular Economy, defines it: "A circular economy has a restorative and regenerative design and aims to keep products, components, and materials in its maximum usefulness and value at all times, distinguishing between technical and biological cycles. This new economic model seeks to decouple global economic development from consuming finite resources" (EMF, 2015).

The objective of the Circular Economy Action Plan proposed for the European Commission in 2020 is to achieve climate neutrality by 2050 and decouple economic growth from resource use while ensuring the long-term competitiveness of the EU and leaving no one behind, addressing Key Product Value Chains: Electronics and ICT (information and communication technology), Batteries and vehicles, Packaging, Plastics, Textiles, Construction and buildings, Food, water, and nutrients.

Regarding batteries and vehicles, crucial for future mobility, the Commission proposed to revise the rules on end-of-life vehicles to promote more circular business models by linking design issues to end-of-life treatment, considering mandatory recycled content for specific materials of components, and improving recycling efficiency. The Commission also proposes a new regulatory framework for batteries, enhancing the sustainability of the emerging battery value chain for electro-mobility and boosting the circular potential of all batteries (European Commission, 2020).

The advancement of transportation infrastructure in tourism plays a crucial role in enhancing the accessibility of tourist destinations. It lowers travel expenses for tourists and significantly influences their decision-making process. Furthermore, it contributes to developing tourism products within destinations and aids in optimizing the overall spatial structure of tourism (Feng, 2023).

Tourism is a driving force of the Spanish economy, accounting for 2022 for 11.6% of GDP with 155.946 million euros and 9.3% of total employment (INE, 2023). This does not include passenger transportation services by road, rail, maritime or air, vehicle rental, or related leisure, which would increase the weight of the Sector significantly. Nevertheless, the Tourism Sector is one of the priority Sectors for the Spanish Government as proposed in the "Circular Spain 2030. Spanish Circular Economy Strategy" (Government of Spain, 2020), along with Construction, Agri-food, Fishing and Forestry, Consumer goods, Textile and clothing, and Industry.

Global transport CO_2 emissions in 2022 were 7.98 Gt, increased by 2.1% (or 137 Mt), also driven by growth in advanced economies. Nonetheless, emissions would have been another 13 Mt higher if all new electric cars on the road had been typical diesel or gasoline cars. Electric car sales surpassed ten million in 2022, making up over 14% of global sales (IEA, 2022).

The year 2022–2023 stood out due to the introduction of pivotal policies in the European Union and the United States. In 2022, 11 nations joined the Global Memorandum of Understanding (MoU) on Zero-Emission Medium and Heavy-Duty Vehicles, elevating the total number of signatories to 27, including emerging markets and developing economies, as illustrated in Fig. 1. These countries share the collective objective of achieving a 100% market share for zero-emission new trucks and buses by 2040. In March 2023, the European Union adopted new CO_2 standards for cars and vans, requiring a 55% and 50% reduction in emissions of new cars and vans by 2030 compared to 2021, and 100% for both by 2035. The new CO_2 standards in the European Union and the Inflation Reduction Act (IRA) in the United States are anticipated to have a substantial influence on the journey toward achieving zero-emission road transportation, according to the IEA (2023).

Global EV Outlook 2023
Catching up with climate ambitions

Policy developments and corporate strategy

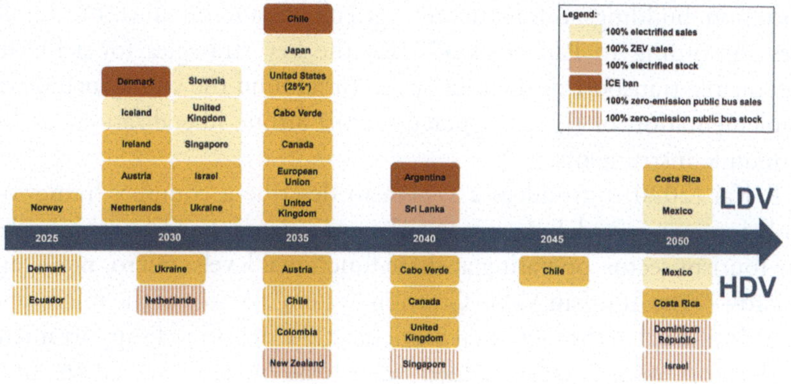

IEA. CC BY 4.0.

* Refers to the share of passenger light-duty vehicle sales accounted for by Advanced Clean Cars II (ACC II) signatories or proposed signatories.

Notes: ICE = internal combustion engine; ZEV = zero-emission vehicle; "electrified" includes hybrid electric vehicles (HEVs) in addition to electric vehicles (EVs) and fuel cell electric vehicles. European Union countries with LDV targets earlier than the EU 2035 target are included separately. Only countries that have legislated or proposed an ICE ban or 100% electrification target have been included. The proposed EU heavy-duty vehicle CO_2 standards include a 100% emission reduction target only for urban buses, and are thus not included in the chart. The Global Memorandum of Understanding (MoU) on Zero-Emission Medium- and Heavy-Duty Vehicles is a pledge and is therefore also not included.

Source: IEA analysis based on announced policies; see the Global EV Policy Explorer for further details.

Zero-emission vehicle targets are now in place in an increasing number of countries, including in emerging markets and developing economies.

Fig. 1 Global zero-emission vehicle mandates and internal combustion engine bans (*Source* International Energy Agency IEA [2023])

An issue tied to tourism revolves around the environmental impact associated with travel, transport in other words. This encompasses aspects such as the alteration of landscapes, interference with ecosystems, the creation of transportation infrastructure, energy consumption, CO_2, and other emissions, primarily driven by local transportation within tourist destinations and the journeys to and from these destinations (Kai, 2020). The amount of emissions from international transport depends on travel mode, fuel efficiency, international business, emission offset initiatives, and externalities for the carbon footprint of global tourism (Pan et al., 2018).

The connection between the tourism activity chain and sustainable development is presented in Fig. 2. To transition to sustainable tourism practices, it is also necessary to "green" or "sustain" various crucial components within the tourism activity chain, including energy, transportation, buildings, infrastructure, agriculture, and intelligent technologies. According to Pan et al. (2018), the key strategies for achieving sustainable transport in the tourism sector around the world include the implementation of (i) green practices, (ii) airline liberalization, or (iii) economic instruments.

P. Kai (2020) introduces a system to describe a complex framework with interconnected links among the core elements and actors within the tourism sector, operating at three functional levels: micro, meso, and macro—"The Tourism Value Creation System". Actors at the micro-level directly add value through their services, at the meso-level support micro-level actors in generating added value, and macro-level actors fulfill specific fundamental functions. Considering all services and providers that directly create or support the tourism service, the system can be illustrated as shown in Fig. 3.

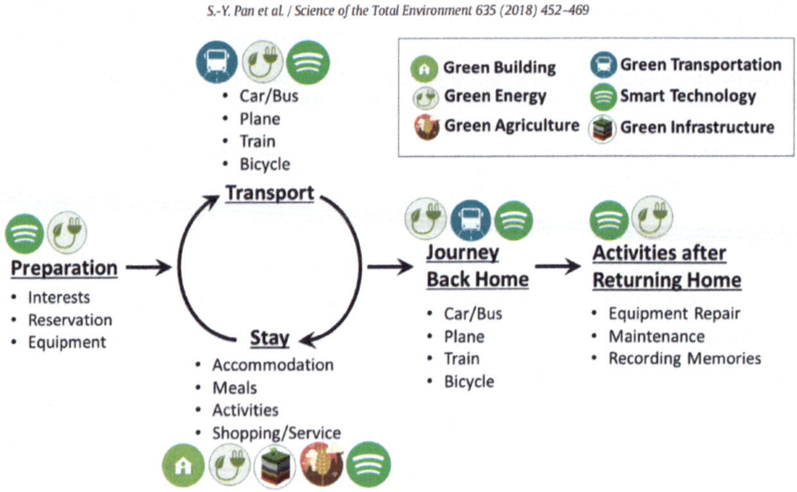

Fig. 2 Tourism chain and its connection with sustainable development (*Source* Pan et al. [2018])

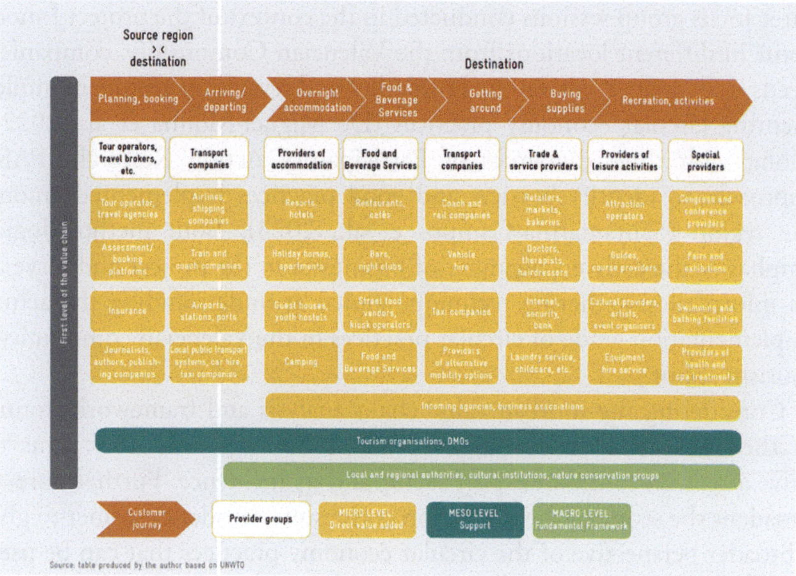

Fig. 3 First value chain level within the tourism value creation system (*Source* P. Kai [2020])

The core of the framework is a "Customer Journey" that describes touchpoints from a tourist traveling from a source region to a destination to identify the services a tourist might demand within the value chain, representing the connection to the possible providers to deliver these services within the supply chain, exhibiting the relevance of Transport in touristic activities (Kai, 2020).

4 Methodology

A qualitative approach was employed to investigate the various aspects of circular activities in the tourism sector to define the extent of transport in the implementation of circular practices.

After conducting a thorough review of existing literature, reports from corporate entities and organizations, as well as insights gathered from three focus group sessions conducted in the context of the project Innoecotur in different locations from the Valencian Community, companies' needs were defined within the hospitality and restaurant sectors in implementing circular economy practices (De Miguel-Molina et al., 2022). Along with three dynamics of Participatory Action Research (PAR) approach, to identify barriers and good practices implemented among the region (Santamarina-Campos et al., 2023). Both methodologies emphasize the early engagement of businesses in the project and serve as an information-gathering technique aimed at understanding the actual implementation grade of circular practices in the Valencian community's tourism sector.

Considering the tourism value chain analysis and frameworks found in the literature review and the project's findings, this work aims to drive attention to the transport sector and its incidence. Furthermore, it broadens the scope of the discussion and results broader customer to give a broader perspective of the circular economy practices that can be used for this purpose by placing the transport flows that can affect them across the customer's touchpoints with accommodation and catering services.

Service process models were utilized to systematically analyze all the stages contributing to a circular model (Geissdoerfer et al., 2017; Kirchherr et al., 2017). To depict the flow of these service processes, the customer journey map (Tueanrat et al., 2021) was employed to provide a more visually engaging representation.

5 Results

Tables 1, 2, 3, 4, 5, 6 and 7 illustrate the primary points of engagement between customers, transport services, and hotel and restaurant services. Furthermore, they outline the possible circular practices that can be implemented while highlighting the transport activities involved in the tourism value chain. Within each process, identify the types of suppliers that can assist companies in adopting these circular practices.

Table 1 Processes associated with the trip (hotels/restaurants)

Process	Elements with which it interacts	Circular practices	Supplier activity
Arrival to the city	Airplane, Cruise, train, bus, private vehicle	Low/0 Carbon print transport, carsharing, electric vehicles	Mobility and sustainable transport
Transfer to the hotel/restaurant	Private vehicle, rented vehicle or public transport (metro, bus, taxi, etc.)	Proposal of sustainable transport through the corporate pages of businesses (e.g. train, electric vehicles, etc.)/Agreements with environmentally responsible transport companies/ Suggest customers to use public transport	Mobility and sustainable transport
Parking	Private vehicle or rented vehicle and parking	Existence of electric chargers in the hotel car park/Bicycles to be rented by hotel guests	Electric vehicle chargers, bicycle manufacturer

Source Authors, based on De Miguel-Molina et al. (2023)

Table 2 Access process (hotels and restaurants)

Process	Elements with which it interacts	Circular practices	Supplier activity
Use of the elevator	Lift	Efficient electrical and lighting systems/ Renewable energy	Renewable energy marketer/LED lighting systems
Use of stairs	Stairs	Efficient electrical and lighting systems/ Renewable energy	Renewable energy marketer/LED lighting systems

Source De Miguel-Molina et al. (2023)

Table 3 Processes associated with the use of the room (hotels)

Process	Elements with which it interacts	Circular practices	Supplier activity
Know the transport services of the hotel	Book or catalog with hotel transport services	Digital system. In case of being physical, be made with paper and recycled materials Shared transport system organized by the hotel for transfers to the main airports and stations as to the main touristic attractions	QR codes, recycled and reusable paper Mobility and sustainable transport
Request for food and drink through room service	Hotel kitchen/ riders (glovo, uber eats, etc.)	Avoid single-use plastics/ Sustainable and reusable utensils and tableware Unify orders of by scheduled times to reduce the transport of food by eating services and the fuel used by motorcycles	Cutlery and utensils made of recycled and reusable materials Food services

(continued)

Table 3 (continued)

Process	Elements with which it interacts	Circular practices	Supplier activity
Personal hygiene	Sanitary hot water, shampoo, soap, lotions, towels, toilet paper, sanitary bags, etc.	Hygiene products developed through sustainable practices/ Transport of sanitary products by sustainable companies (electric vehicles, low carbon print, ...)	Water reuse systems, renewable energy, green chemicals, reusable packaging, green textiles Transport companies of sanitary products
Whitewash	Laundry inside the hotel or outsourced to a supplier	Machines with energy certification/ Minimum water consumption/ Supplier with sustainable standards/Low environmental impact detergent/Reuse of washing water/ If outsourced supplier, electric cars or an environmentally friendly transport	Water reuse systems, use of renewable energy, use of green chemicals External supplier

Source Authors, based on De Miguel-Molina et al. (2023)

6 Discussion

This research constitutes an integral component of the initial stages of the development of the Innoecotur project. Consequently, the hypotheses presented herein are subject to forthcoming validation. Moreover, a portion of the research is actively conducted in collaboration with key stakeholders within the tourism sector through case studies. Consequently, the model outlined in this study has been introduced to hotels

Table 4 Processes associated with table food service (restaurants)

Process	Elements with which it interacts	Circular practices	Supplier activity
Going and return transport	Carsharing, taxi sharing or public transport (metro, bus, taxi, etc.)	Proposal of sustainable transport through the corporate pages of businesses (e.g. bus, metro, electric vehicles, etc.)/Agreements with environmentally responsible transport companies/Suggest customers to use public transport	Mobility and sustainable transport
Food & Beverage suppliers	Inventory	Sustainable suppliers, unification of the buys to reduce the transport	Food suppliers

(continued)

Table 4 (continued)

Process	Elements with which it interacts	Circular practices	Supplier activity
Use of the bathroom	Sanitary water, soap, paper, hand dryer, etc.	Hygiene products developed through sustainable practices/Avoid single-use plastics/ Water consumption reduction systems (e.g. aerators in faucets, pushbuttons in bathroom faucets, small toilet cisterns)/Water consumption awareness/ Transport of sanitary products by sustainable companies (electric vehicles, low carbon print, ...)	Water reuse systems, renewable energy, green chemicals, reusable packaging Transport companies of sanitary products
Cleaning/ waste	Chemicals, gloves, garbage bags, spare cleaning products, produced waste	Use of cleaning products made with sustainable criteria (e.g. easily recyclable garbage bags)/Cleaning chemicals with low impact on the environment/ Reusable or returnable packaging/ Containers to separate waste Used of supplier/ waste companies with sustainable practices	Water reuse systems, renewable energy, green chemicals, reusable packaging, green textiles Transport/waste companies

Source Authors, based on De Miguel-Molina et al. (2023)

Table 5 Check out processes (hotels)

Process	Elements with which it interacts	Circular practices	Supplier activity
Return transfer	Transfer from the hotel to the bus/train station, airport or port	Private vehicle, rented vehicle or public transport (metro, bus, taxi, etc.)	Proposal of sustainable transport through the corporate pages of businesses (e.g. train, electric vehicles, etc.)/ Agreements with environmentally responsible transport companies/Suggest customers to use public transport

Source Authors, based on De Miguel-Molina et al. (2023)

Table 6 Other

Process	Elements with which it interacts	Circular practices	Supplier activity
Bicycles	Bicycles and where bicycles are located	Promote their use/Offer parking for own and guest bicycles/ Manufacture of bicycles using circular practices	Bicycle producers

Source De Miguel-Molina et al. (2023)

and restaurants, with a particular focus on small and medium-sized enterprises (SMEs) and various suppliers operating within their supply chains.

The tables developed as a result of this project are the development of the primary tables outlined in the Innoecotur project (De Miguel-Molina et al., 2022), where the transport was missed. Adding this variable and, in concrete for this work, highlighting only the interference of transport in each one of the topics previously studied before opening the scope to other transport fluxes that were not considered before, as previously mentioned, the transport fluxes have a significant influence (UNO, 2021) in the circular economy in tourism, which is not usually considered when studying this field.

Table 7 Cross-cutting actions to hotels and restaurants

Process	Elements with which it interacts	Circular practices	Supplier activity
Suppliers	Supplier management	Promoting the procurement of goods and services from suppliers that have environmental certificates/ Prioritizing local suppliers/ Collaborating to improve supplier practices	Supplier evaluation and risk analysis systems
Customer and employee awareness	Communication elements	Posters/ Conferences & Events/ Sustainability in Advertising/ Communicating Sustainable Practices/ Integrating Sustainability into Business Strategy	Environmental consulting
Waste management	Containers/Waste collection/Waste management	Waste separation containers/ Return of returnable materials to suppliers/ Composting bin/ Manage the end of life of utensils and furniture	Waste managers

Source Authors, based on De Miguel-Molina et al. (2023)

This work should be understood as the first step in the development of a research Thesis on the importance of transport for the circular economy in tourism, being part of the establishment of the first inputs in the model created for the case study of a touristic city, centered in hotels and service restaurants.

In further studies the relevance of transport will be added to all the value chain proposition, going from the construction of the tourism infrastructure, and the implications of the transport and the circular economy in those, to the final transportation of passengers, as shown in this work.

7 Limitations

The qualitative data collected through the Focus Groups and the Participatory Action Research (PAR) are methodologies with an intrinsic bias related to selecting participants and developing the activity, even though rigor has been ensured in their execution. In this case, participants the stakeholders within the tourism sector (from hotels, restaurants, and providers in each dynamic) that exclusively specific stakeholders within the tourism sector (from hotels, restaurants, and providers in each dynamic) are involved as participants that exclusively pertain to the Valencian Community in Spain. Consequently, it is essential to note that the outcomes of this study may not need to be generalizable to other geographical regions. The findings from this research were utilized to create a platform designed to assist hotels and restaurants in locating a wide range of suppliers offering diverse solutions with various sustainable approaches. This platform aims to facilitate the adoption of circular initiatives within the Valencian Community.

Furthermore, the addition of the transport perspective in this initiative has been studied inside the research group, and it's been developed in the new stages of the project as learned during the development of a doctoral thesis working in the research group.

8 Conclusion

As pointed out during the development of this work, when studying circular economy models, transport is usually missed or reduced to the transport of water waste for recycling. Still, as presented in the results, transport can be studied from other perspectives, such as logistics, which is crucial for tourism and should be implemented in the studies of circular economy as a significant part of it.

Therefore, these results aim to open the scope of the studies and serve as the first stages of the further development of the survey of circularity in transport, with a focus on tourism, that could be opened to other sectors.

Transport fluxes have a significant influence on pollution as, when examined as in the results tables, they can be adapted, optimized, and reduced to reduce pollution but also play a crucial role in the circularity of logistics, as it is needed to present a broader view when talking about circularity and understanding that minimizing the environmental impact of transport is a circular practice that can be achieved by lowering transport fluxes, making them more efficient, or using other types of biofuels, for example.

Understanding that circular practices not only significantly consist of recycling or reusing waste or materials but also the interference of topics not directly related but with significant impact, like transport, should be crucial when facing further research.

For the development of the big picture of the impact of transport on tourism circular practices, it is necessary to develop a more comprehensive study from the bottom to the top. It starts with the building processes of the infrastructure that allows tourism, to the actual transport of the tourists and the logistics of hotels and restaurants. Also, transportation fundamentally, learning other means of transport, such as airplanes and cruises, will show the importance of transportation and its effect on tourism.

References

Conselleria d'Agricultura, D. R. (2018). *Estrategia Valenciana de cambio climático y energía 2030. Generalitat Valenciana*. https://agroambient.gva.es/documents/163279113/163282680/ESTRATEGIA+VALENCIANA+DE+ENERG%C3%8DA+Y+CAMBIO+CLIM%C3%81TICO/4aa4c80d-bc14-4401-a6ac-a40030b5992b

Conselleria d'Agricultura, m. a. (2015). *I Plan Valenciano de Producción Ecológica 2016–2020.* https://agroambient.gva.es/documents/163228750/163232590/I+PLA+VALENCI%C3%80%20DE+PRODUCCI%C3%93%20ECOL%C3%92GICA.pdf/96c71dcb-3b4a-4687-a039-81de15d1b6db

De Miguel-Molina, B., De Miguel-Molina, M., Santamarina-Campos, V., & Segarra-Oña, M. (2022). *Informe de necesidades del sector turístico para la transición a la economía circular*. https://doi.org/10.5281/zenodo.6325274

De Miguel-Molina, M., Sánchez-Planelles, J., Trujillo-Adriá, Y., & Silva-Cardenas, B. (2023). *A model to explore circular economy activities in hotels and restaurants.* https://doi.org/10.4995/BMT2022.2022.15459

Ellen MacArthur Foundation—EMF. (2015). *Towards a circular economy: Business rationale for an accelerated transition.* https://ellenmacarthurfoundation.org/towards-a-circular-economy-business-rationale-for-an-accelerated-transition

European Commission. (2018). *Accompanying the document Proposal for a Regulation of the European Parliament and of the Council setting CO_2 emission performance standards for new heavy duty vehicles.* Commission Staff Working Document Impact Assessment. https://eur-lex.europa.eu/legal-content/EN/TXT/?uri=CELEX%3A52018SC0185

European Commission. (2020). *A new Circular Economy Action Plan For a cleaner and more competitive Europe.* Communication from the Commission to the European Parliament, the Council, the European Economic and Social Committee and the Committee of the Regions. https://eur-lex.europa.eu/legal-content/EN/TXT/?qid=1583933814386&uri=COM:2020:98:FIN

Feng, X. (2023). Coupling and coordinated development of traffic accessibility and regional tourism economy. *Research in Transportation Business & Management, 49*, 101010. https://doi.org/10.1016/j.rtbm.2023.101010

Florido, C., Jacob, M., & Payeras, M. (2019). How to carry out the transition towards a more circular tourist activity in the hotel sector. The role of innovation. *Administrative, 9*(2), 47. https://doi.org/10.3390/admsci9020047

Geissdoerfer, M., Savaget, P., Bocken, N., & Hultink, E. (2017). The circular economy—A new sustainability paradigm? *Journal of Cleaner Production, 143*, 757–768.

Government of Spain. (2020). *España Circular 2030. Estrategia Española de Economía Circular.* https://www.miteco.gob.es/content/dam/miteco/es/calidad-y-evaluacion-ambiental/temas/economia-circular/espanacircular2030_def1_tcm30-509532_mod_tcm30-509532.pdf

IEA. (2022). *Global CO_2 emissions by sector, 2019–2022.* IEA. https://www.iea.org/data-and-statistics/charts/global-co2-emissions-by-sector-2019-2022

IEA. (2023). *Global EV Outlook 2023: Catching up with climate ambitions.* https://iea.blob.core.windows.net/assets/dacf14d2-eabc-498a-8263-9f97fd5dc327/GEVO2023.pdf

INE—Spanish Statistical Office. (2023, December). *INEbase/Services/Hotel Industry and Tourism/Spanish Tourism Satellite Account/Latest data.* INE. https://www.ine.es/dyngs/INEbase/en/operacion.htm?c=estadistica_C&cid=1254736169169&menu=ultiDatos&idp=1254735576863#:~:text=Spanish%20Tourism%20Satellite%20Account.,Latest%20data&text=Tourism%20activity%20reached%20155%2C946%20million,%2C%209.3%25%20of%20total%20employment. Retrieved January 2, 2024.

Jorge-Vázquez, J., & Náñez Alonso, S. (s.f.). *La economía colaborativa en el sector de la movilidad y el transporte: hacia la configuración de un modelo sostenible.* XVIII Congreso Internacional de Investigadores en Economía Social y Cooperativa La Economía Social: herramienta para el fomento del desarrollo sostenible y la reducción de las desigualdades. Tecnocampus de Mataró: UPF. https://www.researchgate.net/publication/344869429_LA_ECONOMIA_COLABORATIVA_EN_EL_SECTOR_DE_LA_MOVILIDAD_Y_EL_TRANSPORTE_HACIA_LA_CONFIGURACION_DE_UN_MODELO_SOSTENIBLE

Kai, P., & Deutsche Gesellschaft für Internationale Zusammenarbeit (GIZ) GmbH. (2020). *The tourism value chain.* https://www.giz.de/en/downloads/giz2020-en-tourism-value-chain.pdf

Kirchherr, J., Reike, D., & Hekkert, M. (2017) Conceptualizing the circular economy: An analysis of 114 definitions, resources. *Conservation Recycling, 127*, 221–232.

Morató, J., Tollin, N., & Jiménez, L. (2017). *Situación y evolución de la economía circular en España.* Fundación COTEC para la innovación.

Pan, S., Gao, M., Kim, H., Shah, K. J., Pei, S., & Chiang, P. (2018). Advances and challenges in sustainable tourism toward a green economy. *Science of the Total Environment, 635*, 452–469. https://doi.org/10.1016/j.scitotenv.2018.04.134

Santamarina-Campos, V., de-Miguel-Molina, M., de-Miguel-Molina, B., & Segarra-Oña, M. (2023). Transición del sector turístico a la economía circular. Necesidades, retos y mejoras. *Zenodo.* https://doi.org/10.5281/zenodo.7706581

Sorin, F., & Einarsson, S. (2020). *Circular economy in travel and tourism: A conceptual framework for a sustainable, resilient and future proof industry transition.* CE360 Alliance. https://www.oneplanetnetwork.org/sites/default/files/from-crm/circular_economy_paper_ce360_fabrice.pdf

Tueanrat, Y., Papagiannidis, S., & Alamanos, E. (2021). Going on a journey: A review of the customer journey literature. *Journal of Business Research, 125*, 336–353.

UNO. (2021). *UNO lidera un proyecto para impulsar la economía circular en la logística y el transporte.* https://www.unologistica.org/uno-lidera-un-proyecto-para-impulsar-la-economia-circular-en-la-logistica-y-el-transporte/

Public Initiatives to Promote CSR and Sustainability: Cooperation as a Key Element for Sustainable Success

Regulation Wave in the Fashion Industry: Media Framing of Legalised CSR

Daria Morozova

1 Introduction

The idea that the era of the fashion industry self-regulation is over has been recently pronounced during the Business of Fashion annual forum for fashion professionals (Kent, 2022a). The speakers have been critical of the fashion companies' claims regarding their commitment to Corporate Social Responsibility (CSR), calling the proclaimed achievements regarding battling air pollution and improving workers' conditions a 'convenient fantasy' (ibid.). The major argument has been that a business company would not sacrifice its revenues by adopting more sustainable, yet more complex and expensive practices (Jaeger & Upadhyay, 2020; Kirchherr et al., 2018). Indeed, greenwashing or the practice of communicating an overoptimistic and misleading message about a company's sustainability-related practices (Torelli et al., 2020) has

D. Morozova (✉)
Glasgow Caledonian University, Glasgow, UK
e-mail: Daria.Morozova@gcu.ac.uk

E. Poveda-Pareja et al. (eds.), *The Strategic Paradigm of CSR and Sustainability*, Palgrave Studies in Governance, Leadership and Responsibility,
https://doi.org/10.1007/978-3-031-58889-1_7

become widespread. According to a recent report by Greenpeace (2023), up to 39% of sustainability claims in the garment, textile and shoe industries might be deceptive (also, Sustainable Brand Platform, 2022). Additionally, the fashion industry is notorious for exploitative labour conditions (Lusty & Richards, 2022) with the coercive labour used for the cotton harvesting in the Xinjiang Uyghur Autonomous Region in China (Zenz, 2023). As a result, there has been a call for tighter regulations for fashion brands (Kent, 2022a).

The voluntary nature of CSR has recently been disputed as more countries have been introducing regulations and standards for CSR policies (Gatti et al., 2019). Similar to greenwashing, false claims by companies have been referred to in research as 'CSR-washing' (Graafland & Smid, 2019). Therefore, the initiatives towards legalisation of CSR have become more common (Berger-Walliser & Scott, 2018). However, there is no agreement on whether this trend has a positive or negative impact on CSR initiatives.

On the one hand, there is evidence that legal regulations can positively impact business practices in both direct and indirect ways (Chen et al., 2018; Peng et al., 2021; Wu et al., 2020). By imposing mandatory regulations, states can put a direct pressure onto the fashion companies pushing them towards greater CSR (Zhang et al., 2022). Previous research (Du & Li, 2020; Habib & Bhuiyan, 2017) argues that financial penalties and a risk of a reputational loss for violating environmental regulations can be an efficient incentive for enterprises. In terms of indirect impact, environmental regulations can steer a brand towards tech-savvy solutions or development of new innovative products that result in higher productivity and business competitiveness (Hu et al., 2020; You et al., 2019).

On the other hand, there is a stream of research that criticises the legalisation of CSR suggesting that it can lead to lower turnover and increase costs for an enterprise (Li & Wu, 2020), add bureaucracy (Rahim et al., 2011) and put companies on the defensive (Halme & Laurila, 2009).

In the fashion industry, tightening regulations are not particularly new. Over a decade ago the focus of this type of legislation was a guarantee of a product's safety. For example, fashion companies needed to follow the so-called Restricted Substances Lists (RSL) to monitor hazardous chemicals harmful for consumers (Greenpeace, 2023). However, recent legislation shifted towards fashion companies' supply chains to monitor labour conditions, breach of human rights, freshwater pollution, etc. In the summer 2021 Israel became the first country to ban the sale of fur for fashion (PETA, 2021). In July 2023, France introduced a new regulation requiring fashion companies to provide a detailed label on a precise climate impact for every sold garment (Eurofins Sustainability Services, n.d.). Further, Germany and Norway have passed due diligence acts demanding companies to demonstrate how they have been working on identifying and eliminating a negative impact (both social and environmental) they might contribute to. Finally, The Netherlands and Britain have initiated an investigation against the fast fashion giants H&M and Boohoo for greenwashing (Deeley, 2022).

Recently, both the US and European Union have been proposing new environmental laws that, if passed, will bring substantial changes into the fashion sector. In New York, the Fashion Sustainability and Social Accountability Act (further the New York Fashion Act) calls for higher transparency of fashion supply chains, meticulous due diligence procedures and strict penalties for environmental harm caused. The EU proposed a 'Strategy for Sustainable Textiles for 2030' focusing on textile circularity and greater brand accountability for produced textile waste.

It is yet unclear whether these proposed regulations will pass, especially given the recent global recession and volatile political landscape. The New York Fashion Act managed to initially secure support by powerful industry players such as Patagonia and Stella McCartney, but a radical 2022 version did not pass the Senate and will need to go through another round. However, if the proposed pieces of legislation eventually pass, they will bring substantial changes into the fashion industry.

Drawing on a concept of framing or portraying a policy issue from a specific perspective while excluding alternative perspectives (Boydstun et al., 2014; Schaffner & Sellers, 2010), this chapter explores how the media has been presenting the New York Fashion Act and other newly proposed regulations to the professional fashion community. Previous studies suggest that news coverage on political and social issues can be a key factor for promoting an agenda for policy changes (Slater et al.,

2008). In addition, media can both increase the relative importance of the discussed issue and alter the public attitudes towards it (ibid.). Finally, by reporting on the opinion of different stakeholders, the media can bring a consensus regarding the policy in question (ibid., p. 367).

A digital platform for fashion professionals (creatives, entrepreneurs and executives) called 'Business of Fashion' (BoF) is selected as a case study. BoF is a B2B resource that provides news on the fashion and lifestyle industry and organises forums to discuss the core developments in fashion. The platform is popular across the US and Europe and offers flexible subscription memberships to its readers.

The rest of the text is structured as follows: first, problematic aspects of CSR in the fashion industry are discussed, followed by a description of the core changes proposed by the pending legislation related to fashion. Next, the relationships between the news coverage and public opinion towards new policies are explained. Further, the concept of framing and the BoF case are presented. Further, the major frames resurfacing on the BoF digital platform between 2021 and 2023 are analysed. Conclusions and some limitations are outlined in the final part of the chapter.

2 What Is Wrong with CSR in the Fashion Industry?

The discussion around CSR in the fashion sector frequently evolves around environmental and human rights issues (Thorisdottir & Johannsdottir, 2020; White et al., 2017). White et al. (2017) argue that actions that fashion brands undertake to promote environmental sustainability and workers' rights are rather aimed at enhancing and protecting a company's reputation (a practice known as greenwashing) (Torelli et al., 2020).

A wave of scandals related to environmental pollution and workers' unfair conditions has shaken the fashion business in recent years (Vänskä & Gurova, 2022) pressing the brands to demonstrate a stronger commitment to social and environmental values. Regardless of this pressure, the existing evidence suggests that fashion brands still fall short of taking corporate social responsibility seriously (CSR) (Thorisdottir &

Johannsdottir, 2020). Though the companies have started to appoint CSR experts, this initiative might look suspicious, taking the overall business model of certain fashion brands. For instance, Boohoo's initiative to appoint Kourtney Kardashian as their 'sustainability ambassador' resulted in a serious backlash from consumers who regard this as misleading and conflictual with genuine sustainability values (Deeley, 2022). However, due to a working business model based on low-cost production of highly fashionable yet short-lived garments, fashion companies lack an incentive to produce clothing responsibly (Thorisdottir & Johannsdottir, 2020).

Environmental Concern

Known as one of the most polluting industries, the fashion sector is responsible for 1.2 billion tons emissions of greenhouse gases, ocean pollution with microplastic, extensive use of coal, water and toxic chemicals (Peleg Mizrachi & Tal, 2022). Critically, it releases billions of tones of textile waste with an expectation of an additional 115,000 km^2 of land used for fibre-growing by 2030 (ibid.).

Various fashion brands have introduced sustainable initiatives, but their authenticity has been questioned. For instance, a common practice is asking consumers to bring their old clothes for recycling. H&M claims that their garments' collecting programme is the world's biggest of its kind (H&M, n.d.). In a nutshell, a consumer is encouraged to bring clothes of any brand they no longer need in exchange of a thank you voucher for their next purchase in H&M. The collected pieces, according to H&M webpage, will be taken over by the brand's business partner to be re-sold in second hands, reused for upcycling if not suitable for re-wear or recycled to make new materials. However, contrary to these claims, a recent investigation by the environmental campaign group Changing Market Foundation (2023), reveals that collected clothes usually end up dumped on the outskirts in Mali, Ghana or another African country.

Another environmentally destructive practice profoundly used by luxury fashion brands is burning their deadstock (Napier & Sanguineti, 2018). The major motivation is to maintain scarcity of luxury garments by preventing them from being sold at discount prices and, thus, maintain their exclusivity (ibid.). Importantly, textile waste and burning as well as manufacturing of clothes occur in developing countries (Abbate et al., 2023). On the other hand, these practices are highly questionable from the perspective of corporate social responsibility compromising the claims of many fashion companies who position themselves as ethical and green (Sagapova et al., 2022).

Working Conditions and Modern Slavery

For the fashion industry, modern slavery and unsatisfying working conditions are still an ongoing issue (Marcketti & Karpova, 2020). Modern-day slavery is a complex term that encompasses a variety of practices, varying from women forced into prostitution to a forced child labour and whole families working for nothing to pay off generational debts (ibid., p. 104).

Modern-day slavery in the fashion industry can be linked, on the one hand, to the phenomenon of globalisation when garment manufacturing shifted from the global West to the global East, mainly to the countries offering lower labour costs (India, China, Pakistan, Bangladesh and Uzbekistan) and weaker regulations (ibid.). Landman (2018) in the analysis of the Global Slavery Index (GSI) suggests there is a connection between a higher GSI and the fashion industry concentrated in the countries with low-cost labour. For example, Clean Clothes Campaign[1] identified such characteristics of modern slavery among Indian fashion factories workers as wage theft, inhuman working conditions and the denial of social security. Uzbekistan is one of the major cotton producers, and it has been reported that over 1 million people could have been forced to work in the fashion sector (Global Slavery Index, 2016).

However, modern slavery in the fashion industry does occur in the West as well: for example, El Monde fashion sweatshop in the US revealed that Thai workers were exposed to inhumane working conditions (Dickson & Warren, 2020). These workers were brought into the

[1] Official webpage of the campaign: https://cleanclothes.org/ (accessed 8 July 2023).

country using fake passports, and these papers were revoked upon arrival into the US. Overall, the Thai workers were forced to work 17–20-hour shifts to sew clothes, completely cut off from the outside word and held captive (ibid.).

To battle the problem, different countries have introduced legislation to control the modern slavery: thus, Australia passed the Australian Modern Slavery Act in 2018, following on from the UK Modern Slavery Act of 2015 and California Transparency in Supply Chains Act of 2012 (Lusty & Richards, 2022). The latter requires both retailers and manufactures doing business in the state and earn over 100 million dollars in annual worldwide sales to report on the steps they undertake to tackle human trafficking and slavery.

Yet, in 2020, Nike and many other global fashion brands were accused of using forced Uyghur labour in China for sourcing their cotton. As a result, consumers boycotted the brands suspected in this practice, whereas European states banned Chinese producers. Meanwhile, Nike released a statement explaining that the company's ties with Xinjiang Uyghur Autonomous Region had been inaccurately reported (Nike XUAR-Statement, 2021). Furthermore, the same statement stipulated that Nike has been trying to improve transparency of its supply chain to guarantee a higher confidence that the materials for their products are responsibly produced (ibid.). Meanwhile, the brand also maintains that due to the fragmentated nature of the global supply chain, it is extremely hard to gain full control over the sourcing and manufacturing of raw materials (ibid.).

Further, Nike provides a Manufacturing map[2] available on their webpage providing detailed information on produced garments (but not raw materials). Regarding labour conditions, Nike's webpage also provides a detailed account on how the brand has been meeting compliance standards, including monitoring risks of modern slavery (Lusty & Richards, 2022). These reports, though informative, do not necessarily simplify consumers' understanding of how sustainable and responsible Nike is. As suggested by Richards et al. (2021), supply chain transparency

[2] Nike's Manufacturing map is available through a link https://manufacturingmap.nikeinc.com/ (accessed 5 June 2023).

that provides wealth of information increases confusion on the ethically driven consumers.

In addition, the fashion sector has become notorious for many other unethical and immoral practices, one of them being harsh conditions for fashion models such as a requirement to stay very thin (Marcketti & Karpova, 2020).

To summarise, CSR in the fashion industry has been traditionally conceptualised through a business model that manufactures clothing with respect to the environment and working conditions (Sagapova et al., 2022). Noteworthy, the responsibility for sustainable improvements has been placed not solely on the brands but also on consumers who have been encouraged to consume more ethically (Zhang et al., 2022). Meanwhile, it is the fashion companies who are expected to adopt marketing techniques that promote greener attitudes among their shoppers—a phenomenon often referred to as 'green marketing' (Goworek et al., 2020). However, this latter practice has been misused by fashion brands who have been promoting pseudo-sustainable garments as ethical and green (Szabo & Webster, 2021). The legislation discussed in this paper is aimed at minimising pseudo-sustainable claims, and the core aspects of these acts will be discussed in the next section.

3 Proposed 'Fashion' Laws

In the US, the Fashion Sustainability and Social Accountability Act, if passed, can make large fashion companies—generating over 100 million dollars per year—will have to map their supply chain across all the production cycle, including all greenhouse gases emissions, chemical use and labour conditions. Additionally, they should explain what they have been doing to reduce the negative impact and to comply with the targets set in the Paris Agreement adopted in 2015 during COP21. In contrast to prior practice when fashion brands were setting the targets themselves, the New York Fashion Act prescribes specific environmental and social targets. For consumers interested in ethical shopping, information on what brands violate the law would be a clear signal which brands to avoid. At the moment, the initial version of the Act did not move forward due to lack of support, otherwise, as suggested by National Law Review (2023) 'would fundamentally alter how the fashion industry operates not only in New York, but globally'.

Next, the Fashion Worker Act was proposed in March 2022. It is aimed at providing stronger labour protection for models and other creatives in the industry such as stylists and makeup artists. According to the proposal, agents will have to pay the creatives within 45 days of a job and ensure there is neither harassment nor discrimination against the worker. Further, agents will be prohibited to change above the market rates for accommodation, and commission fees cannot go over 20%. With penalties up to 3,000 dollars in case of violation, the Fashion Worker Act can improve working conditions for a certain group of the industry workers. This proposed legislation passed was passed by the New York Senate Labor Committee in May 2023, but still needs to be passed through both chambers of the New York State Legislature.

In the European Union, 'Strategy for Sustainable Textiles for 2030' was published in March 2022. Though quite broad, many aspects of these regulations would directly affect the fashion industry through focusing on higher textile circularity and greater responsibility of fashion companies (Paton, 2022). One proposed measure, among others, is a so-called digital product passport that should contain core information of garment's materials (and what share of them can be recycled), durability, reparability, etc. Also, the regulations require businesses to report publicly on the destruction of unsold goods. If passed, these measures are supposed to be put into action by 2025. This regulation, though the same across the EU member states, will prescribe different penalties in individual countries. However, any garment that does not comply with these requirements would not be sold in the EU market, so there will be tremendous consequences for the industry (Paton, 2022). Importantly, the proposed regulations target the companies whose messages about their sustainable principles might be misleading.

In addition, there are other important pieces of legislation currently proposed in the EU, including 'Empowering Consumers in the Green

Transition Directive' and 'Green Claims Directive'[3] targeting greenwashing. However, this paper will focus on those discussed above as they have been under media scrutiny the most.

4 Media and Policy: The Concept of Framing

A link between media coverage and policy has been a research focus in media and political studies, though there is a critique towards the existing concepts due to 'a lack of clarity and consistency' (Nisbet & Huge, 2006, p. 6). In what follows, the relationships between media and policy are discussed, followed by several theoretical frameworks for analysing them. Finally, a case of Business of Fashion, a digital platform for a fashion community will be presented.

Link Between Media and Policy

Looking at the role of the media and its relationships with policy decision-making is not particularly new. Previous research is political science has confirmed that by emphasising a certain agenda, media contributes to shaping public perceptions on the issue in question (Smith et al., 2016; Stephens et al., 2009). Especially when it comes to complex things like technology and innovation, media framing can contribute to better public understanding by providing an expertise of recognisable experts (Smith et al., 2016). Furthermore, media outlets are often uncritically perceived by the public (Grabe et al., 2000; Luhmann, 2000). Overall, though a relationship between public perception and media coverage is multi-layered, a systematic analysis of media coverage can help clarify where a public opinion might be directed, especially when it comes to complex issues like climate change (Stephens et al., 2009). Particularly for those environmental issues that are hard to observe or

[3] More information on this proposed legislation can be found on: https://environment.ec.europa.eu/strategy/textiles-strategy_en (accessed 6 June 2023).

detect, media has confirmed to have a strong impact on the readers (Smith et al., 2016).

Furthermore, previous research suggests that the media can have an impact on information disclosed by companies: thus, it can deter businesses from withholding bad news (An et al., 2020) or prompts them to enhance corporate values (Dang et al., 2021). As far as the media coverage on the environmental issues are concerned, the studies, though limited (see Zhang et al., 2022), argue that the media exhibits control over companies' reporting on their pollution behaviours (Tang & Tang, 2016). Wang and Zhang (2021) in the study of over 500 polluting events in China discover that the companies exposed by the media have been prompted to adhere to greener options. Next, research by Kong et al. (2020) proposes that media coverage increases business efforts to adopt and promote environmental values.

To summarise, the relationships between policy and media have been described as a 'conveyer belt' (Smith et al., 2016, p. 54) with media playing a role as a delivery mechanism for political agenda to the public. Further, Soroka (2002) suggests that media can have an impact on policymakers as they are also relying on media. Meanwhile, Baum and Potter (2008) conclude that the influence is reciprocal: while policymakers might use the media strategically, media can have an impact on legislative decisions as well (Herbst, 2002; Kral, 2003). Kiss' study (2013), for instance, argues that media coverage has influenced the adoption of policies prohibiting certain chemicals in plastic creation. Finally, media reporting on environmental problems can influence business sustainability practices. According to King and Lenox (2001), media helps the public and other stakeholders involved to make more weighted judgements on companies' actions, thus, steering companies towards more sustainable solutions.

Agenda Framing in the Media

Agenda-setting (Edberg & Tarasova, 2016) and framing (Boykoff, 2007; Goffman, 1974) are major theoretical frameworks applied to analyse the relationships between the media, policy and social change. By applying the agenda-setting theory, media studies have explored to what extent the media influences voters' opinions (Bryant & Miron, 2004). These studies are testing a similarity between the top stories and a public's opinion. Agenda-setting framework has confirmed a particularly strong connection between the media reporting and public opinion when it comes to environmental issues that are hard to observe such as pollution, global warming and energy supply (Hansen, 2011; Smith et al., 2016). In this case, the media can 'step in as the main source of information' (Hansen, 2011, p. 170). Additionally, a study by Trumbo (1995) argues that the media agenda-setting can have a stronger effect on policymakers than public.

Framing is one of central concepts in political communication meaning a situation when a policy is portrayed from one specific perspective (Boydstun et al., 2014). As Entman (1993, p. 52) puts it:

> Framing essentially involves selection and salience. To frame is to select some aspects of a perceived reality and make them more salient in a communicating text, in such a way as to promote a particular problem definition, causal interpretation, moral evaluation, and/or treatment recommendation for the item described.

As follows from the quote above, framing, while calling attention to some aspects of an issue in question obscures the others (Smith et al., 2016). Further, Smith et al. (2016, p. 54) summarise the core aspects of using the frame analysis in the following way: 'Framing studies highlight how journalists serve as critical agents within a complex social system, reporting on disturbances within social and natural systems by developing a frame or interpretation of social events'. Therefore, analysing frames (and their dynamic) is crucial for identifying directions towards which a public opinion is steered, especially with spread of digital platform (Boydstun et al., 2014). Existing scholarships admit that framing has had a significant influence on how policy is viewed by the public (Chong & Druckman, 2007) as well as how it is applied in practice (Baumgartner & Mahoney, 2008).

To simplify the analysis, Boydstun et al. (2014) develop a frames' codebook that can be applied for analysing policies and laws: for example, economic frames (costs and benefits); moral frames (duty, honour and anything linked to ethics); fairness and equality (equality between individuals and groups); health and safety; quality of life, etc. The authors suggest applying the frames from the codebook to each of the selected articles and emphasise that a separate article can fall into several frame categories. However, the frame that dominates the storyline of the concrete piece should be regarded as the main one (Boydstun et al., 2014).

In addition to the frames, the tone of the articles is an important characteristic to analyse. Boydstun et al. (2014) differentiate between three types of tones: positive, neutral and negative. For the positive tone, a sympathetic approach to the issue in question is typical, while the negative tone implies an unempathetic and critical portrayal (ibid.). As per the neutral tone, it balances between the positive and negative tones (ibid.). However, previous research also suggests that media coverage of the environmental issues in a 'balanced' tone might lead to downplaying the severity of the climate change problem (Boykoff & Boykoff, 2004).

Business of Fashion

The Business of Fashion (BoF) is an online news platform for the fashion professional community such as creatives, executives and entrepreneurs. Founded in 2007 in London, it was initially financed by its founder Imran Amed, but managed to secure an investment by Index Ventures, LVMH, Carmen Busquets and Felix Capital, who together hold a minority stake in the business (Fashion ABC, n.d.). Regardless of the presence of some powerful fashion industry players among the investors, BoF maintains they are free from the investors' influence and commercial pressure (ibid.).

BoF is positioned as a B2B resource and offers several types of subscription packages.[1] In addition to publishing materials on the fashion industry, BoF provides access to current open vacancies in the fashion industry, organises events such as VOICES (a professional forum that unites major actors from the fashion industry). Furthermore, BoF publishes annually an influential 'The state of Fashion' report co-authored with McKinsey & Company.

In 2018, BoF had 400,000 newsletter subscribers along with over a million visits per month (Fashion ABC, n.d.). The majority of their users were coming from the US, followed by the UK, India and Italy (Similarlab, n.d.). The gender distribution among the users was 60 and 40% for females and males, respectively; and the largest age groups were 25–34 y.o., 18–24 y.o. and 35–44 y.o. (ibid.). Given BoF focus on the professional community, it is a suitable case for analysing framing of the proposed legislation on tightening the control over sustainability and working conditions in fashion.

A search using keywords was carried out on the BoF platform.[4] The search period was set between February 2021 (when the New York Fashion Act was introduced) and November 2023. Based on a keyword search,[5] 36 articles were initially retrieved. However, upon reading the articles, 28 were selected because they were discussing the new laws in detail, while eight remaining were eliminated as the regulations were mentioned in text only sporadically. Though the number of articles is limited, it is noteworthy these are extensive analytical texts. For details on the selected articles, see Table 1.9 in Appendix section.

5 Framing the New Fashion Legislation: The Case of BoF

In this section, five major frames that have emerged in BoF articles are discussed. The analysis starts with the capacity and resource frame that discusses the lack of time left to tackle the environmental and social problems in the fashion industry. Next, the economic frame communicates challenges and opportunities that businesses might face under new regulations. The morality frame raises an issue of accountability in

---

[4] Business of Fashion was accessed using Glasgow Caledonian University subscription.

[5] Keywords for search included 'law', 'regulations', 'act', 'New York Fashion Act', 'bill'.

CSR in fashion. Further, contextual differences between different countries are outlined under the political frame. Finally, the quality-of-life frame brings forward precarity of creative labour in the fashion industry.

Capacity and Resources Frame

According to Boydstun et al. (2014, p. 7), capacity and resource frame is focusing on availability or lack of various resources, including financial, special, physical, etc. Based on BoF articles published between 2021 and 2022, time left for tackling environmental and labour problems in the fashion industry is scarce. Specifically, there is urgency to pass tougher regulations because *'we do not have the leisure of time to get this right'* (Bedat, 2021). Though acknowledging some progress in recent years, BoF texts go as far as stating that the state regulations are an essential—if not the only one left—leverage to drive sustainable change (Bedat, 2021; Kent, 2022b). This frame presented in BoF resonates with a perspective that sustainability is neither luxury nor choice, but a necessity (Sagapova et al., 2022).

The use of this frame is in line with the authoritarian environmental governance paradigm (Xie et al., 2017) that refers to the implementation of environmental regulations to control the environmental behaviour of business enterprises (Zhang et al., 2022). This framework is contrasted against the market-based environmental regulations that encourage businesses to adhere to more environmental practices through market signals such as adjustment of energy prices (Peng et al., 2021).

Economic Frame

BoF discusses economic opportunities that companies might pursue under new regulations. The general tone is positive and highlights that fashion companies will need to innovate in order to stay competitive. For example, the platform cites a fashion expert who maintains that a contemporary and innovative fashion brand cannot be a part of the zeitgeist if ignoring the climate and biodiversity crises (BoF Studio, 2023). Another pro-regulation argument presented in the articles is to create *'a more level playing field for brands already investing in operating more responsibly'* (BoF Studio, 2023). Otherwise, smaller innovative brands that have been operating responsibly are put into misadventures position compared to those companies that manufacture cheaply yet benefit from greenwashing (ibid.).

The articles imply that new legislation will prompt fashion companies to adopt innovative technology, for instance, newer and more sustainable materials (BoF Studio, 2023). Drawing on an example of the fashion companies that started to manufacture using sustainable viscose, BoF suggests that this innovation brought a recognition from consumers (BoF Studio, 2023). The relationship between sustainable practices adopted by a company and its competitiveness has been a popular research topic, though the findings are inconclusive (Hermundsdottir & Aspelund, 2021). Initially, sustainable innovations have been perceived as cost drivers that required high investments yet took a long time to payback (Dey et al., 2019). Meanwhile, recent studies argue that a growing share of companies associate sustainability with higher profitability and efficiency (Bacinello et al., 2019; Cherrafi et al., 2018; Dey et al., 2019).

Interestingly, BoF promotes the idea that the fashion industry is inevitable moving towards tougher regulations (Deeley, 2021; Kent, 2023), so getting adopted to the upcoming changes beforehand will add competitive advantage to business.

Moral Frame

Moral frame is characterised by addressing issues like duty, honour, righteousness or anything connected to ethics and social responsibility (Boydstun et al., 2014). This is the only frame in the analysis that features the negative tone (ibid.). For example, Esponnette (2022) discusses whether the measures stipulated by the New York Fashion Act are enough to enhance sustainability. The author uses a creative metaphor when comparing the proposed measures with an act of killing someone and merely reporting about it: *'Tell people you have taken someone's life and you'll walk away without even a slap on the wrist. Shucks,* *you may even get applause for publicising it. <…> Sound crazy? Well, when it comes to fashion's social and environmental impact, we don't even hold the industry to the standards of this low-bar scenario*' (Esponnette, 2022). Hence, the idea of 'sustainability report' as a positive practice is called into question.

Further, recent research compares business reporting on environmental impact to greenwashing (Torelli et al., 2020). In a similar vein, BoF material argues that there is no hope to stop climate change if accountability of the companies only goes as far as reporting (Deeley, 2021). As a result, tightening regulations in the industry are portrayed as leading to higher accountability (ibid.). Importantly, this moral frame is consistent with other frames adopted by BoF.

The notion of accountability has expanded beyond governmental bodies and is now concerning non-state organisations that affect development—a concept referred to as 'new accountability agenda' (Goetz & Jenkins, 2002). However, fashion companies who report on their sustainable initiatives might employ their own terms and definitions that eventually lead to confusion, and a lot of sustainability-related terms are sloppy (ibid.). The key supporting point towards regulations, as presented by BoF, is that the law will provide rigid and well-defined standards for everyone—something that has been discussed in research as well (Glavič & Lukman, 2007).

Political Frame

Boydstun et al. (2014, p. 7) define the political frame as the one that touches upon any political considerations surrounding the discussion, for example, vote trading, political manoeuvring and lobbing. Recently, there has been a concern over how companies may resort to lobbying to minimise their economic costs (Favotto & Kollman, 2021). Kinderman (2011), for instance, stresses that it has become more challenging to distinguish between genuine ethical behaviour by companies and their lobbying activity.

In February 2023, BoF discusses a record spending on lobbying in the fashion industry in the US (Kent, 2023). BoF links this trend to the unprecedented wave of sustainability-related laws in the country. In 2017, the platform explains, the fashion industry spent an equal amount of money to influence federal lawmakers from passing a border adjustment tax that would have increased the import costs. The article also criticises a local initiative by The Council of Fashion Designers of America (CFDA) who published a series of basic recommendations for 'practical, effective and workable' regulation of environmental sustainability and labour standards (Kent, 2023). However, BoF labels this proposal as yet another attempt by the industry to divert attention from real challenges.

Indeed, Den Hond et al. (2014, pp. 801–806) confirm that companies' CSR and lobbying activity might be in conflict if the same business agrees to decrease its greenhouse gas emissions, yet is lobbying against tighter emission regulations. This contradiction might be damaging for companies' reputations (Lock & Seele, 2016) which resonates with BoF stance on lobbying in fashion: *'(c)ompanies seen to lobby against policies that would further environmental or social goals they've committed to (individually or as members of industry trade groups) face new reputational hazards'* (Kent, 2023).

In contrast, BoF piece on Copenhagen Fashion Week (BoF Studio, 2023) discusses how various industry actors (entrepreneurs, designers, executives and NGO representatives) come together to discuss development of the circular economy model, with particular emphasis on consumers' expectations. For example, BoF cites one of the attendees of the Fashion Week who proposes: *'[By] having an eye-to-eye level conversation between stakeholders — industry, politicians and other stakeholders from research, social aspects, etcetera — I strongly underline the need for us to try to develop such culture within the ecosystem. We need to discuss with each other how can we redesign [the fashion industry]'* (BoF Studio, 2023).

Noteworthy, Knudsen (2017) explores the difference between CSR frameworks in the US and Europe. Specifically, while the US is focusing on the legal framework and regulations, the European context presents 'government-led processes that facilitate discussion and learning among a range of key stakeholders' (p. 179). For the latter framework, a stronger emphasis on consumers' expectations is placed.

Quality-of-Life Frame

In 2023, BoF draws attention to the Fashion Workers Act that is aimed to provide greater protection to creative professionals in the industry, including models. Modelling work, regardless its symbolic value, has been criticised for an extreme precarity. For instance, Wissinger (2007) identifies a risk of a short-term contract with no guarantee of longer employment. Additionally, '(m)odels must be flexible and adapt to peripatetic travel, unpredictable schedules, and a wide variety of situations. Because of the lack of guaranteed work, a model might find him or herself working every day for months, without a break, trying to ride the wave before it ends' (ibid., p. 257).

BoF article (Mzizi, 2023), on the one hand, brings forward several cases when models have been exploited by their agents. These stories, with names of the models or influencers mentioned, vary from non-payment to sexual abuse. Noteworthy, the article does mention agents' defensive position that they are only intermediaries between models and fashion brands and have been unfairly singled out by the proposed act. Yet, the focus is still on a power misbalance between the agents and their models, with a complex hierarchy within the fashion industry critically scrutinised. In the article dating 2023 (Mzizi, 2023), opinions of the industry activists and NGO representatives are mentioned: for example, one of them is quoted saying that fashion is work built on the backs of underprivileged young people. Overall, BoF discussion on labour condition in the fashion sector goes beyond a more established narrative on manufacturing workers (Marcketti & Karpova, 2020).

6 Conclusions

This chapter is looking at the media framing of the proposed fashion legislation on sustainability and labour conditions in the US and EU. For instance, the New York Fashion Act, if passed, will target large fashion corporations with striker rules regarding mapping of the supply chains, adverse impact disclosures and environmental impact reductions. Also, the Fashion Workers Act aims to bring greater protection to industry creatives such as models whose working conditions can be described as precarious. In the EU, a broader legislative scheme that impacts several industries has been introduced; however, the textile waste reduction will be addressed through the digital product passport. Overall, if these regulations pass, the way fashion brands communicate their CSR may change.

While decisions are still pending, this chapter is analysing how the professional media platform 'Business of Fashion' has been framing these laws. Business of Fashion is a B2B digital platform focusing on the industry news for creatives, executives and entrepreneurs. Previous research suggests that media framing can prioritise certain views regarding legislation and promote them to the public (Boydstun et al., 2014). Drawing on the codebook developed by Boydstun et al. (2014), this chapter identifies the core frames on recent fashion-related regulations disseminated by the platform.

Overall, BoF adopts a positive tone towards the proposed laws. Interestingly enough, reinforced control by the state is presented as a necessary leverage for controlling the industry. Progress towards sustainability is portrayed as slow, therefore, urgent measures such as new legislation are seen as desirable. However, a critical tone towards the regulations does appear: specifically, the articles question whether the proposed measures will have any effect on enterprises, apart from making them produce yet another sustainability report. Additionally, the regulations are presented as a unifying document that will set clear boundaries for everyone.

As far as economic frame is concerned, BoF portrays tighter regulations as a trigger for innovative practices that can eventually improve companies' competitiveness. Also, regulating is framed as fair since it might level the market when free riders who have been luring consumers through greenwashing will have to adjust their business models and compete with truly sustainable brands on equal terms.

Contextually, despite a growing sense of urgency regarding the needed shift in the fashion business, there is a variation in legislation across countries: while in the US the proposed measures target the fashion industry directly, the European Union sticks to a more general legal framework aimed at improving Europe's ecological footprint (Paton, 2022).

An acknowledged limitation of this study is the complexity of relationships between media coverage and public perceptions of the phenomenon in question. Due to methodological choices, this study does not suggest any conclusive arguments regarding the actual influence of BoF discourse surrounding the proposed regulations. Furthermore, other important news outlets such as Forbes, Vogue Business and The New York Times could have been included in the analysis. Though recognising these limitations, this paper calls for further investigation into the discussion on the upcoming legislation. Since the New York Act has not yet been passed, understanding the discourse around this act might be important for further understanding of the progress with its enactment.

Appendix

See Table A.1.

Note

1. Further details available on the BoF official webpage: https://www.businessoffashion.com/memberships/packages/ (accessed 6 June 2023).

Table A.1 List of articles selected for analysis, published in business of fashion between June 2021 and November 2023

#	Date of publishing	Article title	Link
1	3 June 2021	Op-Ed | Only Government Can Make Fashion Sustainable	https://www.businessoffashion.com/opinions/sustainability/op-ed-only-government-can-make-fashion-sustainable/
2	15 June 2021	The Sustainability Regulations That Could Reshape Fashion	https://www.businessoffashion.com/articles/sustainability/the-sustainability-regulations-that-could-reshape-the-fashion-industry/
3	7 January 2022	New York Fashion Act to Test Brands' Appetite for Sustainability Regulation	https://www.businessoffashion.com/articles/sustainability/new-york-fashion-act-to-test-brands-appetite-for-sustainability-regulation/
4	18 January 2022	Op-Ed | Why I Support New York's Fashion Act	https://www.businessoffashion.com/opinions/sustainability/op-ed-why-i-support-new-yorks-fashion-act/
5	19 January 2022	Advocacy Groups Push to Toughen New York Fashion Act	https://www.businessoffashion.com/news/topics/advocacy-groups-push-to-toughen-new-york-fashion-act/
6	21 January 2022	Op-Ed | New York's Fashion Act? More Like Fashion Won't Act	https://www.businessoffashion.com/opinions/sustainability/op-ed-new-yorks-fashion-act-more-like-fashion-wont-act/

(continued)

Table A.1 (continued)

#	Date of publishing	Article title	Link
7	25 March 2022	New York Bill Would Give Fashion Models More Labour Protections	https://www.businessoffashion.com/news/workplace-talent/new-york-bill-would-give-fashion-models-more-labour-protections/
8	17 May 2022	The Traceability Tech Aiming to Unlock a More Sustainable Industry	https://www.businessoffashion.com/articles/technology/state-of-fashion-technology-report-sustainability-supply-chain-traceability/
9	3 June 2022	New York's Push to More Tightly Regulate Fashion Lapses into Next Year	https://www.businessoffashion.com/news/sustainability/new-yorks-push-to-more-tightly-regulate-fashion-lapses-into-next-year/
10	8 June 2022	Resale and Rental Companies Band Together to Lobby for Circular Fashion Policies	https://www.businessoffashion.com/news/sustainability/resale-and-rental-companies-band-together-to-lobby-for-circular-fashion-policies/
11	9 September 2022	The Paradox of Kourtney Kardashian Selling Sustainability	https://www.businessoffashion.com/articles/sustainability/boohoo-kourtney-kardashian-barker-sustainability-ambassador-influencer-greenwashing/
12	23 September 2022	Corporate Climate Action Hits Its Limits	https://www.businessoffashion.com/articles/sustainability/corporate-climate-commitments-voluntary-regulation-fashion-sustainability/

(continued)

Table A.1 (continued)

#	Date of publishing	Article title	Link
13	17 November 2022	Patagonia, Reformation Back Toughened New York Fashion Act	https://www.businessoffashion.com/news/sustainability/patagonia-reformation-back-toughened-new-york-fashion-act/
14	2 December 2022	Fashion's Age of Self-Regulation Is Over	https://www.businessoffashion.com/articles/sustainability/end-fashion-self-regulation-greenwashing-labour/
15	5 January 2023	Beyond 'Blah Blah Blah': Fashion's Sustainability Priorities for 2023	https://www.businessoffashion.com/articles/sustainability/2023-sustainability-climate-risk-regulation-circularity-recycling-degrowth-worker-rights/
16	13 January 2023	On Labour Rights, You Get What You Pay For	https://www.businessoffashion.com/articles/sustainability/workers-rights-labour-fashion-h-and-m-gap-purchasing-practices/
17	13 January 2023	Fashion Isn't Ready for the Regulation Coming for It	https://www.businessoffashion.com/articles/sustainability/france-regulation-fashion-law-waste-recycling-transparency-louis-vuitton-gucci-zara-nike/
18	3 February 2023	Fashion Is Spending More to Shape Regulation	https://www.businessoffashion.com/articles/sustainability/fashion-lobby-policy-regulation-sustainability-environment-labour/

(continued)

Table A.1 (continued)

#	Date of publishing	Article title	Link
19	6 February 2023	How Can the Fashion Industry Accelerate Systems Change?	https://www.businessoffashion.com/articles/sustainability/copenhagen-fashion-week-executive-insights-sustainability-innovation-systems-change/
20	16 February 2023	How Can Fashion Rethink the End-of-Life of Products?	https://www.businessoffashion.com/events/sustainability/bof-live-how-can-fashion-rethink-the-end-of-life-of-products/
21	12 April 2023	Activists Renew Push for Fashion Workers' Rights Bill	https://www.businessoffashion.com/articles/sustainability/activists-renew-push-for-fashion-workers-rights-bill/
22	17 April 2023	When Marketing Gets Political	https://www.businessoffashion.com/articles/sustainability/rothys-bottle-bill-new-york-recycling/
23	30 May 2023	In Copenhagen, Regulators and LVMH's Luxury-Only Climate Pact	https://www.businessoffashion.com/articles/sustainability/global-fashion-summit-copenhagen-regulation-louis-vuitton-antoine-arnault/
24	21 July 2023	What if Fashion Went on Strike?	https://www.businessoffashion.com/briefings/marketing-pr/what-if-fashion-went-on-strike/
25	22 August 2023	What Big Brands' Sustainability Reports Won't Tell You	https://www.businessoffashion.com/opinions/sustainability/fashion-sustanability-reporting-wont-tell-you-esg/

(continued)

Table A.1 (continued)

#	Date of publishing	Article title	Link
26	25 August 2023	What American Fashion Wants From Sustainability Regulation	https://www.businessoffashion.com/articles/sustainability/american-fashion-lobby-sustainability-regulation-cfda-aafa-california/
27	15 September 2023	In New York, From Fashion Week to Climate Week	https://www.businessoffashion.com/articles/sustainability/new-york-climate-week-fashion-week/
28	8 November 2023	Millions of Luxury Products Now Come With Unique Digital Passports. Here's What That Means	https://www.businessoffashion.com/articles/technology/millions-of-luxury-products-now-come-with-unique-digital-passports-heres-what-that-means/

References

Abbate, S., Centobelli, P., Cerchione, R., Nadeem, S. P., & Riccio, E. (2023). Sustainability trends and gaps in the textile, apparel, and fashion industries. *Environment, Development and Sustainability*, 1–28.

An, Z., Chen, C., Naiker, V., & Wang, J. (2020). Does media coverage deter firms from withholding bad news? Evidence from stock price crash risk. *Journal of Corporate Finance*, *64*, 101664.

Bacinello, E., Tontini, G., & Alberton, A. (2019). Maturity in sustainable innovation and corporate social responsibility: Implications in business performance. *Brazilian Journal of Management/Revista de Administração da UFSM*, *12*.

Baum, M. A., & Potter, P. B. (2008). The relationships between mass media, public opinion, and foreign policy: Toward a theoretical synthesis. *Annual Review of Political Science, 11*, 39–65.

Baumgartner, F. R., & Mahoney, C. (2008). Forum section: The two faces of framing: Individual-level framing and collective issue definition in the European Union. *European Union Politics, 9*(3), 435–449.

Bedat, M. (2021, June 3). *Op-Ed | Only government can make fashion sustainable*. Business of Fashion.

Berger-Walliser, G., & Scott, I. (2018). Redefining corporate social responsibility in an era of globalization and regulatory hardening. *American Business Law Journal, 55*(1), 167–218.

BoF. (2023, February 16). *How can fashion rethink the end-of-life of products?* Business of Fashion.

BoF Studio. (2023, February 6). *How can the fashion industry accelerate systems change?* Business of Fashion.

Boydstun, A. E., Hardy, A., & Walgrave, S. (2014). Two faces of media attention: Media storm versus non-storm coverage. *Political Communication, 31*(4), 509–531.

Boykoff, M. T. (2007). From convergence to contention: United States mass media representations of anthropogenic climate change science. *Transactions of the Institute of British Geographers, 32*(4), 477–489.

Boykoff, M. T., & Boykoff, J. M. (2004). Balance as bias: Global warming and the US prestige press. *Global Environmental Change, 14*(2), 125–136.

Bryant, J., & Miron, T. (2004). Theory and research in mass communication. *Journal of Communication, 54*(4), 662–704.

Changing Markets Foundation. (2023). *Take-Back Trickery. An investigation into clothing take-back schemes.* https://changingmarkets.org/take-back-trickery/#:~:text=Between%20August%202022%20and%20July,them%20to%20a%20Boohoo%20scheme. Retrieved July 25, 2023.

Chen, H., Hao, Y., Li, J., & Song, X. (2018). The impact of environmental regulation, shadow economy, and corruption on environmental quality: Theory and empirical evidence from China. *Journal of Cleaner Production, 195*, 200–214.

Cherrafi, A., Garza-Reyes, J. A., Kumar, V., Mishra, N., Ghobadian, A., & Elfezazi, S. (2018). Lean, green practices and process innovation: A model for green supply chain performance. *International Journal of Production Economics, 206*, 79–92.

Chong, D., & Druckman, J. N. (2007). Framing public opinion in competitive democracies. *American Political Science Review, 101*(4), 637–655.

Dang, T. L., Huynh, T. H., & Nguyen, M. T. (2021). Media attention and firm value: International evidence. *International Review of Finance, 21*(3), 865–894.

Deeley, R. (2021, June 15). *The sustainability regulations that could reshape fashion.* Business of Fashion.

Deeley, R. (2022, September 9). *The Paradox of Kourtney Kardashian selling sustainability*. Business of Fashion.

Den Hond, F., Rehbein, K. A., de Bakker, F. G., & Lankveld, H. K. V. (2014). Playing on two chessboards: Reputation effects between corporate social responsibility (CSR) and corporate political activity (CPA). *Journal of Management Studies, 51*(5), 790–813.

Dey, B. K., Sarkar, B., Sarkar, M., & Pareek, S. (2019). An integrated inventory model involving discrete setup cost reduction, variable safety factor, selling price dependent demand, and investment. *RAIRO-Operations Research, 53*(1), 39–57.

Dickson, M., & Warren, H. (2020). A look at labor issues in the manufacturing of fashion through the perspective of human trafficking and modern-day slavery. *The Dangers of Fashion: Towards Ethical and Sustainable Solutions*, 103–124.

Du, W., & Li, M. (2020). Assessing the impact of environmental regulation on pollution abatement and collaborative emissions reduction: Micro-evidence from Chinese industrial enterprises. *Environmental Impact Assessment Review, 82*, 106382.

Edberg, K., & Tarasova, E. (2016). Phasing out or phasing in: Framing the role of nuclear power in the Swedish energy transition. *Energy Research & Social Science, 13*, 170–179.

Entman, R. M. (1993). Framing: Toward clarification of a fractured paradigm. *Journal of Communication, 43*(4), 51–58.

Esponnette, B. (2022, January 21). *Op-Ed | New York's Fashion Act? More like fashion won't act*. Business of Fashion.

Eurofins Sustainability Services. (n.d.). *Climate impact labels on clothing becomes law*. https://sustainabilityservices.eurofins.com/news/climate-impact-labels-on-clothing-becomes-law/#:~:text=Environmental%20AGEC%20labelling%20Decree%20in,comply%20in%202024%20and%202025. Retrieved July 8, 2023.

Fashion ABS. (n.d.). *The Business of Fashion*. https://www.fashionabc.org/wiki/the-business-of-fashion/#:~:text=The%20website%20has%20grown%20to,400%2C000%20subscribers%20to%20the%20newsletter. Retrieved July 6, 2023.

Favotto, A., & Kollman, K. (2021). Mixing business with politics: Does corporate social responsibility end where lobbying transparency begins? *Regulation & Governance, 15*(2), 262–279.

Gatti, L., Vishwanath, B., Seele, P., & Cottier, B. (2019). Are we moving beyond voluntary CSR? Exploring theoretical and managerial implications of mandatory CSR resulting from the new Indian companies act. *Journal of Business Ethics, 160*, 961–972.

Glavič, P., & Lukman, R. (2007). Review of sustainability terms and their definitions. *Journal of Cleaner Production, 15*(18), 1875–1885.

Global Slavery Index. (2016). *Global Slavery Index Report*. https://www.oas.org/ext/en/security/crime-prevention-network/Recursos/Multimedios/the-global-slavery-index-2016#:~:text=The%20Walk%20Free%20Foundation's%202016,some%20form%20of%20modern%20slavery. Retrieved July 9, 2023.

Goetz, A. M., & Jenkins, R. (2002). *Voice, accountability and human development: The emergence of a new agenda* (No. HDOCPA-2002-04). Human Development Report Office (HDRO), United Nations Development Programme (UNDP).

Goffman, E. (1974). *Frame analysis: An essay on the organization of experience*. Harvard University Press.

Goworek, H., Oxborrow, L., Claxton, S., McLaren, A., Cooper, T., & Hill, H. (2020). Managing sustainability in the fashion business: Challenges in product development for clothing longevity in the UK. *Journal of Business Research, 117*, 629–641.

Graafland, J., & Smid, H. (2019). Decoupling among CSR policies, programs, and impacts: An empirical study. *Business & Society, 58*(2), 231–267.

Grabe, M. E., Zhou, S., Lang, A., & Bolls, P. D. (2000). Packaging television news: The effects of tabloid on information processing and evaluative responses. *Journal of Broadcasting & Electronic Media, 44*(4), 581–598.

Greenpeace. (2023). *Greenwash Danger Zone. 10 years after Rana Plaza* (Report). https://www.greenpeace.de/publikationen/Greenpeace_Report_Greenwash_Danger_Zone.pdf. Retrieved July 8, 2023.

Habib, A., & Bhuiyan, M. B. U. (2017). Determinants of monetary penalties for environmental violations. *Business Strategy and the Environment, 26*(6), 754–775.

Halme, M., & Laurila, J. (2009). Philanthropy, integration or innovation? Exploring the financial and societal outcomes of different types of corporate responsibility. *Journal of Business Ethics, 84*, 325–339.

Hansen, A. (2011). Communication, media and environment: Towards reconnecting research on the production, content and social implications of environmental communication. *International Communication Gazette, 73*(1–2), 7–25.

Herbst, S. (2002). How state-level policy managers "read" public opinion. In J. Manza, F. L. Cook & B. Page (red.). *Navigating public opinion: Polls, Policy, and the future of American Democracy* (pp. 171–183).

Hermundsdottir, F., & Aspelund, A. (2021). Sustainability innovations and firm competitiveness: A review. *Journal of Cleaner Production, 280*, 124715.

Hu, J., Pan, X., & Huang, Q. (2020). Quantity or quality? The impacts of environmental regulation on firms' innovation–Quasi-natural experiment based on China's carbon emissions trading pilot. *Technological Forecasting and Social Change, 158*, 120122.

Jaeger, B., & Upadhyay, A. (2020). Understanding barriers to circular economy: Cases from the manufacturing industry. *Journal of Enterprise Information Management, 33*(4), 729–745.

Kent, S. (2022a, December 2). *Fashion's age of self-regulation is over*. Business of Fashion.

Kent, S. (2022b, January 7). *New York Fashion Act to test brands' appetite for sustainability regulation*. Business of Fashion.

Kent, S. (2023, February 3). *Fashion is spending more to shape regulation*. Business of Fashion.

Kinderman, D. P. (2011). Why do some countries get CSR sooner, and in greater quantity, than others? The political economy of corporate responsibility and the rise of market liberalism across the OECD: 1977–2007.

King, A. A., & Lenox, M. J. (2001). Does it really pay to be green? An empirical study of firm environmental and financial performance: An empirical study of firm environmental and financial performance. *Journal of Industrial Ecology, 5*(1), 105–116.

Kirchherr, J., Piscicelli, L., Bour, R., Kostense-Smit, E., Muller, J., Huibrechtse-Truijens, A., & Hekkert, M. (2018). Barriers to the circular economy: Evidence from the European Union (EU). *Ecological Economics, 150*, 264–272.

Kiss, S. J. (2013). Legislation by agenda-setting: Assessing the media's role in the regulation of bisphenol A in the US states. *Mass Communication and Society, 16*(5), 687–712.

Knudsen, J. S. (2017). How do domestic regulatory traditions shape CSR in large international US and UK firms? *Global Policy, 8*, 29–41.

Kong, G., Kong, D., & Wang, M. (2020). Does media attention affect firms' environmental protection efforts? Evidence from China. *The Singapore Economic Review, 65*(3), 577–600.

Kral, A. (2003). *Print media impact on state legislative policy agendas*. Louisiana State University and Agricultural & Mechanical College.

Landman, T. (2018). Out of the shadows: trans-disciplinary research on modern slavery. *Peace Human Rights Governance, 2*(2), 143–162.

Li, J., & Wu, D. (2020). Do corporate social responsibility engagements lead to real environmental, social, and governance impact?. *Management Science, 66*(6), 2564–2588.

Lock, I., & Seele, P. (2016). The credibility of CSR (corporate social responsibility) reports in Europe. Evidence from a quantitative content analysis in 11 countries. *Journal of Cleaner Production, 122*, 186–200.

Luhmann, N. (2000). *The reality of the mass media* (p. 1). Stanford University Press.

Lusty, N., & Richards, H. (2022). Modern slavery legislation and the limits of ethical fashion. *Cultural Studies*. https://doi.org/10.1080/09502386.2022.2103165

Marcketti, S. B., & Karpova, E. E. (2020). *The dangers of fashion: Towards ethical and sustainable solutions*. Bloomsbury Publishing.

Mzizi, Y. (2023, April 12). *Activists renew push for fashion workers' Rights Bill*. Business of Fashion.

Napier, E., & Sanguineti, F. (2018). Fashion Merchandisers' Slash and Burn dilemma: A consequence of over production and excessive waste? *Rutgers Business Review, 3*(2).

National Law Review. (2023). *New York's fashion sustainability and social accountability act—Round 2 underway*. https://www.natlawreview.com/article/new-york-s-fashion-sustainability-and-social-accountability-act-round-2-underway. Retrieved July 9, 2023.

Nike XUAR-Statement. (2021). *XUAR-Statement*. https://admin.about.nike.com/media/files/949e2527-4f64-4a37-af44-8467064deb8f/XUAR-Statement.pdf. Retrieved July 9, 2023.

Nisbet, M. C., & Huge, M. (2006). Attention cycles and frames in the plant biotechnology debate: Managing power and participation through the press/policy connection. *Harvard International Journal of Press/Politics, 11*(2), 3–40.

Paton, E. (2022, September 30). The new laws trying to take the anxiety out of shopping. *The New York Times*. https://www.nytimes.com/2022/09/30/fashion/fashion-laws-regulations.html. Retrieved July 6, 2023.

Peleg Mizrachi, M., & Tal, A. (2022). Regulation for promoting sustainable, fair and circular fashion. *Sustainability, 14*(1), 502.

Peng, B., Chen, S., Elahi, E., & Wan, A. (2021). Can corporate environmental responsibility improve environmental performance? An inter-temporal analysis of Chinese chemical companies. *Environmental Science and Pollution Research, 28*(10), 12190–12201.

PETA. (2021). *Breaking: Israel becomes first country ever to Ban Fur*. https://www.peta.org/blog/israel-bans-fur/. Retrieved July 8, 2023.

Rahim, R., Jalaludin, F. W., & Tajuddin, K. (2011). The importance of corporate social responsibility on consumer behaviour in Malaysia. *Asian Academy of Management Journal, 16*(1).

Richards, C., Hurst, B., Messner, R., & O'Connor, G. (2021). The paradoxes of food waste reduction in the horticultural supply chain. *Industrial Marketing Management, 93*, 482–491.

Sagapova, N., Buchtele, R., & Dušek, R. (2022). The Fashion industry and its problematic consequences in the green marketing era a review. In *SHS Web of conferences* (Vol. 135, p. 01011). EDP Sciences.

Schaffner, B. F., & Sellers, P. J. (2010). Winning with words. *The Origins and Impact of Political Framing*.

Similarlab. (n.d.). *The Business of Fashion*. Available at: The Business of Fashion. https://www.similarweb.com/website/businessoffashion.com/#overview. Retrieved July 6, 2023.

Slater, M. D., Long, M., Bettinghaus, E. P., & Reineke, J. B. (2008). News coverage of cancer in the United States: A national sample of newspapers, television, and magazines. *Journal of Health Communication, 13*(6), 523–537.

Smith, H. M., Smith, J. W., Silka, L., Lindenfeld, L., & Gilbert, C. (2016). Media and policy in a complex adaptive system: Insights from wind energy legislation in the United States. *Energy Research & Social Science, 19*, 53–60.

Soroka, S. N. (2002). Issue attributes and agenda-setting by media, the public, and policymakers in Canada. *International Journal of Public Opinion Research, 14*(3), 264–285.

Stephens, J. C., Rand, G. M., & Melnick, L. L. (2009). Wind energy in US media: A comparative state-level analysis of a critical climate change mitigation technology. *Environmental Communication, 3*(2), 168–190.

Sustainable Brand Platform. (2022). *The EU strategy for sustainable textiles*. https://sustainablebrandplatform.com/magazine/market-trend/18/the-eu-strategy-for-sustainable-textiles.html. Retrieved July 9, 2023.

Szabo, S., & Webster, J. (2021). Perceived greenwashing: The effects of green marketing on environmental and product perceptions. *Journal of Business Ethics, 171*, 719–739.

Tang, Z., & Tang, J. (2016). Can the media discipline Chinese firms' pollution behaviors? The mediating effects of the public and government. *Journal of Management, 42*(6), 1700–1722.

Thorisdottir, T. S., & Johannsdottir, L. (2020). Corporate social responsibility influencing sustainability within the fashion industry. A systematic review. *Sustainability, 12*(21), 9167.

Torelli, R., Balluchi, F., & Lazzini, A. (2020). Greenwashing and environmental communication: Effects on stakeholders' perceptions. *Business Strategy and the Environment, 29*(2), 407–421.

Trumbo, C. (1995). Longitudinal modeling of public issues: An application of the agenda-setting process to the issue of global warming. *Journalism and Communication Monographs, 152*.

Vänskä, A., & Gurova, O. (2022). The fashion scandal: Social media, identity and the globalization of fashion in the twenty-first century. *International Journal of Fashion Studies, 9*(1), 5–27.

Wang, K., & Zhang, X. (2021). The effect of media coverage on disciplining firms' pollution behaviors: Evidence from Chinese heavy polluting listed companies. *Journal of Cleaner Production, 280*, 123035.

White, C. L., Nielsen, A. E., & Valentini, C. (2017). CSR research in the apparel industry: A quantitative and qualitative review of existing literature. *Corporate Social Responsibility and Environmental Management, 24*(5), 382–394.

Wissinger, E. (2007). Modelling a way of life: Immaterial and affective labour in the fashion modelling industry. *Ephemera: Theory and Politics in Organization, 7*(1), 250–269.

Wu, W., Liu, Y., Wu, C. H., & Tsai, S. B. (2020). An empirical study on government direct environmental regulation and heterogeneous innovation investment. *Journal of Cleaner Production, 254*, 120079.

Xie, R. H., Yuan, Y. J., & Huang, J. J. (2017). Different types of environmental regulations and heterogeneous influence on "green" productivity: Evidence from China. *Ecological Economics, 132*, 104–112.

You, D., Zhang, Y., & Yuan, B. (2019). Environmental regulation and firm eco-innovation: Evidence of moderating effects of fiscal decentralization and political competition from listed Chinese industrial companies. *Journal of Cleaner Production, 207*, 1072–1083.

Zhang, Y., Zhang, R., & Zhang, C. (2022). Insight into the driving force of environmental performance improvement: Environmental regulation or media coverage. *Journal of Cleaner Production, 358*, 132024.
Zenz, A. (2023). Coercive labor in the cotton harvest in the Xinjiang Uyghur autonomous region and Uzbekistan: A comparative analysis of state-sponsored forced labor. *Communist and Post-Communist Studies, 56*(2), 1–32.

Strategic Planning for a Smart Sustainable City Model: The Importance of Public Administration and Enterprises Cooperation

Inmaculada Martín-Rojo

1 Introduction

The purely materialistic view of the company is now a thing of the past. Today, the medium and long-term survival of a company is linked to the concept of sustainability in a broad sense: environmental, economic, and social.

In this line, Corporate Social Responsibility (CSR) emerges as a voluntary response of companies and institutions in favor of sustainable development, which can be defined as that which "meets the needs of the present without compromising the ability of future generations to meet their own needs" (World Commission on Environment and Development, 1987). Corporate Social Responsibility is the commitment of organizations to contribute to sustainable economic development by working with employees, their families, the local community, and society

I. Martín-Rojo (✉)
University of Málaga, Málaga, Spain
e-mail: icmartin@uma.es

E. Poveda-Pareja et al. (eds.), *The Strategic Paradigm of CSR and Sustainability*, Palgrave Studies in Governance, Leadership and Responsibility,
https://doi.org/10.1007/978-3-031-58889-1_8

at large to improve their quality of life (World Business Council on Sustainable Development, 1998).

Following these approaches, organizations must generate added value for society through their activity, going beyond the restricted vision of achieving maximum economic profit, because even the achievement of maximum profit projected over an unlimited period of time implies guaranteeing the adaptation of the company to its environment, satisfying the expectations of stakeholders, not only in the economic sphere, but also in the social and environmental spheres. Thus, the results of companies should be measured considering three magnitudes: economic, social, and environmental, in order to offer a joint positive value.

If we add to all this the continuous changes in which today's society lives and the new economic movements, we find ourselves with a New Economy whose objective is sustainability and at the same time to improve people's lives with collaborative methods. This so-called New Economy encompasses among others the following aspects (Martín-Rojo, 2018, pp. 107–108):

- Common Good Economy: it proposes new indicators of success for both private and public organizations at the municipal level, considering the importance of implementing tools to create a "Common Good Balance Sheet".
- Collaborative economy: it is based on new information and communication technologies that allow the creation of social networks and portals where people can interact on a massive scale, with or without monetary compensation.
- Circular Economy: it is the economy that is committed to recycling, moving from a linear economy that produces, uses, and throws away, to a circular model in which waste can be used again as raw material.
- Green Economy: aims to generate profitability from environmental protection and preservation.
- Blue Economy: proposed by Gunter Pauli, it goes a step further than the Green Economy, which is sometimes unsustainable from an economic point of view. It is based on the premise that basic needs must be met with the local resources available, creating multiple

benefits, employment, and social capital, in short, offering more with less.

- Economics of Happiness: analyses the effect of macroeconomic fluctuations on people's happiness. This study involves social scientists (sociologists, psychologists, economists) who suggest that, once primary needs are met, policy measures should be oriented toward increasing people's satisfaction, and not just economic growth.

All this justifies and marks the interest of this work to analyze the strategic planning for a Sustainable Smart City model, considering public and private cooperation.

First, a review of the existing literature will be made, and the conceptual framework will be presented. Then, some city models will be analyzed, following the case study methodology. With this information, some guidelines will be given to define what kind of city model we want, to develop a strategic planning; and the variables to be considered in order to carry out a strategic planning for a sustainable city model will be identified. All of this in accordance with the United Nations Sustainable Development Goals for 2030.

Thus, the main contribution of this paper is to identify the variables to be considered, to carry out sustainable and Smart city strategic planning, based on published city index and city case studies and developing some implications for researchers, business manager, and public managers.

2 Conceptual and Theoretical Background

Sustainability City, Smart City, and Smart Sustainable City are unique terms, though they can be interrelated.

The concept of Sustainability Development has been applied to city planning since the early 1990s. Richardson defines sustainable urban development as "a process of change in the built environment which fosters economic development while conserving resources and promoting the health of the individual, the community, and the ecosystem" (1989, p. 14). The strategic process of sustainable urban development seeks to create healthy, livable, and prosperous human environment with minimal demand on resources (water, energy, etc.) and minimal impact on the environment (pollution, toxic waste, etc.). According, a sustainable city strategy is one of many urban planning approaches worthy of implementation to ensure long-term city growth and development (Alshuwaikhat et al., 2022).

The rise of technologies sets up another concept: Smart City. There are many definitions of this term, but one of the most thorough is that a Smart City is "an innovative city that focuses on applying the next generation ICT to all walks of life, and hence performs in a forward-looking and participatory way in governance, economy, people, mobility, environment, and living on the basis of the intelligent combination of endowments and activities of independent and aware citizens, to ensure socio-economic development, quality of life, the intelligent management of natural resources, and the efficient operation of infrastructures and facilities"(Bibri, 2018a, p. 766).

In Smart City models, smart sustainability includes concepts such as the use of renewable energies, sustainable resource management, circular economy, and environmental protection (Della Corte et al., 2017; Ribes & Baidal, 2018). Bulchand-Gidumal (2022) proposes a Smart Destination Wheel framework, and some of the pillars in this Wheel are entrepreneurship & innovation and productivity & employment, regarding enterprises, but not only governance, mobility, infrastructures, education, or health & safe, which are aspects related to Public Administration. It justifies the importance of Public Administration and enterprises cooperation.

The concept of Smart Sustainable Cities has emerged as a result of three global trends: the importance of sustainability, the spread of urbanization, and the rise of Information and Communication Technologies—ICT. It is a new term that has developed in the last decade, alongside the growth of technology, sustainability, and sustainable development concepts (Alshuwaikhat et al., 2022). As expressed by Höjer and Wangel (2015), the interconnection of the concepts: sustainability, urbanization, and ICT has converged under what is labeled "Smart Sustainable City". Accordingly, the term "Smart Sustainable City" is used to describe "a city that is supported by the pervasive presence and massive use of advanced ICT, in connection with various urban systems and domains and how these intricately interrelate and are coordinated to improve economic and societal outcomes" (Bibri, 2018b, p. 4).

Smart Sustainable City is a new emerging concept that combines urban sustainability and smartness, "both aspects should be considered simultaneously. Its emergence can be seen both as: (a) a response to the critics of such Smart city solutions that are contradictory to sustainability, and (b) as an attempt to address the needs of the currently highly digitalized cities, more comprehensively than the traditional concept of sustainability" (Huovila et al., 2019, p. 2).

The clarification of these terms will address the implementation challenges of Smart Sustainable Cities' strategies.

A Smart Sustainable City is a complex system that must interrelate the built environment (land use, urban design, transport, human activities) with the pervasive computing. Therefore, the goals seeking to become a Smart Sustainable City are:

- The economic, societal, and environmental sustainability;
- The destination accessibility; and
- The innovation and application of ICT.

Nevertheless, although these goals coexist in contemporary cities, as expressed by Bibri (2018b, p. 7), "sustainable urban development as a long-range objective for achieving the aim of urban sustainability is worthy for urban planners, as they need a strategic process to achieve the status of sustainable cities, to increase the contribution of Smart cities to sustainability, and to spur the development of Smart sustainable cities". Hence the need of a strategic planning involving Public Administration, enterprises, and diverse stakeholders (research institutes, universities, local population, etc.). It justifies the importance of Public Administration and enterprises cooperation.

Strategic city planning can be defined as a systematic, creative, and participatory process that lays the foundations for long-term integrated action, defines the future model of development, formulates strategies and courses of action to achieve this model, establishes a continuous system of decision-making, and involves local actors throughout the process (Slack et al., 2018). There are several urban change factors:

economic change factors, societal change factors, technological change factors, urban planning change factors, governance change factors, and environmental change factors. To deal with the complexity, diversity, and uncertainty of contemporary cities and at the same time interpret their growing challenges, the city must be conceptualized as an evolving functional ecosystem (Fernández-Güell et al., 2016). Thus, the municipal strategic planning must be elaborated in terms of the stakeholders, type of projects developed, and the global trends they were addressing (Fernandez-Anez et al., 2018). Therefore, in this process Public Administration and private companies must be involved, since this cooperation is needed to achieve smart cities that are also sustainable.

3 Methodology

The 2030 Agenda of the United Nations is committed to sustainable development in a broad sense: environmental, economic, and social. Along these lines, the model of cities for 2030 must be created, in accordance with sustainable development, creating wealth and employment, but preserving the natural and cultural heritage of the regions and in a socially responsible manner.

In addition, there are other social trends and demands, such as:

- Accessibility, which is necessary for people with permanent or temporary disabilities or older people.
- The use of new information and communication technologies—ICTs.
- Health and hygiene safety, which has become a priority in the wake of the COVID-19 pandemic.
- The search for health and well-being in a stressful society.
- Contact with nature, especially for those living in big cities.

This paper aims to identify the variables to be considered to carry out sustainable and smart city strategic planning.

There is a large variety of indicator frameworks and tools to assess either urban sustainability or smartness. Huovila et al. (2019) identify following indicator standards on Smart Sustainable Cities:

- ISO 37120:2018 sustainable development of communities—indicators for city services and quality of life.
- ISO/DIS 37122:2018 sustainable development in communities—indicators for Smart Cities.
- ETSI TS 463 key performance indicators for sustainable digital multiservice cities.
- ITU—T Y.4901/I.1601 key performance indicators related to the use of information and communication technology in Smart Sustainable Cities.
- ITU-T-Y.4902/I.1602 key performance indicators related to the sustainability impacts of information and communication technology in Smart Sustainable Cities.
- ITU—Y.4903/I.1603 key performance indicators for Smart Sustainable Cities to assess the achievement of sustainable development goals.

According to these indicators, the triple bottom line of sustainability can be analyzed: people (social sustainability), planet (environmental sustainability), and prosperity (economic sustainability). And, as expressed by Huovila et al. (2019), two urban smartnesses can be distinguished: hard smartness related to tangible assets, such as technology or physical infrastructure (transport water, energy…) and soft smartness related to social, cultural, and human capital (knowledge, governance, innovation, economy, inclusion an equity…).

Other authors as Akande et al. (2019) make use of indicators suggested by the United Nations Economic Commission for Europe (UNECE) and the International Telecommunications Union (ITU) to rank European capital cities based on how Smart and Sustainable they are, and show this visual representation of the UNECE-ITU Smart Sustainable Cities Framework (Fig. 1).

Considering these indicators and the research of these authors, two indexes have been selected to identify the variables in carrying out sustainable and smart city strategic planning: the Cities in Motion Index (IESE Business School, 2022) and the Arcadis Cities Index (Batten, 2022). Finally, this research has been completed with case studies from cities such as New York—USA (Alshuwaikhat et al., 2022; Balsas, 2022),

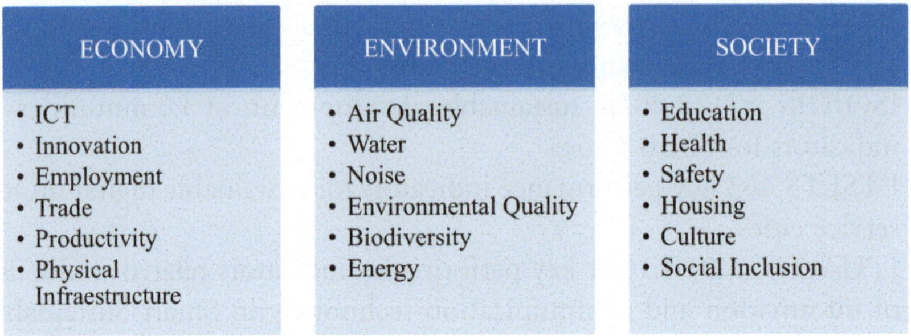

Fig. 1 Visual representation of the UNECE-ITU Smart Sustainable Cities Framework (*Source* Own elaboration)

Rotterdam—Netherlands (Moraci et al., 2018), Gothenburg—Sweden (Bibri, 2018b), Singapore (Alshuwaikhat et al., 2022), Riyadh—Saudi Arabia (Alshuwaikhat et al., 2022; Klingmann, 2022), and Malaga (Spain); these cities have been selected because they are in different continents (American, Asian, and European continents) and they are also really diverse from each other, although they are in the indexes analyzed in prominent positions, in certain dimensions.

The IESE Cities in Motion Index compared 183 cities to determine the world's smartest and more sustainable cities for 2022; it presents a ranking of cities according to the following dimensions:

- Economy
- Human capital
- Social cohesion
- Environment
- Urban planning
- International profile
- Technology
- Mobility and transportation
- Governance.

The Arcadis Sustainable Cities Index 2022 ranks 100 of the world's cities based on three pillars of sustainability: planet, people, and profit. The indicator details are:

- Planet pillar: air pollution, bicycle infrastructure, energy consumption and renewable energy share, green spaces, greenhouse gas emissions, public policy, sustainable transport incentives, waste management.
- People pillar: quality of public transport infrastructure, cost of broadband, crime (homicide and theft rates), education, health, income inequality, Wi-Fi availability, and work-life balance.
- Profit pillar: Access to reliable electricity, affordability, connectivity, ease of making business, economic development, employment, green finance, job quality, and commercial transport infrastructure (Table 1).

Both indexes consider aspects related to Public Administration—social cohesion, mobility and transportation, governance, urban planning—and others to private companies—economy, technology, human capital—this is the reason why the cooperation between Public Administration and enterprises is so important, to achieve a balanced city on an environmental, social, and economic level.

The study of these indexes has been completed and the results have been compared with the aforementioned research on cities such as New York, Rotterdam, Gothenburg, Singapore, Riyadh, and Malaga. Specifically in the case of Malaga, we have participated in the process of developing the Strategy for Malaga 2020 and the Strategy for Malaga 2030, which aims to design a Smart Sustainable City.

With all this information, the aim is to formulate a strategic planning model for Smart Sustainable Cities.

Table 1 Comparison between IESE Cities in Motion Index and Arcadis Sustainable Cities Index

Arcadis Sustainable Cities Index	IESE Cities in Motion Index
Planet Pillar	Environment, Urban planning
People Pillar	Social cohesion, Mobility and transportation, Governance
Profit pillar	Economy, International profile, Human capital, Technology

Source Own elaboration

4 Case Study Results: Special Reference to the Case of Malaga

According to the ***IESE Cities in Motion Index 2022 (Instituto de Estudios Superiores de Empresa-IESE-)***, considering all the dimensions, the top ten cities are:

1. London (United Kingdom)
2. New York (USA)
3. Paris (France)
4. Tokyo (Japan)
5. Berlin (Germany)
6. Washington (USA)
7. Singapore (Singapore)
8. Amsterdam (Netherlands)
9. Oslo (Norway)
10. Copenhagen (Denmark).

However, not all of them are in the top positions in dimensions such as environment, social cohesion, or urban planning, as presented in Table 2.

London tops the overall ranking thanks to its performance in the dimensions of human capital (rank 1), international profile (rank 1), urban planning (rank 1), governance (rank 2), and mobility and transportation (rank 4); but does not perform as well in the dimensions of social cohesion (rank 25) and environment (rank 17).

New York ranks second due to its performance in the dimensions of economy (rank 1), mobility and transportation (rank 1), urban planning (rank 2), human capital (rank 3), and international profile (rank 3); but it performs poorly in social cohesion (rank 121) and environment (rank 105).

Therefore, though these are the top ten cities of this ranking, not all of them are Smart and Sustainable Cities. In fact, only one of them: Copenhagen, has a top position in the dimension of social cohesion (rank 4), and only two of them perform very well in environment: Oslo (rank 2) and Copenhagen (rank 3).

Table 2 Ranking by dimension

City	Economy	Human capital	Social cohe-sion	Environment	Governance	Urban plan-ning	International profile	Technology	Mobility and transportation
London	7	1	25	17	2	1	1	18	4
New York	1	3	121	105	10	2	3	6	1
Paris	9	5	67	49	17	34	2	27	3
Tokyo	2	10	41	25	9	112	6	9	62
Berlin	94	7	40	21	3	5	14	39	7
Washington	11	4	73	131	8	9	41	7	37
Singapore	20	40	31	78	24	26	4	4	58
Amsterdam	38	35	48	14	40	13	18	10	20
Oslo	25	18	21	2	11	33	18	10	20
Copenhagen	46	45	4	3	20	23	25	22	31

Source IESE Cities in Motion Index (2022)

Nonetheless, it is interesting to study other cities such as Rotterdam, which is not among the top ten of the ranking, but performs very well in the dimension of urban planning (rank 4).

Regarding the ***Arcadis Sustainable Cities Index 2022***, the top ten cities considering all the positions and their rank in each pillar—planet pillar, people pillar, and profit pillar—are presented in Table 3.

According to this index, the top ten cities of the profit pillar are in USA, but none of them are in the top ten ranking in planet pillar and people pillar. However, there are cities, such as Rotterdam, which are not in the top ten position in the overall index, but perform very well in planet pillar (rank 10) and people pillar (rank 8). Thus, it was interesting to compare these indexes with case studies of some cities.

In the ***case study of Rotterdam***, though it is not in the top ten ranking of these indexes in overall dimensions or pillars, it is a great example of adaptation to climate change and ranks 4 in urban planning (IESE Cities in Motion Index, 2022). The theme of urban resilience has been under the attention of the municipality in the last twenty years. The Rotterdam Adaptation Strategy (City of Rotterdam, 2013) charts the course by which Rotterdam has planned to adapt to the consequences of climate change and shows how residents, businesses, and the city can gain maximum benefit from it. Rotterdam practice, in its adaptation strategy, focuses on anticipating climate change (Moraci et al., 2018).

Table 3 Top ten cities of the Arcadis Sustainable Cities Index 2022

Overall Sustainable Cities Index	Planet	People	Profit
1. Oslo	1. Oslo	1. Glasgow	1.Seattle
2. Stockholm	2. Paris	2. Zurich	2. Atlanta
3. Tokyo	3. Stockholm	3. Copenhagen	3. Boston
4. Copenhagen	4. Copenhagen	4. Seoul	4. San Francisco
5. Berlin	5. Berlin	5. Singapore	5. Pittsburgh
6. London	6. London	6. Vienna	6. Tampa
7. Seattle	7. Tokyo	7. Tokyo	7. Dallas
8. Paris	8. Antwerp	8. Rotterdam	8. Chicago
9. San Francisco	9. Zurich	9. Madrid	9. Baltimore
10. Amsterdam	10. Rotterdam	10. Amsterdam	10. Miami

Source The Arcadis Sustainable Cities Index 2022. www.arcadis.com

In the ***case study of Gothenburg***, it is neither in the top ranking of these indexes in overall dimensions nor pillars, but ranks 4 in environment (IESE Cities in Motion Index, 2022). The Project Gothenburg 2050 aims to draw up and develop long-term visions for the Sustainable City in Sweden, which, as part of a sustainable society, could motivate a faster development toward sustainability. The Project specifies energy and environment targets as part of a sustainable society with the principle of equity (Bibri, 2018b). To this aim, different stakeholders are involved in cooperation: universities, energy companies, city governments, Public Administration, and research councils.

On the other hand, the ***case study of New York*** shows that though this city ranks second on all dimensions (IESE Cities in Motion Index, 2022), it performs poorly in social cohesion (rank 121) and environment (rank 105). New York is a smart city, in fact advanced technology and innovation have become essential for the city's development (Alshuwaikhat et al.,; 2022); but it is not a social and environmental sustainable city, though the city leaders are working to improve it by 2050, and there are studies on how to plan it, especially in the district of Hudson Yard (Balsas, 2022).

The ***case study of Singapore*** is similar; it is among the top ten cities of IESE Cities in Motion Index 2022 because it ranks 4 in technology and international profile, but must improve in environment, governance, urban planning, and social cohesion. There are studies that recommend strategies for covering housing, health, education, and emigration (Alshuwaikhat et al., 2022).

These case studies show that a balanced city is not only a smart one, but a smart and sustainable one. As expressed by Bibri (2021), the data-driven technologies and solutions offered by Smart Cities as an approach to urban development are to be applied in the operational management and development planning of sustainable cities in ways that enable them to continually make and monitor their progress toward achieving the goals of sustainability. As a result, in the last years there has been research about strategies to design Smart Sustainable Cities, considering social and environmental sustainability, some of them applied to Chinese cities with a technology development, but also a social and environmental sustainable development (Liu et al., 2021).

In addition, the experience of these cities analyzed helps to elaborate strategies to become a Smart Sustainable City, for instance ***the case of Riyadh—Saudi Arabia*** (Alshuwaikhat et al., 2022; Klingmann, 2022).

Finally, ***the case of Malaga (Spain)***, a city that has changed a lot in the last 30 years, has been analyzed. The I Strategic Plan of the city of Malaga (1992–1996) started with the elaboration of a diagnosis based on an analysis of weakness, opportunities, threats, and strengths—SWOT. The II Strategic Plan considered aspects such as globalization, governance, sustainability, and people as the center of all activity. Later, Strategy Malaga 2020 was suggested as an integrated sustainability development strategy. These strategic plans of the city of Malaga have been evolving with the social changes that have taken place, to adapt the city to them. Nowadays, Malaga is a Smart City, but the Strategy Malaga 2030 is being designed according to the Sustainable Development 2030 goals of the United Nations; the priorities are to achieve a smart, sustainable, and inclusive growth, and to get it, strategic projects in different areas have been planned:

- Malaga International Capital of Culture.
- Malaga International Tourist Capital.
- Creative Malaga.
- Educator Malaga.
- Malaga of Knowledge and Innovation.
- Malaga Airport and Port.
- Sustainable Mobility.
- Energy Efficiency and Climate Change.
- Healthy Life.
- Local Governance.
- Integrated and Integrative Malaga, looking for inequality and poverty between different neighborhoods.

A relationship is detected between these planning strategic projects and the dimensions considered in the IESE Cities in Motion Index, as shown in Fig. 2.

In addition, these strategic plans have been elaborated according to the opinion of stakeholders—university, local government, private

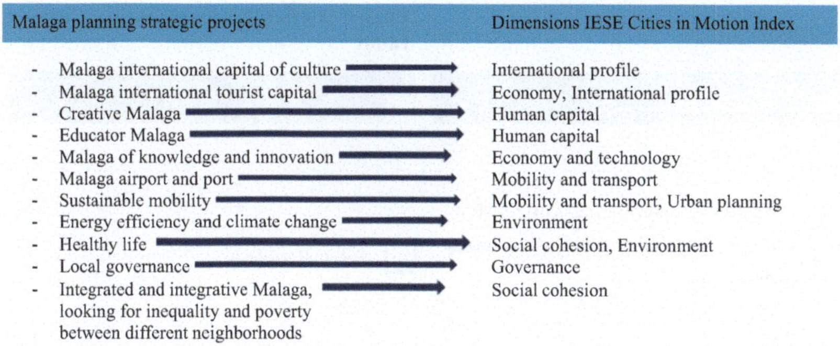

Fig. 2 Relationship between Malaga planning strategic projects and the dimensions considered in the IESE Cities in Motion Index (*Source* Own elaboration)

companies, labor unions, and professionals—in an attempt to cooperate between the Public Administration and private enterprises. Thus, the contributions of sixteen working groups, made up of professionals and experts from the city government, universities, private companies, and trade unions, were considered, as well as the ideas of citizens who responded to surveys.

Five strategic lines are contemplated:

- Malaga, Education and Citizenship;
- Malaga, Global and Inclusive;
- Innovative and Digital Malaga;
- Sustainable and Coastal Malaga;
- Malaga of Culture; and
- Sustainable and Coastal Malaga.

The relationship between these strategic lines and the three pillars of sustainability of the Arcadis Sustainable Cities Index is shown in Fig. 3.

Each line develops a series of strategic objectives, in turn collected in eighty-two projects, among which are projects related to Circular Economy, Green Economy, and Blue Economy, to address problems such as climate change. The aim is to make Malaga a smart, sustainable, and resilient city.

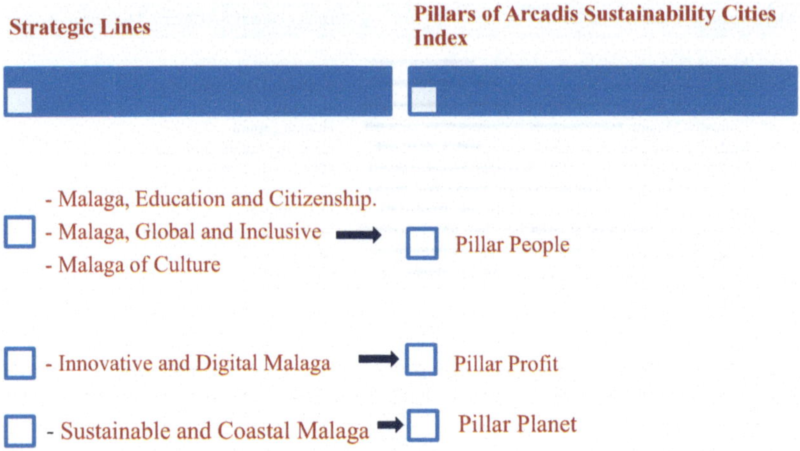

Fig. 3 Relationship between Strategy Malaga 2030 strategic lines and the three pillars of sustainability of the Arcadis Sustainable Cities Index (*Source* Own elaboration)

5 Discussion

The urban and demographic growth of destinations justifies the need for sustainable management not only by private companies, but also by the Public Administrations that govern these municipalities. Likewise, the urban space must be a well-connected territory, with internal and external accessibility, allowing the coexistence of the daily life of its residents.

Considering the new trends that are giving way to a New Economy, it should be noted that the new information and communication technologies have favored the development of collaborative economies, with or without monetary consideration.

With regard to the Green and Blue Economy, although their development is the responsibility of private enterprises, Public Administration can act as catalysts for them, with programs to support the development of businesses that are committed to the use of locally available resources and by implementing environmental protection and preservation measures in the municipalities.

Furthermore, economic movements such as the Economy of the Common Good or the Economy of Happiness are based on the assumption that in areas where basic needs are already covered, Public Administration should adopt policies focused on satisfying the local population and improving their quality of life.

In short, this New Economy that we mentioned in the introduction to this chapter favors the existence of Smart Sustainable Cities.

In the case studies analyzed, we see that there are Smart Cities that are not socially and environmentally sustainable; and there are other cases of cities that are more socially and environmentally sustainable, but less economically sustainable. There really must be a balance in the city model to achieve a Smart Sustainable City.

Malaga is one of the most balanced cases. Malaga's strategic planning is based on:

- Public–private cooperation.
- It takes into account the opinion and demands of stakeholders.
- It develops projects according to their corresponding Sustainable Development Goals 2030.
- These projects relate to the Economy of Common Good and Happiness (for instance, Integrated and integrative Malaga, looking for inequality and poverty between different neighborhoods, Local governance, Healthy life, Creative Malaga, Educator Malaga); Blue Economy and Green Economy (for example, Sustainable mobility, Energy efficiency and climate change); Collaborative Economy (for instance, Malaga International Capital of Culture, Malaga International Tourist Capital, Malaga of Knowledge and Innovation, Malaga Airport and Port).

According to the "VI Business Climate Barometer. Foreign investment in Malaga" (2023b) elaborated by the Area of Innovation and Urban Digitalization and Promotion of Technological and Business Investment and Attracting Investment of Malaga City Council, in recent years there has been an increase in foreign investment in Malaga. Among the most important assets that have contributed to this are the quality of life and infrastructure, the support of the Public Administration to make Malaga a city that invests in technology and innovation, and legal stability and security.

In short, Malaga has been reformulating its strategies over the last 30 years and is currently orienting its strategies toward 2030 based on 4 axes: ecological transition, digitalization, training and employment, and social and territorial cohesion, in an attempt to become a Smart Sustainable City.

Although the case of Malaga seems to be an example to follow, there is no single model of a city, as it is necessary to consider the climatological, geographical, demographic, economic, etc. conditions of each place, as has been shown in other cases such as Gothenburg, with excellent urban planning and adapting to climate change.

Considering all the cases analyzed, we conclude that there is no single model of success, but that it is necessary to define what type of city we want to develop. However, according to the parameters of the New Economy and the dimensions analyzed in the Arcadis Sustainable Cities Index 2022 and IESE Cities in Motion Index 2022, the most sustainable cities are those that are committed to Social Cohesion, Environment, Urban Planning and Mobility and Transportation, boosting local economies, and if we add Technological Development to achieve these objectives, we will have achieved a Smart Sustainable City.

6 Conclusions

The strategic planning of a city must start from an analysis of the evolution of the city and its environment to identify weaknesses and strengths of the city and threats and opportunities of its environment—SWOT. But strategic management also implies having a vision of the future, defining what kind of city model we want, following the SWOT analysis, in order to design specific projects. Furthermore, it is necessary to carry out a process of continuous adaptation of strategic planning, given the continuous changes (new technologies, pandemics such as COVID-19, etc.).

In line with the Europe 2020 Strategy's key priorities of smart growth, sustainable growth, and inclusive growth, the UN's 2030 Sustainable

Development Goals, and the changing environment in the wake of the COVID-19 pandemic, cities need to plan strategically to achieve a balance between economic development, social justice, environmental friendliness, and urban governance, relying on new technologies. This is the only way to achieve Smart Sustainable Cities.

However, there is no single model for a successful city, as each city has different strengths and weaknesses and an environment with different opportunities and threats, although all strategic planning should be focused on making cities more digital, sustainable, and resilient to the changes and challenges of the future. It will only be achieved with the cooperation of Public Administration and private enterprise, considering the demands of stakeholders.

From this study we can draw implications for researchers, business managers, and public managers. Researchers must analyze the strengths, opportunities, threats, and weaknesses of a destination to develop a strategic city plan. To implement this plan, it is necessary that business managers develop smart and sustainable actions in their companies, related to the Collaborative Economy, Circular Economy, Green Economy, Blue Economy, etc. In addition, public managers will oversee carrying out actions related to urban planning, social cohesion, mobility and transportation, governance, or international profile.

References

Akande, A., Cabral, P., Gomes, P., & Casteleyn, S. (2019). The Lisbon ranking for smart sustainable cities in Europe. *Sustainable Cities and Society, 44*, 475–487.

Alshuwaikhat, H. M., Adenle, Y. A., & Almuhaidib, T. (2022). A lifecycle-based smart sustainable city strategic framework for realizing smart and sustainability initiatives in Riyadh City. *Sustainability, 14*(14), 8240.

Balsas, C. J. (2022). Retaining social and cultural sustainability in the Hudson river watershed of New York, USA, a place-based participatory action research study. *Journal of Place Management and Development, 15*(3), 336–354.

Batten, J. (2022). *The Arcadis Sustainable Cities Index 2022.* On line www.arcadis.com

Bibri, S. E. (2018a). A foundational framework for smart sustainable city development: Theoretical, disciplinary, and discursive dimensions and their synergies. *Sustainable Cities and Society, 38*, 758–794.

Bibri, S. E. (2018b). Backcasting in futures studies: A synthesized scholarly and planning approach to strategic smart sustainable city development. *European Journal of Futures Research, 6*(1), 1–27.

Bibri, S. E. (2021). The underlying components of data-driven smart sustainable cities of the future: A case study approach to an applied theoretical framework. *European Journal of Futures Research, 9*(1), 1–14.

Bulchand-Gidumal, J. (2022). Post-COVID-19 recovery of island tourism using a smart tourism destination framework. *Journal of Destination Marketing & Management, 23*, 100689.

Butlin, J. (1989 [1987]). *Our common future. By World commission on environment and development* (p. 383). Oxford University Press.

CIEDES. (2023) *Business Climate Barometer. Foreign investment in Malaga.* Promalaga Publications.

City of Rotterdam. (2013). *Rotterdam climate change adaptation strategy.* Rotterdam Climate Initiative.

Della Corte, V., D'Andrea, C., Savastano, I., & Zamparelli, P. (2017). Smart cities and destination management: Impacts and opportunities for tourism competitiveness. *European Journal of Tourism Research, 17*, 7–27.

Fernandez-Anez, V., Fernández-Güell, J. M., & Giffinger, R. (2018). Smart city implementation and discourses: An integrated conceptual model. The case of Vienna. *Cities, 78*, 4–16.

Fernández-Güell, J. M., Collado-Lara, M., Guzmán-Arana, S., & Fernández-Anez, V. (2016). Incorporating a systemic and foresight approach into smart city initiatives: The case of Spanish cities. *Journal of Urban Technology, 23*(3), 43–67.

Höjer, M., & Wangel, J. (2015). Smart sustainable cities: Definition and challenges. In *ICT innovations for sustainability* (pp. 333–349). Springer International Publishing.

Huovila, A., Bosch, P., & Airaksinen, M. (2019). Comparative analysis of standardized indicators for Smart sustainable cities: What indicators and standards to use and when? *Cities, 89*, 141–153.

IESE Business School. (2022). IESE Cities in Motion Index 2022.

Klingmann, A. (2022). Re-scripting Riyadh's historical downtown as a global destination: A sustainable model? *Journal of Place Management and Development, 15*(2), 93–111.

Liu, J., Zhao, Y., Lin, T., Xing, L., Lin, M., Sun, C., Zeng, Z. & Zhang, G. (2021). Analysis of sustainability of Chinese cities based on network big data of city rankings. *Ecological Indicators, 133*, 108374.

Martín-Rojo, I. (2018). Sustainable management of tourism companies and destinations: The new economy. *Journal of Corporate Social Responsibility, 28*, 103–122.

Moraci, F., Errigo, M. F., Fazia, C., Burgio, G., & Foresta, S. (2018). Making less vulnerable cities: Resilience as a new paradigm of smart planning. *Sustainability, 10*(3), 755.

Ribes, J. F. P., & Baidal, J. I. (2018). Smart sustainability: A new perspective in the sustainable tourism debate. *Investigaciones Regionales-Journal of Regional Research, 42*, 151–170.

Richardson, N. (1989). Land use planning and sustainable development in Canada.

Slack, E., Cuadrado-Roura, J. R., Fernández Güell, J. M., Rojas, E., Bird, R., Klink, J., Lefévre, C., Subirats, J., Brugué, Q., Monzón, A., & Etchegaray, A. (2018). *Governing the metropolis: Principles and cases*. IDB Publications (Books).

World Business Council on Sustainable Development. (1998). Stakeholder dialogue on CSR. Netherlands.

Implementation of the Sustainable Development Goals (SDGS) in Municipalities with Less Than 2,500 Inhabitants: The Agenda Marca Pueblo Project

Jaime de Pablo Valenciano, Francisco Javier García Corral, José Luis Caparrós Martínez, Juan Milán García, and Rosa María Martínez Vázquez

1 Introduction

The Basis of the Sustainable Development Goals (SDGs) and Their Relationship with the 2030 Agenda

On September 25, 2015, the United Nations General Assembly adopted the 2030 Agenda for Sustainable Development, consisting of 17 Sustainable Development Goals (SDGs) and 169 targets (United Nations, n.d.). This global action plan aims to achieve sustainable development in economic, social, and environmental dimensions (Glass & Newig, 2019; Gusmão et al., 2018). It is based on the principles of universality, integration, and indivisibility, directly applying to all countries and stakeholders. It recognizes and emphasizes the importance of equality among

J. de Pablo Valenciano (✉) · F. J. García Corral · J. L. Caparrós Martínez · J. Milán García · R. M. Martínez Vázquez
University of Almería, Almería, Spain
e-mail: jdepablo@ual.es

F. J. García Corral
e-mail: fgc423@ual.es

E. Poveda-Pareja et al. (eds.), *The Strategic Paradigm of CSR and Sustainability*, Palgrave Studies in Governance, Leadership and Responsibility,
https://doi.org/10.1007/978-3-031-58889-1_9

diverse actors, ranging from civil society to the private sector and international organizations, ensuring the development of everyone (Colglazier, 2015; Sachs, 2012).

This initiative represents a historic opportunity for global reorientation toward sustainability, inclusivity, and resilience. Achieving this requires a significant transformation of productive and consumption models, acknowledging that human development has conditioned global sustainability (Bossel, 1999). Cooperation emerges as a fundamental pillar, both internationally and among actors closest to the citizenry (Berrone et al., 2016). From municipalities to smaller capitals, it is crucial to demonstrate that being small is not an obstacle to engaging in sustainability-related actions (Terama et al., 2019).

The SDGs constitute a universal call to end poverty, protect the planet, and ensure global peace and prosperity (United Nations Development Programme, n.d.). Their objectives and targets are interrelated with daily challenges such as inequality, environmental degradation, peace, and justice (United Nations, n.d.). Originating from a participatory and inclusive process involving governments, civil society, the private sector, and academia, they reflect aspirations and priorities at a general level. They acknowledge and preserve different realities, promoting both culture and opportunities for cooperation and solidarity (Scheyvens et al., 2016; Xiao et al., 2018).

The evolution from the Millennium Development Goals (MDGs), established in 2000 and culminating in 2015, gave rise to the SDGs. This shift in cooperative principles highlighted existing inequalities and the need to address structural and systemic issues hindering sustainable development. Nevertheless, the MDGs had structural deficiencies, necessitating a more detailed process for effectiveness (Patole, 2018).

J. L. Caparrós Martínez
e-mail: jlcapa@ual.es

J. Milán García
e-mail: jmg483@ual.es

R. M. Martínez Vázquez
e-mail: rosamaria@ual.es

The SDGs are designed for global implementation regardless of the level of development. This necessitates a focus on monitoring, evaluation, and accountability, crucially establishing a connection from local implementation to global impacts. This proves challenging as the SDGs are conceived globally, but their implementation occurs at the level of specific projects, emphasizing an upward approach (Thacker et al., 2019).

This evolution toward the SDGs poses a significant challenge but also an unparalleled opportunity for transformation and reflection on the future of the planet. It calls for collaboration among all actors to contribute positively to this path.

Therefore, the proposed development and cooperation imply an observation from the starting point of local development, viewed as a participatory and decentralized process leveraging endogenous resources and potentialities without compromising the environment (Colglazier, 2015; Robert et al., 2005). This approach involves actions from all actors with a democratic bottom-up vision. A new decentralization is thus proposed as a fundamental aspect for governance, helping overcome existing obstacles, as political and fiscal separation poses significant challenges in local democracy (Faguet & Pöschl, 2015; Smoke, 2019; Zhang et al., 2016).

Undoubtedly, municipalities play a leading role in the implementation of the SDGs. They constitute the best-positioned government to convey the vision of the three pillars of sustainability to local communities (Echebarria et al., 2014). Participation at this level offers benefits such as democratic legitimacy, social acceptance, promotion of cooperation, building trust, fostering equity and good governance, and empowering marginalized communities and groups (Amer et al., 2015; Kolk et al., 2017). Therefore, local leaders must be strengthened, as their role is crucial, and public administration must be robust and unequivocal to make lasting decisions (Beisheim et al., 2017; Feiock, 2009; Tummers & Bakers, 2014).

In recent times, the Agenda 2030 has garnered significant interest, especially in the wake of the COVID-19 pandemic, prompting global institutions such as the UN, the European Union, and numerous governments worldwide, including Spain, to consider a green exit from the crisis as the primary strategy for economic reconstruction that safeguards both our health and the health of our planet. A clear alignment exists between the SDGs and the policies of ecological transition and demographic challenge pursued by the Next Generation EU funds of the European Recovery Plan.

However, as evident, this is a complex process not without challenges for actors. The greatest failure would be not achieving the United Nations Sustainable Development Goals by 2030, signifying a threat to our survival (IPCC, 2018). In a more detailed breakdown, the part closest to the citizenry, such as local governments, sees the need for an expansion of financial and technical resources for these projects with a more precise focus than never before. The implementation of the SDGs in many municipalities will require increased investments in infrastructure and public services. Moreover, addressing economic, social, and gender inequality in each municipality is crucial to ensure that the benefits of the SDGs reach all segments of the local population. In turn, greater coordination and articulation of all actors are necessary to achieve greater synergy, and therefore, there must be a continuous process of measurement and monitoring of interventions and established indicators (Swain, 2018). A shared comprehensive strategic vision is essential, highlighting the specific potentialities of each area and strengthening management and relationship capabilities to facilitate collaboration with other actors if necessary. This makes it a complex process that can be both individual and plural but, above all, must be efficient and transparent, promoting innovation and new technologies (Camussi et al., 2018).

This is a challenge that requires broad political and social commitment, as it represents an opportunity to improve management and contribute to the sustainable development of all communities. The effectiveness of these projects is greatly influenced by their design and structure, but one must not forget the socio-ecological-economic context in which they exist. If there is limited collaboration or a lack of citizen awareness from the outset, efficiency will be significantly reduced (Gómez-Martín et al., 2020a).

Nevertheless, it is crucial not only to highlight the more challenging aspects but also to showcase the wide range of possibilities and effects that will become evident in the territory (Suganthi, 2018). Thus, local governments can benefit from improved management by aligning their plans and policies in a globalized world with shared goals, entering a dynamic of resources and alliances that they could not previously observe individually. They can make better use of their resources through long-term planning that identifies existing synergies and compensations for use to help find a proper balance, such as in their protected areas (Calliari et al., 2019; Gómez-Martín et al., 2020b).

Another opportunity lies in the commitment to Local Sustainability. The Agenda 2030 represents a formal declaration by the municipality in favor of sustainable development, raising awareness among the actors involved in its territory. The creation of a local action plan, establishing objectives and goals, monitoring indicators, as well as outlining responsible parties and required resources, serves as an excellent roadmap to achieve a more inclusive, environmentally sustainable municipal management.

Furthermore, there is a significant promotion of public–private partnerships. Facilitating the construction of alliances with other administrations or key agents, such as the private sector and civil organizations, can strengthen the financial, technical, and knowledge capacity of municipalities (Berrone et al., 2019; Emerson, 2003; Ordonez-Ponce et al., 2021; Zheng et al., 2008).

Following this is citizen participation and transparency. The Agenda 2030 represents a stimulus for the participation of the local population, providing an opportunity to involve citizens in planning and developing sustainable solutions that cater to local needs. Additionally, innovation and technology must be mentioned, offering the opportunity for cities and municipalities to leverage intelligent technological solutions to promote sustainable development. Lastly, there is the exchange of best practices. This initiative offers the opportunity for municipalities to learn from each other, sharing successful experiences in the implementation of the SDGs.

In summary, the path toward achieving the SDGs requires a collective effort, with municipalities playing a pivotal role. As local governments navigate the challenges, it is essential to recognize the potential benefits and positive impacts that can be realized in the pursuit of sustainable development. The road ahead demands a comprehensive and transparent approach, underpinned by collaboration, innovation, and a commitment to the principles of the 2030 Agenda for Sustainable Development.

2030 Agenda and the Marca Pueblo Project

The Marca Pueblo Project began in 2019 with the participation of the Almeria municipalities of Alcóntar, Almócita, Líjar, Lubrín, Olula de Castro, Purchena and Serón. In the next two phases, the towns of Abla, Abrucena, Fondón, Laroya, Laujar de Andarax, Padules, and Tahal were incorporated. All have the characteristic of being municipalities with less than 2,500 inhabitants with depopulation problems located in the inland areas of the province.

Therefore, they unanimously present the need to fix the population and seek to reactivate rural environments from all possible axes of action. This currently implies the need for the population to participate in the territorial strategy, taking them into account at all times from a bottom-up approach to make the decisions that concern them.

Based on this bottom-up vision, the Marca Pueblo methodology was carried out or is being carried out in a first phase that each villa has individually, consisting of initially combining the collection and processing of data with a diagnosis, and with the implementation of a strategic analysis from the perspective of sustainability. The purpose reached is to demonstrate that the realities of the municipalities are different, being necessary for development to propose different strategies depending on the differentiation observed.

It is necessary for this the innovative character in the activities to be carried out, the revaluation of the natural and cultural heritage, the entrepreneurial spirit, the technological development, the applications of new technologies, the endogenous resources, and the revaluation of the role of women in these environments. All this, obviously, framed in this integral and multisectoral approach of networking and cooperation.

Once these diagnoses have been made and there is a differentiated strategic plan, the objective in the next phase becomes the implementation of the application of the SDGs in the projects to be carried out at the municipal level. The objective is to take advantage of the methodology established in the Marca Pueblo Project, to lay the foundations that lead to the implementation of the 2030 Agenda in each of the municipalities of the project.

The desired future is that each of the municipalities of the project have a municipal strategy to fight against rural depopulation, in which all the local actors of the municipalities participate and whose main lines of action are to increase prosperity, social inclusion, and environmental sustainability at the municipal level.

2 The Theoretical and Methodological Basis

The Question at Hand, Can Our Small Municipalities Contribute to Sustainability and the Fulfillment of the SDGs?

It has been evident that small municipalities play a key role in achieving these Sustainable Development Goals (SDGs). They constitute a significant part of the social and economic fabric of the country, and their territories host rich biodiversity and environmentally valuable spaces. As an illustrative example, some of their contributions to the most relevant SDGs are complemented:

- SDG 2 (Zero Hunger) and SDG 12 (Responsible Consumption and Production)

In these rural areas and small municipalities, historically sustainable agricultural and livestock models have been developed, with moderate levels of intervention, such as organic and ecological farming, crop diversification, or extensive grazing. These practices promote the efficient use of natural resources, resulting in high-quality production.

- SDG 7 (Affordable and Clean Energy) and SDG 13 (Climate Action)

Rural municipalities can and should play a leading role in the planet's energy transition. Generally, their territories have enormous potential to harness resources such as solar, wind, or hydroelectric energy within an energy model that is fair to the local population and does not harm the conservation of the natural heritage of these areas. Additionally, they must address the effects of Climate Change, such as droughts, floods, or soil erosion, by implementing adaptation measures like sustainable water management, reforestation, or soil conservation.

– SDG 8 (Decent Work and Economic Growth)

A large portion of Spanish rural municipalities face the global phenomenon of rural depopulation, making them the focus of initiatives to promote local economies. Moreover, the global COVID-19 pandemic has prompted institutions like the UN or the European Union, and the Spanish government to consider a green recovery or "Green Deal", benefiting our rural areas. Administrations should explore alternatives to return some of the environmental benefits provided by rural areas, either through compensation actions or through the promotion of green, forestry, livestock, and agroecological employment. The exit from the health crisis also opens up new opportunities for the economy of these areas, such as the expected population migration for telecommuting, increased rural tourism, or the likely delocalization of companies and services.

– SDGs related to access to basic services by the population

Currently, any plan or strategy to combat rural depopulation aims to ensure equitable and fair access to basic public services for the population, including:

- Adequate healthcare (SDG 3—Good Health and Well-being).
- Adequate water supply and sanitation (SDG 6—Clean Water and Sanitation).
- Digital connectivity and industrial infrastructure (SDG 9—Industry, Innovation, and Infrastructure).
- Public education services for all age groups (SDG 4—Quality Education).

The Methodological Approach of the Marca Pueblo Project

As a methodology of the Marca Pueblo Project, a multiple basic idea was proposed for the sustainable development of the municipality that considered the economic, sociological, anthropological, environmental and cultural aspects. To do this, and following the local development methodology (de Pablo et al., 2022), the research part is divided into three broadly related stages: data collection, diagnosis, and strategic analysis (see Table 1).

These three stages are carried out sequentially through in-house analysis and meetings in each municipality. Thus, after various sessions and interviews, along with a municipal correction process, a series of objectives to be achieved are determined, highlighting what makes that particular municipality unique. Consequently, a foundational strategy is extracted, developed, and planned to achieve differentiation. Also, parameters are established to generate synergies among different sectors to diversify and enhance the town. It is essential to present the products and services that will be offered, the value proposal for the target audience, and its segmentation. Additionally, calculating the necessary resources and activities for municipal functioning is crucial. Furthermore, it is relevant to take into account the ideological, environmental, and the mechanical or planning structure that may have already begun to be outlined.

In the present text, a series of general conclusions from the various phases conducted will be presented. Thus, it will start by showcasing the sample taken superficially, beginning with the breakdown of the province and its constituent regions. Subsequently, a detailed examination will be conducted for each, featuring the analyzed municipalities. In a concise manner, a SEPO analysis of overall sustainability will be carried out from all municipalities. To conclude, a classification of the best practices implemented in each of these towns will be continued.

Table 1 Line of research followed

Data collection and processing	Various sources of information are used (municipal databases, interviews with experts, population surveys...) It seeks to integrate the information extracted and check the impact of publications on the municipality The case study and field experience method are used to dialogue with local actors, preserve information, improve implementation of plans, strengthen local cooperation and promote sustainable development
Diagnostic methodologies	Various diagnostic methodologies are used, such as the PNI (positive, negative and interesting) method, the SWOT (strengths, weaknesses, opportunities, and threats) analysis, the SEPO (*succès, echecs, potentialités et obstacles*//successes, stumbles, potentialities and obstacles) method, the Flying Balloon, the PESTEL analysis and the Business Model Canvas These methodologies enable the understanding of the current situation, identification of problems and opportunities, and the development of appropriate strategies
Strategic analysis methodologies	The strategic approach is used to define the vision, mission, values, and strategic lines of the municipality It also employs the competitive agenda, which combines internal and external resources, and the Logical Framework Approach, which identifies the means needed to achieve the objectives

Source Own elaboration

3 The Results of the Almeria Projection

Sample Selection and Characterization

The province of Almería is located southeast of the Iberian Peninsula and has an area of 8,774 km^2. According to census data in 2022, it had a population of 731,792 inhabitants, which makes it one of the most thriving provinces (Instituto Nacional de Estadística, 2023). At a general level, it is characterized by its Mediterranean climate and its wide natural and cultural wealth. Economically, its agricultural and industrial activities, as well as its tourist importance, can be emphasized. The latter is especially due to its abundant resources, including over 200 km of coastline and protected areas such as the Cabo de Gata-Níjar Natural Park, the Maritime-Terrestrial Natural Park of Alborán, or the Sierra Nevada National Park. Additionally, there are places of interest such as the geological formations of the Tabernas Desert, or the mountain ranges of Los Filabres and Alhamilla (Diputación de Almería, n.d.).

The province is subdivided into counties, each grouping several municipalities with similar characteristics. Within the Marca Pueblo Project, the regions of Alpujarra Almeriense, Filabres-Tabernas, Levante Almeriense, and Valle del Almanzora would be particularly reflected (see Fig. 1). Within them, as previously mentioned, 14 municipalities are involved (see Table 2).

The region of the Alpujarra Almeriense is a historical and cultural region formed by 22 municipalities that are distributed between the mountains of Gádor, Lújar, La Contraviesa, and Sierra Nevada. It is characterized by its mountain landscape through which it crosses the Andarax River and its tributaries. It stands out for its architecture of white houses with flat roofs generated by its long history, which has seen from the Iberians to the Moors, passing through the Romans, the Visigoths, and the Arabs. Within this region in the project would be the municipalities of Almócita, Fondón, Laujar de Andarax, and Padules.

Continuing, would be the region of Los Filabres-Tabernas as an area of great diversity and contrast especially landscape. It is located in the center-west of the province, bordering other regions of Almeria and the province of Granada. It is formed by 18 municipalities of which in the study would be Abla, Abrucena, Olula de Castro, and Tahal.

For its part, the region of Levante Almeriense is located at the eastern end of the province, bordering to the north with the province of Murcia, to the east with the Mediterranean Sea, to the south with the region of western Almeria and to the west with the region of Los Vélez. It has an area of 1,976 km^2 and in it you can enjoy much of the beaches and coves. In the project is the municipality of Lubrín.

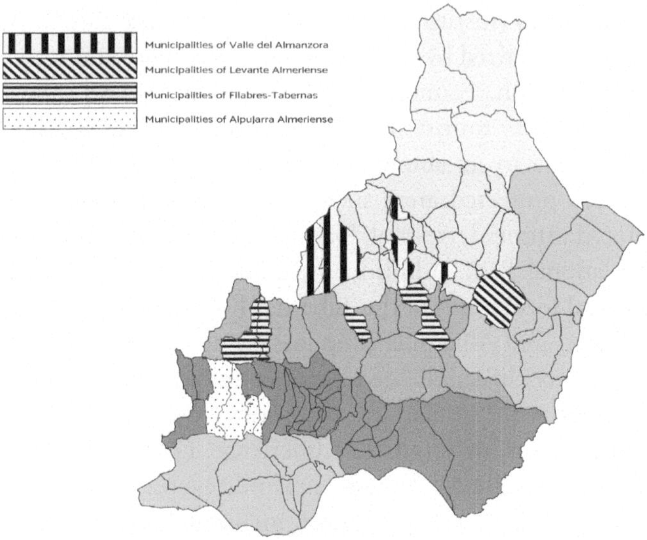

* By location, from left to right:
Valle del Almanzora: Alcóntar, Serón, Purchena (its territory is divided into two overlapping parts), Laroya and Líjar
Levante Almeriense: Lubrín
Filabres-Tabernas: Abrucena, Abla, Olula de Castro and Tahal
Alpujarra Almeriense: Laujar de Andarax, Fondón, Almócita and Padules

Fig. 1 Map of regional division with the municipalities of the project highlighted (*Source* Own elaboration)

Finally, it would be the region of Valle del Almanzora located in the northwest of the province. It extends along the course of the Almanzora River, the backbone river that gives it its name, from its source in the Sierra de Los Filabres to its mouth in the Mediterranean Sea. It is an area composed of 27 municipalities of great landscape, cultural and economic diversity, of which Alcóntar, Laroya, Líjar, Purchena, and Serón participate. Although like all, it enjoys a great historical heritage and natural wealth, it is possibly best known for the marble industry, which has made this region a world reference in the natural stone sector.

Table 2 Member municipalities during Marca Pueblo Project

Municipality	County	Surface area (km^2)	Distance to the capital (km)	Total population	Average age
Abla	Filabres-Tabernas	45.2	61.2	1,247	49.5
Abrucena	Filabres-Tabernas	83.6	63.2	1,221	49.9
Alcóntar	Valle del Almanzora	93.8	87.7	538	53.8
Almócita	Alpujarra Almeriense	30.8	47.0	201	50.7
Fondón	Alpujarra Almeriense	91.1	56.0	1,045	49.4
Laroya	Valle del Almanzora	21.7	70.1	200	46.5
Laujar de Andarax	Alpujarra Almeriense	92.7	59.2	1,587	46.4
Líjar	Valle del Almanzora	28.2	70.0	383	52
Lubrín	Levante Almeriense	138.1	68.7	1,457	53
Olula de Castro	Filabres-Tabernas	33.6	50.7	192	55.3
Padules	Alpujarra Almeriense	26.5	46.2	424	54.1
Purchena	Valle del Almanzora	56.6	81.2	1,550	44.5
Serón	Valle del Almanzora	166.2	78.2	2,062	49.5
Tahal	Filabres-Tabernas	94.5	55.2	346	52.5

Source Own elaboration based on data collected from Sistema de Información Multiterritorial de Andalucía (2023)

Result of the Diagnoses Carried Out: Key Aspects Identified for Sustainability

Successes (Past+Positive)

The municipalities in general have the following noteworthy aspects:

- A wide network of approved and secondary trails on relevant websites. They are also complemented by routes such as the almond tree route, unique routes approved on horseback.

- A wide environmental landscape diversity (from desert to mountain).
- It has an excellent state of municipal conservation.
- It has a wide network of cultural and industrial heritage to use: Remains of oil mills, hydraulic mills, cisterns, rafts.
- There is a wide range of tourist accommodation.
- It is a province with a wide historical importance ranging from cave paintings to today, with some that have qualifications such as assets of cultural interest.
- Extensive own infrastructures: scenic spaces, swimming pool, gym, pavilion, pharmacy, doctor's office, Guadalinfo center, school for the first ages minimum, fiber optic network in all urban centers except one, water networks and some with their own treatment plant, banks or minimum has an ATM for banking operations.
- Active attitude.
- Fight for the recovery of their traditions.
- Active aging activities, crafts, reinforcement for children.
- All have active associations.
- Importance of the role of women in rural areas.
- Implementation of a development strategy based on the enhancement of endogenous resources.
- There are municipalities that are national references in the use of renewable energies with even some awards.
- The use of Rural Employment Schemes (former PER).
- Numerous patron saint and general festivities.
- It is committed to the fight against depopulation and the search for more sustainable models of life.
- City Councils active as Local Development Agents.
- Rapid adaptation to extreme situations such as adaptation to the pandemic.

Stumbles (Past+Negative)

- Little digital update except for a few cases that show outdated websites or a low use of RRSS or telematic means of communication with the citizen.

- Lack of entrepreneurship or entrepreneurial culture generally, being in a particular region a wide dependence on its most important sector, eliminating the corresponding entrepreneurial spirit.
- Problems with water such as water management or storage.
- Low activity usually of associations more dedicated to young people.
- Agriculture used especially for subsistence.
- Average ages higher than the provincial.
- Significant population loss.
- There is no correct urban update in many ways: for example, neglect of homes in the historic center, or new buildings that break the municipal aesthetics.
- Uses of some more overexploited endogenous resources without thinking about their consequences.
- Historical delay in certain infrastructures, such as the Marble Highway-Baza/Purchena Section.
- Abandonment and deterioration of the ethnographic heritage of the Sierra (Cortijadas, eras, balates, mining infrastructures, etc.).
- Poor use of forest resources.
- Lack of unity between nearby peoples.
- Complex development due to protected area regulations.
- Lack of urban and industrial land.
- Youth exodus.
- Need for improvement in leisure activities, especially those focused on young people.
- Public transport problems.
- Internal struggles between the municipalities themselves and their lack of overall vision.
- A strategic plan was not visualized.
- Budget constraints that hinder project implementation.
- Resistance by certain local actors to changes or updates due to their own interests.
- Extensive bureaucracy for any procedure and complicated coordination between entities.
- Neglect for the follow-up of the actions carried out, not visualizing the reasons for various failures.

Potentialities (Future+Positive)

- Arrangement and enhancement of cultural elements that are available but are in disuse or wasted.
- Unique locations.
- Promotion of tourism as active and cultural, since there are adequate conditions for athletes, guided tours, museums.
- New collaboration networks not previously visualized such as the University of Almeria.
- Business development support centers are available.
- A new way of union extra-regional view through projects with other entities such as the present Marca Pueblo.
- Development of shared cultural weeks.
- Rise of new healthier life models.
- The Circular Economy as a central pillar in development.
- The existence of funds such as the European New Generation Funds.
- The rise of new ways of working, such as teleworking.
- Promotion of the agricultural sector benefiting Local Trade.
- Carrying out inventories of unique elements for their better conservation and use.
- Review, updating or assembly of renewable energy infrastructures (wind and solar) aimed at achieving energy self-sufficiency at least in municipal facilities and buildings, if it has not yet been achieved.
- Updating the leisure and cultural services provided to join the digital world.
- Start-up of coworking centers in the urban area.
- Ideal areas to implement Wi-Fi areas in public spaces that may be needed for certain issues such as tourist updating through the use of Qr codes.
- New development thinking based on a bottom-up approach.
- Existence of a good road network that connects the municipalities quickly with provincial capitals.
- Not only the municipalities of the project have unique locations, but the province in general has its own characteristics that differentiate it from the rest.

Obstacles (Future+Negative)

- Water resources.
- Climate change and desertification.
- Pandemics.
- Plans drawn up in areas of greater economic weight, such as desalination plants that will not supply some areas.
- Formations with a high fragility against environmental disturbances (pests and fires).
- Risk of erosion and fires caused by the abandonment of traditional uses.
- The deterioration that will be caused to the small rural settlements and the high mountain villages.
- The possible loss or simple deterioration of essential public services of regional competence (health, education and public transport).
- Loss of interest in the rural world.
- In general, and due to the size, the deficit of conventional leisure possibilities more focused on the early ages.
- The costs of maintenance and management of the network of infrastructures and municipal facilities.
- Problems in the availability of housing and tourist accommodation.
- Possible relocation of certain public administrative services.
- Maintenance with a low budget, especially municipalities with less than 1,000 inhabitants.
- The difference in development between the regions of the province itself.
- Deficit of undeveloped urban land pockets and the complex development of spatial planning plans.
- Non-adequacy of funding for cooperation or development programs.
- General ignorance of the province even for its own inhabitants. Concern only for the capital and the nearest nuclei especially of coast.

Typification of Good Practices and Lessons Learned

Currently, development projects have been developed in each of the municipalities, but without going into a breakdown linking them with the corresponding SDGs as a tool or orientation plan. To focus the work carried out, a list of projects of each of the municipalities by regional grouping will be made, as well as their link to the corresponding SDGs in order to begin to contextualize the good practices already carried out by local government institutions (see Tables 3, 4, 5 and 6).

4 Discussion

Description of the Last Phase of the Project: The People's Brand Agenda

Planning is a key element that promotes cooperation and dialogue among development actors and strengthens the capacity of local actors for strategic management. In addition, it helps to mobilize local society and establish mechanisms and methodologies for comprehensive territorial planning (Fudis, 2018). Planning also helps reduce uncertainty and risks by setting clear goals and providing a path to achieve them, which improves the coordination of activities and increases efficiency in the management of tasks and resources (Garrido, n.d.).

As basic ideas for the correct adaptation of the sustainable municipal strategy to the SDGs since they have been analyzed and their differentiating factor is beginning to be known, two central objectives are proposed:

1. Develop an open forum in a municipal manner that specifies and involves civil society directly with its actions and its future.
2. Develop accordingly, a guide of strategic plans in which to frame a posteriori all the projects that arise, both individually and collectively.

Table 3 Alpujarra Almeriense County

Municipality	Projects	SDGs
Almócita	'Reforestation' in which neighbors have planted more than 1,000 trees to reforest La Alpujarra	15
Almócita	'Energy Self-Sufficiency, Pro-Consumption Community and Elimination of Wiring in Facades': The creation of a Pro-Energy Consumption community that will start from the installation of municipal and neighborhood photovoltaic panels, together with the installation of batteries for energy storage. It is also linked to an update of the wiring in the area	7 8 10 11 12 15 17
Almócita	"Cohousing" of a community self-managed by the inhabitants themselves for small families with whom to share common spaces	10 11 17
Almócita	Project of municipal ecological housing in cession of use	10 11 15 17
Almócita	The new buildings and the rehabilitation of the next ones will be in an ecological way and with an intelligent multifaceted use for the settlement of entrepreneurs and provide possibilities of teleworking	8 9 11 17
Fondón	Multiple investments have been made thanks to the Provincial Cooperation Plan for these years	9
Laujar de Andarax	It has proceeded to the renovation of the market, including new tiling, floors, electric lighting and LED installations, sanitation	12 8 11
Padules	A new shelter has been created in the old water tank	8 9
Padules	In turn, the municipality has proceeded to the installation of photovoltaic panels in municipal buildings to save energy and has updated the new lighting with LED bulbs	7

Source Municipal meetings within the Project, Almócita City Council (n.d.), Laujar de Andarax City Council (n.d.)

Objective 1: Develop a Local Action Forum or Open Consultation Forum

The Local Forum 2030 Agenda will be a tool that will address issues at the personal, group, community, and global levels. It is based on several theoretical and practical approaches rooted in democracy, with the aim

Table 4 Filabres-Tabernas County

Municipality	Projects	SDGs
Abla	'Abla a pie' is a project whose objective is to create a new entrance area to the municipality. It is included in the Urban Public Space Regeneration Program (PREPU) and has an investment of €330,516	11
Abla	It has set itself the goal of innovation and long-term development in Abla: to establish a friendly town before 2029	16
Abla	An improvement has been made in the sewerage network of the north and south, with an investment of €800,000	6
Abrucena	Update project in which a new Tourism Development Plan has been created. It aims to advance with an orderly development of tourism at the local level with public and private aid	8
Abrucena	This town is the only one in the province to participate in the "Holapueblo" project by Red Eléctrica Group, IKEA, and AlmaNatura. Its objective is to find new inhabitants and companies to reactivate inland municipalities	8 10
Olula de Castro	The municipality has completed the installation of LED lighting and solar panels thanks to the collaboration of the Diputación de Almería with an investment close to €100,000. You will thus have a saving of 50% in consumption	7 9 17
Olula de Castro	A place has been adapted to turn it into an artisanal nougat factory, symbol and outstanding product of the town	8
Tahal	A call has been created for different positions, such as cultural promoter, as well as the selection of different cleaning bodies	8 4 11
Tahal	A grant has been obtained to extend a ship for cultural use inside the hull	4 9
Tahal	An 841 kW photovoltaic plant has been installed in the village	7 13
Tahal	In order to improve some services, a municipal shelter has been set up	8 9
Tahal	Projects have been carried out to improve certain municipal roads	9
Tahal	The municipality is part of the "Life Alchemia" project for the treatment of water with natural radioactivity	6

Source Municipal meetings within the Project, Tahal City Council (n.d.), Som Energía (n.d.)

Table 5 Levante Almeriense County

Municipality	Projects	SDGs
Lubrín	The municipality has obtained funding to carry out the project "Social Connection" that will help 30 inhabitants. The €50,000 is destined to reactivate socioeconomic activity and fight against depopulation	3 8
Lubrín	Another project is its new trademark "Lubrin, natural legacy" to jointly promote agri-food products and publicize their own	12 8
Lubrín	At the same time, several updates are being carried out in municipal infrastructures with a value of about €160,000 by the Junta de Andalucía	9
Lubrín	The Provincial Council of Almería has announced the final approval of the General Urban Planning Plan of the municipality of Lubrín	16 17

Source Municipal meeting within the Project

of managing and transforming relationships and organizations. It seeks to create a space for discussion about its community future.

As environments of action will be the municipalities themselves and their neighborhoods, having already started from the basis of a previous municipal analysis in the other phases of the project. Therefore, they have an idea of demographic changes, employment situations, the complexities of communications, or access to housing. As such, it is especially noteworthy to note that it is assumed that hostilities do not materialize toward the new inhabitants who have arrived in the municipalities looking for a development opportunity, although not all the nuclei described above are equally integrated.

The forum aims to structure with the participants sitting in the same room and at the same level, also counting on people who represented different positions or roles in municipal development. During the course of the session, depending on the number of attendees, a possible change of positions will be proposed to separate profiles that could first be sitting together and thus try to further enrich the close dialogue. All this through open call sessions actively promoted in the municipality, either through physical or telematic channels.

This is materialized methodologically through participation in five instances:

Table 6 Valle del Almanzora County

Municipality	Projects	SDGs
Alcóntar	The municipality is updating its approach to tourism and are carrying out renovations and restorations in environments such as "La Torre del Ramil"	8
Alcóntar	Beautification project of the public space with an investment close to €100,000	11
Alcóntar	The creation of a Senior Horizontal Community is proposed as an ambitious project for the care of its elderly	3 8 9
Alcóntar	The improvement of the wastewater treatment is proposed since the project of the wastewater treatment plants (WWTP) within the core is tendered	6
Laroya	An update of the lighting by solar street lamps has been carried out and improvements have been made in municipal facilities	7
Laroya	The municipality has received a grant of €150,000 for the rehabilitation of housing in a sustainable way	10 11
Laroya	Improvements to the rural school and roads have been developed	4 9
Líjar	The municipality of Líjar has begun to carry out actions to update municipal spaces	16 9
Líjar	To improve local tourism, a municipal building is being rehabilitated and will be used for this purpose	8 9
Líjar	Within the framework of the PFEA, the construction and restoration of a park and health-promoting has been promoted, as well as the adaptation of Almazara Street and a series of new facilities	3 9 11
Purchena	The municipality now has the installation of a defibrillator in the Sports City of Los Juegos Moriscos	3
Purchena	The operation of a bar restaurant in the pool area has been tendered for the 2023 season	8
Purchena	The Public Library has been awarded for its project "Biblioteca de Acogida" thanks to its link with immigrant children and at risk of exclusion	10 16
Purchena	The municipality is in the European project "Communal Green Decisions" on good practices in the environment funded mostly by the European Commission Erasmus program	15 4 17
Purchena	Work has begun on the development of the nursing home. It involves an investment of €540,000	3 8 10 9

(continued)

Table 6 (continued)

Municipality	Projects	SDGs
Serón	The elaboration of the Historical Park project will be carried out from which they have obtained about €7,000 from the European Union	8 16 17
Serón	The municipality is in the European project "Communal Green Decisions" on good practices in the environment funded mostly by the European Commission Erasmus program	15 13 17
Serón	The installation of renewable electric generators for self-consumption has been carried out in certain places of the town	7 13

Source Municipal meeting within the Project, Laroya City Council (n.d.), Purchena City Council (n.d.)

– **First Instance: Institutional and Stakeholder Analysis**

It will be the space that aims to identify the supra-municipal administrations whose decisions may have repercussions on the 2030 Agenda, as well as the key agents of the municipality (Assets and Liabilities). Emphasis will be placed on the usefulness of the diagnostics carried out in the early phases of the Marca Pueblo project to map current local action regarding the SDGs, pursuing a "four helices" approach (business, civil society, knowledge sector and government). It will begin with a meeting that will present the objectives of the forum and the political decision to continue with the successive sessions.

– **Second Instance: Creation of Local Forum 2030 Agenda**

In this instance, the questions posed by everyone in the first meeting are shown, the generated proposals are presented and new proposals are added. It will be the first major space for dialogue and exchange aimed at strengthening the role of the population in the formulation and implementation of the 2030 Agenda. It should encourage debate among municipal managers, main local actors, and the technical team of the Marca Pueblo project. After the appropriate meetings, this forum will prepare a Draft Strategic Scorecard in which the selected SDGs and proposed measures for each of them will be included. You can already begin framing them in the different plans.

– **Third Instance: Campaign "Participate 2030"**

In a more local way and for greater dissemination, a new visualization is proposed through multiple participation instruments agreed as the most appropriate for each municipality (online or street surveys, participatory workshops, advisory council, jury, descriptive posters exhibited in public places, RRSS, etc.). It is intended to gather as many contributions and opinions as possible regarding the proposals emanating from the 2030 Agenda Forum, as well as possible new ones. This will allow you to create a Results Report.

– **Fourth Instance: Strategy Elaboration for the Local 2030 Agenda**

Participants will be able to identify the most feasible projects for the coming years. These projects will stem from their ideas in collaboration with other areas such as government, while always taking into account the emerging demands. It is therefore already intended as an objective to translate the global SDGs into an agenda that adapts to the local context. In it, the following will be presented to the Local Forum:

I. Diagnosis of the municipal situation regarding each of the 17 SDGs.
II. Proposal of strategic lines, action programs, and necessary actions.
III. Proposed Monitoring Plan.

– **Fifth Instance. Publication and Official Presentation of the Local 2030 Agenda**

It is intended, as mentioned, to publicize and share knowledge, showing society the sustainability strategy proposed by the municipality through the dissemination of the content of the municipal 2030 Agenda. This Agenda would include a publication related to the municipal 2030 Agenda, a presentation phase to the general population through an act at the University of Almería and an act of presentation to the local population through the organization of local conferences.

Objective 2: Delimitation of the Municipal Action Plan

Thus, and with the corresponding bases established and published, the municipalities will be able to establish in their mandate a series of plans that will have already begun to be outlined, but that will be developed definitively with actions in a transversal and sectoral way (see as an example Annex A: Example of a spatial planning matrix). These projects will be regarded as management and participatory inclusion tools based on the community's recognition of the territory through a new paradigm of unity and relationship with the environment (Baca-Tavira & Herrera-Tapia, 2016; Betancurth et al., 2020; Padilla, 2020).

Therefore, in a more dynamic manner, it is proposed to frame individual projects within framework action plans that encompass the future of territorial development. These general guidelines have already been adapted to the municipal reality and are linked to one or several sustainable objectives in order to better assess their impact and evaluation (an example can be seen in "Annex A: Example of a spatial planning matrix"). These framework plans are a direct consequence of the previous base analyses that, by virtue of the municipal need, will be able to adapt correctly to their situation, especially the sectoral aspect that gives greater emphasis to existing needs.

For this objective, it is proposed to mainly draw strategic general guidelines in a comprehensive manner within the corresponding plans. These guidelines will encompass different aspects: social action (focusing on inclusion and equality), economic action (with a vision of the current situation and its potential development), environmental approach (generally, while also delving into specific actions such as renewables), municipal digitalization basics (enabling the observation of municipal impact and technological situation), and an urban plan (responsible for land and potential growth).

The Vision of Sustainability and Its Importance for Local Development

Therefore, we see how throughout the work, the concept of sustainability for development is fundamental, as it must be based on the premise that it is necessary to meet the needs of current inhabitants without compromising the future (Hashimoto et al., 2019; Huaranca et al., 2019; Mohanty et al., 2016). Sustainable local development will draw from various concepts, with the solid foundation being the participation of all local actors, both public and private, in the creation and implementation of their plans. Thus, the importance of that comprehensive strategic vision with a bottom-up approach is once again emphasized (Fiorino, 2010).

As some examples of contributions from sustainable local development and activities or projects framed within these plans, we can find:

- the promotion of agroecological production and the preservation of indigenous seeds, as well as the use of Sustainable Food Systems (SFS),
- the use and promotion of renewable energies through, perhaps, the creation of own parks installation of plates with a community nature,
- draw up a plan for the existing environmental and cultural heritage and establish guidelines for its proper maintenance,
- integral and own management of waste together with the generation of shared places for the own elaboration of compost,
- organization of workshops on entrepreneurship, particularly focused on utilizing local resources,
- exploration of digital advancements and the adoption of cleaner and more efficient technologies,
- improvements in transport networks, especially public transport, as well as the implementation of a collective transport system,
- projects related to Green Infrastructures.

Municipal SDG Indicators and Their Sustainability

To check the status and evolution of the current global situation, a series of indicators have been created that must be observed temporarily. It is equally important to analyze both the current situation and the desired evolution of the objectives. But depending on the specific case, it is possible that these indicators may require variation depending on their own factors such as the level of application, the area or environment, actors, or even the level of development.

In Spain, the AROPE indicator is used to identify people at risk of poverty or social exclusion, combining factors such as income, consumption, and employment. As well as to guarantee free, equitable, and quality primary and secondary education, the dropout rate is addressed. In recent years, 26% of the Spanish population was at risk of poverty or social exclusion (Instituto Nacional de Estadística, 2022), 8.0% of GDP was allocated the previous year to Health (Ministerio de Sanidad, 2021), or the dropout rate had decreased, although it is higher than the average in the EU.

With regard to gender equality and the creation of equal opportunities between men and women in all social, economic and political spheres, there are still cultural patterns and inequalities in employment, pay and gender-based violence. Economic inequality, as measured by the Palma index, shows that it has not been reduced despite economic growth.

At the environmental level, Spain has improved its sustainable and efficient resource management and resource productivity, but still faces challenges in terms of resource waste and recycling rates. The percentage of energy produced from renewable sources, which has risen to more than 40%, has improved dramatically. However, Spain still relies heavily on coal (Ember Climate, 2022).

Finally, there is the trajectory in development cooperation that seems to require an update and creation of new policies and stable and consistent resources in the strengthening of development cooperation.

However, as mentioned, these indicators must be adapted to a more local public in these cases to, on a smaller scale, be able to assess whether their current situation is improving or if, on the contrary, the state average only disguises the situation depending on the different scales. Therefore, it is necessary to require an adaptation of the indicators according to what is sought so that their evaluation is carried out in the most correct way possible (see as an example "Annex B: Municipal indicators presented as a factor of municipal development").

5 Conclusions

The UN's 2030 Agenda for Sustainable Development is a global plan of 17 Sustainable Development Goals (SDGs) and 169 targets to end poverty, protect the planet, and improve the lives of people around the world. These SDGs cover the economic, social, and environmental dimensions in a complete way, but their implementation requires a major transformation of the production and consumption model, as well as cooperation at all levels.

Municipal governments will play a fundamental role in the implementation of the SDGs since they are the administration closest to the population of a territory. Their participation contributes to democratic legitimacy, equity, and good governance. Even so, they are not without challenges, such as the need for financial and technical resources, the reduction of inequality and coordination between actors. Along with this, it is important to remember that measurement and monitoring systems must be in place to evaluate progress. However, carrying out actions within the framework of the SDGs also offers opportunities such as improving local management, promoting sustainability, fostering public–private partnerships, involving citizens, promoting innovation and technology, and sharing good practices.

But as we have seen, we must always start from the importance of sustainability. It is essential to meet the needs of current inhabitants without compromising the future, while maintaining a balance between the economic, social, and environmental pillars. To do this, it is necessary to assess the situation continuously. To evaluate it and observe whether or not there is evolution, a series of indicators have been established that must be observed temporarily. However, it is important to note that indicators may vary depending on specific factors. Therefore, it is important to adapt the indicators at the local level to assess whether the current situation is improving or whether the global or state average obscures the existing disparities at different scales.

With the Marca Pueblo Project, 14 municipalities in Almeria with different characteristics have been analyzed, aiming to promote sustainable development and improve municipal management. This has been based on a bottom-up approach in which citizen participation, transparency, and cooperation are key.

From the past to the present, the municipalities involved have seen how various successes have been achieved. Among them, it can be highlighted that a wide network of projects has been developed, or they have preserved in excellent condition their cultural heritage ranging from cave paintings to assets of cultural interest from just a few centuries ago such as industrial ones. They are also villas that have large infrastructures of their own such as scenic spaces, swimming pools, gyms, and comply with all basic services. This makes them participatory and committed actors who fight for the recovery and development of their environment, both culturally and environmentally.

Currently, they have focused on a development strategy based on the enhancement of their endogenous resources thanks to a differentiation. But they need to go a step further. The last phase of the Project, called "The People's Brand Agenda", aims to make planning the central element of development and to strengthen strategic management capacity at the local level.

And to achieve an adequate adaptation of this sustainable municipal strategy to the SDGs, two main objectives are proposed: the creation of a local action forum or open consultation forum and the elaboration of a guide of strategic plans to frame the proposed projects.

The local action forum will be a space for discussion and participation. It seeks to involve civil society in decision-making and management of the community's future. The process will consist of five instances that will allow to gather contributions and opinions from the population, generate proposals, and develop a municipal action plan that adapts to the local context and is aligned with the SDGs.

This will lead us to the corresponding line of municipal action, which will be framed in action plans. These will be adapted to the municipal reality and linked to one or more sustainable objectives, differentiating between general cross-cutting actions and more specific sectoral actions according to their situation.

Annex A: Example of a Spatial Planning Matrix

	Transverse						Sectorial					
	Strategic plan	Inclusion, equality and social progress plan	Economic boost plan	Climate change resilience plan	Municipal update Plan 2.0	Urban review plan	Digital literacy plan	Energy and climate plan: based on renewables	Waste and recycling plan	Intra and extra-municipal mobility plan	Sustainable promotion and tourism plan	Cultural and rural spirit plan
Goal 1: No Poverty	x	x	X									
Goal 2: Zero Hunger	x											
Goal 3: Good Health and Well-being	x	x	X	x	x	x						
Goal 4: Quality Education	x	x			x		x					
Goal 5: Gender Equality	x	x	X									
Goal 6: Clean Water and Sanitation	x	x						x				
Goal 7: Affordable and Clean Energy	x			x		x		x	x			

(continued)

(continued)

	Transverse						Sectorial						
	Strategic plan	Inclusion, equality and social progress plan	Economic boost plan	Climate change resilience plan	Municipal update Plan 2.0	Urban review plan	Digital literacy plan	Energy and climate plan: based on renewables	Waste and recycling plan	Intra and extra-municipal mobility plan	Sustainable promotion and tourism plan	Cultural and rural spirit plan
Goal 8: Decent Work and Economic Growth	x		X	x								
Goal 9: Industry, Innovation and Infrastructure	x		X			x		x			x	
Goal 10: Reduced Inequality	x	x					x					X
Goal 11: Sustainable Cities and Communities	x	x	X	x	x	x		x	x	x		
Goal 12: Responsible Consumption and Production	x			x							x	

(continued)

(continued)

	Transverse						Sectorial					
	Strategic plan	Inclusion, equality and social progress plan	Economic boost plan	Climate change resilience plan	Municipal update Plan 2.0	Urban review plan	Digital literacy plan	Energy and climate plan: based on renewables	Waste and recycling plan	Intra and extra-municipal mobility plan	Sustainable promotion and tourism plan	Cultural and rural spirit plan
Goal 13: Climate Action	x	x		x				x	x		x	
Goal 14: Life Below Water	x			x								
Goal 15: Life on Land	x			x				x	x			
Goal 16: Peace and Justice Strong Institutions	x	x										
Goal 17: Partnerships to achieve the Goal	x											X

Source Own adaptation based on the Practical Guide to elaborate the local 2030 Agenda of the Diputació de Barcelona (year 2021)

Annex B: Municipal Indicators Presented as a Factor of Municipal Development

SDG	Benchmark indicator
1. No Poverty	– Average Income – Assistance to people at risk of poverty or homeless
2. Zero Hunger	– Average Income
3. Good Health and Well-being	– Analysis of health centers (number, occupation, difficulty in attending, operating days...) – Air Quality Index of the municipality – Surface for pedestrian use – Km. of bike lane or trails – Life expectancy men – Life expectancy for women
4. Quality Education	– Review of schools (levels, difficulty to continue...) – School dropout rate – Places in early childhood education from 0 to 3 years – People who have passed at least secondary education – People with University Studies
5. Gender Equality	– Number of contracts made to both genders depending on the level – Revisions of family care equity in field meetings (number of hours per week perhaps?) – Average personal income (differentiated by gender) – Percentage of women in the Municipal Corporation – Victims of violence against women

(continued)

(continued)

SDG	Benchmark indicator
6. Clean Water and Sanitation	– Review of the aforementioned infrastructures and possible updating depending on the needs – Domestic water consumption per inhabitant per day – Sanitary qualification of drinking water – Houses in the municipality connected to the sanitation network that have adequate wastewater treatment systems – Homes in the municipality not connected to the sanitation network but with adequate wastewater treatment systems
7. Affordable and Clean Energy	– Operational projects of renewable energies and their visualization in the municipality (apathy for the installation, etc.) – Household electricity consumption per inhabitant and year – Total energy consumption of local government – Share of renewable energy in total final energy consumption
8. Decent Work and Economic Growth	– Attendance at CADEs and innovation and entrepreneurship seminars – Unemployment rate (youth—adult and differentiated by gender) – Persons employed in establishments of the municipality
9. Industry, Innovation and Infrastructure	– Number of companies set up and maintenance of existing ones – Generation of companies. Net balance of establishments
10. Reduced Inequality	– Protected housing stock – Demand for Protected Housing – Immigration rate

(continued)

(continued)

SDG	Benchmark indicator
11. Sustainable Cities and Communities	– Artificial flooring – Area occupied by parks, gardens and urban green areas – People with some degree of dependency in the municipality – Places in residential centers for the elderly – Places in day centers for the elderly – Meetings of the face-to-face mechanisms of citizen participation
12. Responsible Consumption and Production	– Recycling rate and review of recycling projects – Generation of household and commercial waste per inhabitant – Green procurement and procurement: number of tenders with environmental clauses – Sustainability education activities – Participants in sustainability education activities
13. Climate Action	– Percentage of production of energy consumption renewable energy sources – Greenhouse gas emissions of the City Council per inhabitant and year
14. Life Below Water	– *
15. Life on Land	– Area of special protection with respect to the total area of the municipality – Municipal investment in ecological restoration projects
16. Peace and Justice Strong Institutions	– Meetings of the face-to-face mechanism of citizen participation of Local Agenda 21 – Municipal plans and programs with the publication of the evaluation of the degree of compliance and results

(continued)

(continued)

SDG	Benchmark indicator
17. Partnerships to achieve the Goal	– Municipal budget for international development cooperation – Number of networks and alliances in which the municipality participates related to sustainable development

*Indicators not developed as all members of the project are inland municipalities
Source Own adaptation

References

Almócita City Council. (n.d.). *Homepage*. http://www.almocita.es/

Amer, W., Ashong, S., & Tiomoko, D. (2015). *Management manual for UNESCO biosphere reserves in Africa: A practical guide for managers*. German Commission for UNESCO.

Baca-Tavira, N., & Herrera-Tapia, F. (2016). Proyectos sociales. Notas sobre su diseño y gestión en territorios rurales. *Convergencia, 23*(72), 69–87.

Beisheim, M., Ellersiek, A., Goltermann, L., & Kiamba, P. (2017). Meta-governance of partnerships for sustainable development: Actors' perspectives from Kenya. *Public Administration and Development, 38*(3), 105–119.

Berrone, P., Gelabert, L., Massa-Saluzzo, F., & Rousseau, H. E. (2016). Understanding community dynamics in the study of grand challenges: How nonprofits, institutional actors, and the community fabric interact to influence income inequality. *Academy of Management Journal, 59*(6), 1940–1964.

Berrone, P., Ricart, J. E., Duch, A. I., Bernardo, V., Salvador, J., Peña, J. P., & Planas, M. R. (2019). EASIER: An evaluation model for public-private partnerships contributing to the sustainable development goals. *Sustainability, 11*(8), 2339.

Betancurth, D. P., Vélez, C., & Sánchez, N. (2020). Cartografía social: construyendo territorio a partir de los activos comunitarios en salud. *Entramado, 16*(1), 138–151.

Bossel, H. (1999). *Indicators for sustainable development: Theory, method, applications* (p. 138). International Institute for Sustainable Development.

Calliari, E., Staccione, A., & Mysiak, J. (2019). An assessment framework for climate-proof nature-based solutions. *Science of the Total Environment, 656*, 691–700.

Camussi, S., Mancini, A. L., & Tommasino, P. (2018). Does trust influence social expenditures? Evidence from local governments. *Kyklos, 71*(1), 59–85.

Colglazier, W. (2015). Sustainable development agenda: 2030. *Science, 349*(6252), 1048–1050.

De Pablo, J., Giacinti, M. A., Martínez, R. M., Milán, J., Oliver, F. J., & Uribe, J. (2022). *Metodología en el desarrollo local sostenible* (2nd ed.). Delta Publicaciones Universitarias.

Diputación de Almería. (n.d.). *Localización y descripción general de la provincial*. https://www.dipalme.org/Servicios/Anexos/Anexos.nsf/E17005A8B38E2A61C125756E0045DAA2/$file/Cap_2_Resumen_descriptivo.pdf

Echebarria, C., Barrutia, J. M., Aguado, I., Apaolaza, V., & Hartmann, P. (2014). Capturing the benefits that emerge from regional sustainability networks: The Castile–La Mancha network of sustainable cities and towns. *Papers in Regional Science, 95*(S1), S27–S49.

Ember Climate. (2022). *Global Electricity Review 2022*. https://ember-climate.org/insights/research/global-electricity-review-2022/

Emerson, J. (2003). The blended value proposition: Integrating social and financial returns. *Environment: Science and Policy for Sustainable Development, 45*(5), 35–51.

Faguet, J. P., & Pöschl, C. (2015). *Is decentralization good for development? Perspectives from academics and policy makers*. Oxford University Press.

Feiock, R. C. (2009). Metropolitan governance and institutional collective action. *Urban Affairs Review, 44*(3), 356–377.

Fiorino, D. J. (2010). Sustainability as a conceptual focus for public administration. *Public Administration Review, 70*(s1), s78–s88.

Fudis. (2018). *Manual de planificación estratégica para el desarrollo local*. https://www.fudis.info/wp-content/uploads/2018/04/MANUAL-DE-PLANIFICACION-ESTRATEGICA-PARA-EL-DESARROLLO-LOCAL.pdf

Garrido, J. (n.d.). *Planificación estratégica y desarrollo local*. https://www.redcimas.org/wordpress/wpcontent/uploads/2012/08/m_JGarrido_PLANIF.pdf

Glass, L. M., & Newig, J. (2019). Governance for achieving the Sustainable Development Goals: How important are participation, policy coherence, reflexivity, adaptation and democratic institutions? *Earth System Governance, 2*, 100031.

Gómez-Martín, E., Giordano, R., Pagano, A., van der Keur, P., & Máñez Costa, M. (2020a). Using a system thinking approach to assess the contribution of nature based solutions to sustainable development goals. *Science of the Total Environment, 738*, 139693.

Gómez-Martín, E., Máñez Costa, M., & Schwerdtner Máñez, K. (2020b). An operationalized classification of nature based solutions for water-related hazards: From theory to practice. *Ecological Economics, 167*, 106460.

Gusmão, R. G., Leal, W., Quelhas, O. L. G., & de Mattos, D. L. (2018). A literature-based review on potentials and constraints in the implementation of the sustainable development goals. *Journal of Cleaner Production, 198*, 1276–1288.

Hashimoto, S., DasGupta, R., Kabaya, K., Matsui, T., Haga, C., Saito, O., & Takeuchi, K. (2019). Scenario analysis of land-use and ecosystem services of social-ecological landscapes: Implications of alternative development pathways under declining population in the Noto Peninsula, Japan. *Sustainability Science, 14*, 53–75.

Huaranca, L. L., Iribarnegaray, M. A., Albesa, F., Volante, J. N., Brannstrom, C., & Seghezzo, L. (2019). Social perspectives on deforestation, land use change, and economic development in an expanding agricultural frontier in Northern Argentina. *Ecological Economics, 165*, 106424.

Instituto Nacional de Estadística. (2022). *Encuesta de condiciones de vida. Últimos datos.* https://www.ine.es/prensa/ecv_2022.pdf

Instituto Nacional de Estadística. (2023). *Almería: Población por municipios y sexo. (2857).* https://www.ine.es/jaxiT3/Tabla.htm?t=2857

IPCC [Intergovernmental Panel on Climate Change]. (2018). *Global warming of 1.5° C: An IPCC special report on the impacts of global warming of 1.5° C above pre-industrial levels and related global greenhouse gas emission pathways, in the context of strengthening the global response to the threat of climate change, sustainable development, and efforts to eradicate poverty.* Intergovernmental Panel on Climate Change.

Kolk, A., Kourula, A., & Pisani, N. (2017). Multinational enterprises and the sustainable development goals: What do we know and how to proceed? *Transnational Corporations, 24*(3), 9–32.

Laroya City Council. (n.d.). *Homepage.* http://www.laroya.es

Laujar de Andarax City Council. (n.d.). *Homepage.* https://www.laujardeandarax.es/

Ministerio de Sanidad. (2021). *Gasto sanitario total: millones de euros, porcentaje sobre el PIB y euros por habitante según los países de Unión Europea (UE-27 +*

Reino Unido). https://www.sanidad.gob.es/eu/estadEstudios/sanidadDatos/tablas/tabla30_3.htm

Mohanty, S. P., Choppali, U., & Kougianos, E. (2016). Everything you wanted to know about smart cities: The internet of things is the backbone. *IEEE Consumer Electronics Magazine, 5*(4), 60–70.

Ordonez-Ponce, E., Clarke, A., & MacDonald, A. (2021). Business contributions to the sustainable development goals through community sustainability partnerships. *Sustainability Accounting, Management and Policy Journal, 12*(6), 1239–1267.

Padilla, M. R. (2020). Los proyectos comunitarios, una visión de desarrollo desde el escenario turístico rural. *Revista Universidad y Sociedad, 12*(3), 14–19.

Patole, M. (2018). Localization of SDGs through disaggregation of KPIs. *Economies, 6*(1), 15.

Purchena City Council. (n.d.). *Homepage.* https://www.purchena.es/

Robert, K. W., Parris, T. M., & Leiserowitz, A. A. (2005). What is sustainable development? Goals, indicators, values, and practice. *Environment: Science and Policy for Sustainable Development, 47*(3), 8–21.

Sachs, J. D. (2012). From millennium development goals to sustainable development goals. *The Lancet, 379*(9832), 2206–22111.

Scheyvens, R., Banks, G., & Hughes, E. (2016). The private sector and the SDGs: The need to move beyond 'business as usual.' *Sustainable Development, 24*(6), 371–382.

Sistema de Información Multiterritorial de Andalucía. (2023). *Andalucía pueblo a pueblo. Datos de las fichas municipales.* https://www.juntadeandalucia.es/institutodeestadisticaycartografia/sima/datos/smex99.xls

Smoke, P. (2019). *Improving subnational government development finance in emerging and developing economies: Toward a strategic approach* (ADBI Working Paper, 921).

Som Energia. (n.d.). *Producción.* https://www.somenergia.coop/es/produccion

Suganthi, L. (2018). Multi expert and multi criteria evaluation of sectoral investments for sustainable development: An integrated fuzzy AHP, VIKOR/DEA methodology. *Sustainable Cities and Society, 43*, 144–156.

Swain, R.B. (2018). A critical analysis of the sustainable development goals. In W. Leal Filho (Ed.), *Handbook of sustainability science and research* (pp. 342–356). Springer International Publishing.

Tahal City Council. (n.d.). *Homepage.* https://www.tahal.es

Terama, E., Peltomaa, J., Mattinen-Yuryev, M., & Nissinen, A. (2019). Urban sustainability and the SDGs: A Nordic perspective and opportunity for integration. *Urban Science, 3*(3), 69.

Thacker, S., Adshead, D., Fay, M., Hallegatte, S., Harvey, M., Meller, H., O'Regan,N., Rozenberg, J., Watkins, G. & Hall, J. W. (2019). Infrastructure for sustainable development. *Nature Sustainability, 2*(4), 324–331.

Tummers, L., & Bakers, V. (2014). Policy implementation, street level bureaucracy and the importance of discretion. *Public Management Review, 16*(4), 527–547.

United Nations Development Programme. (n.d.). *Objetivos de Desarrollo Sostenible*. https://www.undp.org/es/sustainable-development-goals

United Nations. (n.d.). *La Agenda para el Desarrollo Sostenible*. https://www.un.org/sustainabledevelopment/es/development-agenda/

Xiao, W., Mills, J., Guidi, G., Rodríguez-Gonzálvez, P., Gonizzi Barsanti, S., & González-Aguilera, D. (2018). Geoinformatics for the conservation and promotion of cultural heritage in support of the UN Sustainable Development Goals. *ISPRS Journal of Photogrammetry and Remote Sensing, 142*, 389–406.

Zhang, P., Zhu, C., & Hu, Y. (2016). Fiscal decentralisation, flat administrative structure, and local government size: Evidence and lessons from China. *Public Administration and Development, 36*, 198–214.

Zheng, J., Roehrich, J. K., & Lewis, M. (2008). The dynamics of contractual and relational governance: Evidence from long-term public–private procurement arrangements. *Journal of Purchasing and Supply Management, 14*(1), 43–54.

Measurement of Circularity for the Generation of Strategic Information in the Implementation of Sustainable Tourism Models

Carlos A. García-Meseguer, Joaquín Sánchez-Planelles, Ángel Peiró-Signes, and Marival Segarra-Oña

1 Introduction

Multiple definitions of the concept of Circular Economy can be found in the scientific literature. In fact, Kirchherr et al. (2017) found 114 definitions from which it follows that through the application of the Circular Economy, the sustainable development of economies is pursued by promoting the use of resources efficiently and continuously, leaving behind linear models consisting of extracting, producing, consuming, and discarding, due to their detriment to the environment.

Early definitions of the Circular Economy concept focused more on waste management through recycling (Demin, 2004), later extending the concept to process optimization and design through reverse logistics (Andersen, 2007).

C. A. García-Meseguer (✉) · J. Sánchez-Planelles · Á. Peiró-Signes · M. Segarra-Oña
Universitat Politècnica de Valencia, Valencia, Spain
e-mail: gestor@iiama.upv.es

E. Poveda-Pareja et al. (eds.), *The Strategic Paradigm of CSR and Sustainability*, Palgrave Studies in Governance, Leadership and Responsibility,
https://doi.org/10.1007/978-3-031-58889-1_10

Over the last decade, the concept has been evolving with the aim of integrating economic activity with the environment in a sustainable way, proposing new business models. Murray et al. (2017) define the Circular Economy as a business model where planning, sourcing of raw materials and materials, production, and reprocessing are designed and managed in both resource and product quality to maximize ecosystem functioning and human well-being. The same authors relate this concept and its application to that of sustainability and its three pillars (environmental, social, and economic).

The evolution of the business model concept seems to gain relevance over the years. After reviewing the concept and analysing its evolution, Kirchherr et al. (2017) define the concept as "an economic system that replaces the end-of-life concept with reduction, alternative reuse, recycling, and recovery of materials in production, distribution, and consumption. It operates at the micro (products, companies, and consumers), meso (eco-industrial parks), and macro (cities, regions, nations, etc.) levels, with the aim of achieving sustainable development by generating environmental quality, economic prosperity, and social equity at the same time". In recent years, the concept of Circular Economy has also been approached as a business strategy and considers the possibility of generating new markets and business models (Chen et al., 2020; Geissdoerfer et al., 2018; Lüdeke-Freund et al., 2019; Pieroni et al., 2019; Webster, 2021).

This notion goes beyond the incorporation of waste reduction or reuse and other circular practices in the usual practices of companies. It implies a new concept of operation that forces redefining business models and considers these concepts throughout the business plan and its development. Therefore, to evolve from linear to circular models, it is important for companies to incorporate the concepts related to the Circular Economy into their business model and new strategic management processes.

Thus, the Circular Economy proposes an economic model that seeks to maximize the value of resources and reduce their environmental impact. This approach focuses on optimizing resources through the reuse, repair, recycling, and redesign of products and materials rather than following the linear model of extract, produce, consume, and discard (Ellen MacArthur Foundation, 2019). The Ellen MacArthur Foundation defines the Circular Economy as an economic and industrial model based on the principles of restoration and regeneration. There are seven concepts or Rs of the circular economy that it identifies: Reduce, Reuse, Redesign, Repair/Rehabilitate, Refurbish/Rework, Return/Recover, and Recycle.

For the application of circular practices, The Ellen McArthur Foundation distinguishes between two types of cycles, biological and technical. In the biological ones organic products and materials are returned to the bioeconomy in the process of regenerating natural systems. The technical cycles are related to products, components, and materials, which remain on the market for as long as possible and with the highest possible quality through the processes of repair and maintenance, reuse, refurbishment, remanufacturing, and, ultimately, recycling. For this foundation, the circular model builds economic, natural, and social capital, and it is based on three principles:

- Eliminate waste and pollution to avoid the negative impacts of economic activity on human health and the environment.
- Maintain products and materials in use, taking into account the designs for this purpose and considering different uses until their final disposal in natural systems.
- Regenerate natural systems, avoiding the use of non-renewable sources and returning valuable nutrients to help soil regeneration.

In recent years, several aspects have become increasingly important. On one hand, and in line with the sustainability strategies and plans that public administrations and companies are promoting, the relationship between the concepts of Circular Economy and sustainable development (sustainability) is one of the aspects to which attention has been paid over the last few years. Sandoval et al. (2017) found that the concept of Circular Economy evolves from the concept of sustainability. They state in their article that the present literature has mostly limited itself to defining the applications of Circular Economy without reviewing its direct connection to the objective of the concept, sustainability. In fact,

Kirchherr et al. (2017) found in their study that there were no definitions that explicitly related the concept of Circular Economy to that of sustainability, especially in its social aspect.

The concept of sustainability encompasses three interrelated aspects: environmental, social, and economic. Environmental sustainability refers to the ability to preserve natural resources and the environment. The Circular Economy can contribute to this aspect by reducing the impact of the environmental footprint by using fewer natural resources and minimizing the production of waste and pollutants. The social aspect refers to ensuring equality, fairness, and equity between people and societies. The role of the Circular Economy with respect to this aspect is articulated through creating sustainable jobs, fostering social inclusion, and ensuring stakeholder participation in decision-making processes. The economic aspect alludes to a long-term sustainable economic growth model, i.e. without harming the environment and people. The application of circularity concepts could contribute to economic sustainability through new business models and innovation opportunities that generate value from waste and discarded resources.

On the other hand, as circular practices are being incorporated into the activities of companies and the conception of business models, there is a need for clear measurement guidelines and methodologies, as well as indicators and metrics that facilitate the adoption of these practices (Cayzer et al., 2017; Kristensen & Mosgaard, 2020; Linder et al., 2017; Niero & Kalbar, 2019) and serve as management tools (Ivars-Baidal et al., 2021).

In recent years, public authorities have tried to promote the change of economic model towards circular or sustainable models, even more so with the commitments made in the 2030 Agenda. For this change of model, one of the sectors which has been focused on due to its impact is the tourism sector. Thus, for example, it is worth mentioning Law 3/2022 of June 15 on urgent measures for the sustainability and circularity of tourism of the Balearic Islands, which obliges certain companies in the tourism sector in that region to implement circularity plans.

With this measure, the Balearic Islands could be considered the first circular tourism destination in the world. Expectations about the results of the application of this law are high, and studies are already underway to evaluate the response of tourist establishments to it and their involvement in the adoption of circular models (Moon et al., 2022).

However, and in spite of this effort towards the implementation of circular models in this sector, there are already authors who question the way in which this model transformation is being implemented. Thus, at the macro level (sectoral and regional) some authors highlight the importance of considering all aspects of sustainability. That is, not only environmental, but also social and economic aspects (Tomassi & Cavagnaro, 2022). To this end, it is important to take into account the interaction of companies with the environment, suppliers, customers, etc. The suitability and capacity of the indicators usually proposed to support the Sustainable Development Goals agenda has also been questioned if the environmental, social, economic, and political particularities of the destinations are not taken into account (Glyptou et al., 2022).

But what problems are tourism companies encountering in their transition to circular models? Are the legislative measures that are being implemented appropriate and sufficient for the transformation of their linear business models into circular ones? Are the indicators and measures proposed in the laws adequate in the elaboration of the circularity plans of the companies?

In order to answer these questions and support companies in their transition towards circular and sustainable business models, the InnoEcoTur initiative has been carried out (in which the authors have participated). Thus, among the objectives of this initiative are to try to clarify the challenges and barriers of tourism companies in the Valencian Community, as well as to develop specific indicators and tools for these companies to facilitate the evaluation of circularity.

In this sense, some authors have noted that indicators specifically designed for the tourism sector are rarely proposed (Arzoumanidis et al., 2021). The World Tourism Organization defends the need to have indicators that can be used as quantitative and synthetic instruments that facilitate the analysis and evaluation of information and that, together with other instruments, allow improving the decision-making process (WTO, 2004). This task may not be easy. The availability of data or agreeing on the same indicators for different destinations that consider both local and global impacts is an example of this (Torres-Delgado & Saarinen, 2014).

2 Sustainability and Circularity: The Tourism Sector

Tourism is one of the largest global industries, accounting for a tenth of the world's GDP and employment.[1] According to the World Tourism Organization, it is predicted that by 2030 the figure of 1.8 billion travellers worldwide will be reached, making the Spanish tourism industry the second most powerful in the world in terms of revenue and one of the most powerful in terms of foreign tourists, with the resulting contribution to the country's GDP and its economic development. Thus, for example, Spain closed 2018 with 82.6 million international tourists, 0.9% more than the previous year, which accounted for 89,678 million euros in expenditure.[1] These visitor figures have allowed the weight of the tourism sector in Spain to increase from 11.7% of total GDP in 2017 with 13,7020 million euros[1] to 12.3% in 2019[2] and from 12.2% of those affiliated to the national economy (2.4 million people) in 2018[1] to 13.7% of those affiliated to the Social Security in 2019.[2] These figures have been maintained after the COVID-19 pandemic. Thus, in 2022 Spain received 71.6 million international tourists who maintained expenditure at 87,061 million euros, exceeding the average expenditure compared to 2019.[3] With these figures, the tourism sector is one of the most important sectors for the Spanish economy at a global level, being even strategic for some territories, as is the case of the Comunitat Valenciana, also contributing to an important part of the regional GDP. Thus,

[1] General guidelines of the Spanish Sustainable Tourism Strategy 2030. Ministry of Industry, Trade and Tourism.

[2] Plan for the Modernisation and Competitiveness of the Tourism Sector. Spanish Government.

[3] Ministry of Industry and Tourism (https://www.mincotur.gob.es/es-es/GabinetePrensa/NotasPrensa/2023/Paginas/En-2022-visitaron-Espa%C3%B1a-71,6-millones-de-turistas-internacionales-que-realizaron-un-gasto-de-87.061-millones-de-euros.aspx#:~:text=In%202022%20visited%20Spain%20C3%B1a%20a%20a,7%2C1%20d%C3%ADas%20of%202019).

in this Region, the tourism sector is considered the main driving force of the economy, and its specific weight has increased continuously since 2011, reaching in 2019 the figure of 15.9% of employees and 15.5% of the total GDP of the region (IMPACTUR Comunitat Valenciana Study, 2020).[4]

However, parallel to this growth in tourism, its environmental impacts have also been growing. Tourism has not only physically transformed tourist areas, but has also generated significant environmental impacts, such as the destruction of ecosystems, a decrease in the quantity and quality of water, impoverishment and contamination of soils, waste generation, environmental, land and sea pollution, etc. According to some studies such as those by Gómez Martín (2017),[5] it is estimated that every million tourists that Spain receives generate 25 million kilos of carbon dioxide, 1.5 million kilos of waste and 300 million litres of wastewater. In addition, 11 million litres of fuel, 300 million litres of water, and 2 million kilos of food are consumed. In the Valencia Region, the consequences of these impacts are even greater due to the regional situation: scarcity of water resources, erosion and loss of biodiversity, not to mention the impacts due to pollution, consumption of energy resources, waste generation, etc.

In recent years, several initiatives have been launched to promote circularity. At the European level, it is worth highlighting the publication in March 2020 of the second Circular Economy Action Plan (European Commission, 2020). This Plan defines actions for key areas on the road to a Circular Economy: plastics, electronic waste, packaging, batteries and vehicles, buildings and construction, water and nutrients, and textiles. Along the same lines, and as a projection of the European initiative, the Spanish Circular Economy Strategy, Spain Circular 2030 (MITECO, 2020), was launched in Spain in 2020. This document identifies six priority sectors of activity to incorporate this challenge for a "Circular Spain", and the tourism sector is one of them. For this axis "Tourism" the Document has defined a series of programmes such as, for example, the Intelligent Tourist Destinations programme, where the

[4] https://www.exceltur.org/wp-content/uploads/2020/12/impactur_VALENCIA-2019.pdf.

[5] Gómez Martín, B. (2017). Challenges for Spanish tourism in the face of climate change.

aspects of action are: the incorporation of technologies, sustainability, the incorporation of innovations, and the increase of accessibility. This sector's characteristics and the value chain's interaction with other sectors mean that its influence and initiatives have a high impact.

There are eight main areas of action on which the efforts of the Spanish Circular Economy Strategy, Spain Circular 2030, and its corresponding action plans will be focused. Thus, the First Circular Economy Action Plan 2021–2023 includes five axes and three lines of action. On one hand, the axes focus on production, consumption, waste management, secondary raw materials, reuse, and water treatment. On the other hand, the three lines are more cross-cutting and address aspects such as training, public awareness, and R&D&I. This plan includes actions by the Spanish Government to incorporate circularity criteria in tourism planning and the conversion of tourist destinations with circularity criteria.

These efforts towards the circularity of the sector can also be seen in component 14 (Plan for the modernization and competitiveness of the tourism sector) of the Recovery, Transformation and Resilience Plan published in June 2021. The main investments are directed towards component 14, which is organized around 4 axes. The first of the axes, "Transformation of the tourism model towards sustainability", with an estimated budget of 1,904 million euros, is articulated through the document "The Strategy for the Recovery, Transformation and Resilience of the Tourism Sector". 1,904 million is articulated through the document "The Strategy for Sustainable Tourism in Destinations", which includes the programme "Tourism Sustainability in Destinations", which includes the programme "Tourism Sustainability Plans in Destinations". The aim is to advance in the transformation of tourist destinations towards a new model based on sustainability in its triple environmental, socio-economic, and territorial dimension as the backbone of the destination according to the definition of the World Tourism Organization. Among other measures, the aim is to promote the adoption of energy efficiency and circular economy strategies in the field of tourism, as well as investment in projects in this same field of the circular economy (reduction, reuse, and recycling of waste; efficient use of water; use of local food and materials, etc.).

Moreover, in recent years, and with the adoption by governments of the 2030 Agenda with its 17 Sustainable Development Goals, the concept of sustainability has become even more pervasive in government policies, including those affecting the tourism sector. In fact, the circular economy is linked to the United Nations Sustainable Development Goal[6] 12, consumption and production, which aims to reduce resource use and pollution and analyses the use of goods throughout their entire life cycle. The successful achievement of this goal requires broad cooperation between all stakeholders, businesses, end consumers, researchers, and policymakers.

Thus, the Spanish government is preparing the Spain Sustainable Tourism Strategy 2030 to lay the foundation for the transformation of the Spanish tourism model, facing the challenges of the sector in the medium and long term and promoting the three pillars of sustainability: environmental, social, and economic. The lines of action of this document should be aligned with those of the Circular Economy Strategy, mainly in relation to the tourism sector and the environmental pillar.

At regional level, efforts to move towards the adoption of circular models are also noteworthy. A few years ago, the Valencian Government published the document "Plan Estratégico del Turismo de la Comunitat Valenciana 2020/2025", which defines a strategic line in Circular Economy: "Transition towards a circular economy in valencian tourism".

Together with the articulation of policies through the aforementioned plans, it is necessary to define effective legislative measures to guide the change in the development model. For example, in a context of resource scarcity, reducing consumption and waste to mitigate some of the environmental burdens of tourism. In fact, the implementation of circular management models in this sector (improving the reuse or effective recycling of waste, reducing consumption, etc.) can have a significant impact on the environment.

In this regard, the new waste law (Law 7/2022 of 8 April on waste and contaminated soils for a circular economy) establishes objectives for municipalities that could not be achieved without the involvement of the tourism sector, especially in tourist areas. This law provides rebates

[6] https://sustainabledevelopment.un.org/sdg12.

on waste taxes for catering establishments that can prove that they have reduced food waste. Agreements with the hotel and catering sector are also proposed, such as the promotion of the use of reusable packaging and offering customers surplus food that has not been consumed, the integration of environmental and waste prevention criteria in the contracting of materials and services.

At the same time, at the regional level, Law 5/2022, of 29 November, on waste and contaminated soils for the promotion of the circular economy in the Valencia Region, proposes, in addition to what is indicated in the state law, the development of regulations to reduce waste and food loss, the obligation of selective collection systems for catering establishments in municipalities with more than 5,000 inhabitants, among others. It also proposes economic spending agreements with strategic economic sectors in the Valencia Region, such as the hotel and catering sector, to encourage the reduction of waste generation and the reuse of products.

However, the efforts made in the Balearic Islands should be noted. In this region the transformation from linear to circular business models has already been addressed through Law 3/2022 of June 15 on urgent measures for the sustainability and circularity of tourism. This Law is aligned with the new Circular Economy Action Plan for a cleaner and more competitive Europe (published in March 2020) within the EU Green Deal, which stresses the importance of circularity especially for regions with large amounts of waste generated as a result of tourism. Circularity has to be the lever that drives the decarbonization of the economy and at the same time decouples the relationship between economic growth and natural resource extraction. The Law obliges tourist establishments in the Balearic Islands belonging to the hotel accommodation groups (hotels, city hotels, flat hotels, and inland tourism accommodation), tourist flats, and rural tourism accommodation (rural hotels and agrotourism) to apply a circularity strategy in order to incorporate the concepts of circularity into their strategic business model, internal processes, and relations with their stakeholders. It includes as objectives the reduction of consumption such as energy or water resources in the value chain of the tourism system, as well as the preferential use of local and ecological products, or reusable products. To this end, it requires that all tourism companies must have a 5-year circular economy plan that must be renewed periodically and be subject to an evaluation every year. The plan must focus on five priority areas, such as water or food consumption, waste generation, or the use of renewable energies.

Thus, for example, among the water-saving measures, these establishments are obliged to have a double push button or flush stop button on toilet cisterns or to instal water-saving devices on taps in washbasins or showers. On the other hand, in order to reduce carbon dioxide emissions, fossil fuel boilers such as fuel oil or diesel are prohibited.

The fifth Additional Provision of the Law establishes that the ministry responsible for tourism must draw up a strategic plan for the circular destination of the Autonomous Community of the Balearic Islands, coordinated by the Tourism Strategy Agency of the Balearic Islands. In the absence of this strategic plan that takes into account the particularities of each island, so as to establish a territorialization of the strategy and objectives that serve as a guide for the sector, companies have to be guided by the Law. Thus, the Law already includes aspects such as the priority areas of action or procedural aspects such as the duration of the Plan, its structure, and the need for evaluation. The Law defines circularity planning and evaluation as essential elements of the circularity plan, for which strategic frameworks and self-diagnosis applications developed for this purpose and recognized by the tourism sector and the Balearic government may be used. However, although the Law mentions some parameters to be measured for each of the four defined areas, it does not include specific evaluation criteria with their numerical targets. It indicates that these should be based on UNE or international standards, certifications issued by entities of recognized prestige in the field, or the strategic frameworks and self-diagnosis applications already mentioned.

Furthermore, the proposed indicators are scarce and are not contextualized to the characteristics of the establishment. These aspects could make it difficult to choose more circular practices to implement.

Through these plans and new legislation, the public administration can address the sector towards circularity. Without these measures that promote the development model towards sustainability by incorporating environmental management criteria and based on circular economy principles, the impact that tourism activity can generate can be considerably high.

To help in this transition in the application of these principles and methodologies in the tourism sector, several guides have been published by some public administrations. Thus, the Ministry of Industry, Trade and Tourism, through the Secretary of State for Tourism, has published the document "Guide for the Application of the Circular Economy in the Spanish Tourism Sector". In addition, the Regional Ministry of Economic Model, Tourism and Labour published the "Guide for the development of the circularity plan of the tourist establishments of the Balearic Islands", which serves as a guideline for companies in the sector for the application of Law 2/2022.

However, despite these efforts, there are aspects that are not being taken into account in the implementation of models based on the circular economy that we believe could be important. On the one hand, both indicators and targets at company level should be based on targets at regional level, taking into account the concept of sustainability in its three aspects, not only environmental sustainability. This would allow the evaluation of measures and policies in cost-benefit terms and optimize impacts by taking into account specific economic and regional aspects. On the other hand, there are other unique aspects that should be analysed in the choice of circular practices to be implemented. For example, the seasonality of the impacts or the impact of the circular practices adopted in the company on the rest of the processes in the value chain (suppliers).

So, in this context, it is a priority to develop indicators, tools, guidelines, measurement and evaluation systems, etc. that allow the evaluation of the indicators and impacts of the actions carried out in the process of implementing circular models that take into account the principles of sustainable economy.

Considering the profound relationship between the concepts of Circular Economy and sustainability, the different methodologies developed for measuring sustainability could be used in the field of Circular Economy. For example, in 2004, with the aim of promoting sustainable tourism, the World Tourism Organization published the guide

"Indicators of Sustainable Development for Tourism Destinations: A Guidebook" (UNWTO, 2004) to provide tourist destinations with tools to develop indicator systems which must inevitably incorporate social, environmental, and economic aspects. Subsequently, in 2013, the European Commission launched the "European Tourism Indicator System" (European Commission, 2013) with the aim of providing tourist destinations with a guide to monitor and evaluate their sustainability. More recently, and aimed at tourist accommodations to provide them with tools for the progressive incorporation of measures to improve their environmental, social, and economic sustainability, the Instituto Tecnológico Hotelero has developed the ITH Model of Tourism Sustainability and Improvement Plans, including a Hotel Sustainability Self-Assessment Test. In recent years, initiatives have also arisen in the field of sustainability certification in tourism establishments (Ecostars or Biosphere Sustainable).

But, paradoxically, although the knowledge acquired and the indicators developed to measure the sustainability of tourism destinations could be useful in implementing circular practices in the tourism sector, it is possible that they do not include all the aspects necessary for implementing circular models.

The sustainability of tourism destinations can be assessed through a variety of indicators, such as water and energy consumption and waste generation. However, the concept of Circular Economy presents in these aspects a broader dimension than sustainability, as it pursues the creation of closed production and consumption systems. As previously shown, this implies changes in business models and the management of the supply chain. Creating a circular model in the tourism sector is going to require the development of a new business model with the respective indicators, tools, knowledge, and data to evaluate its implementation, i.e. the efficiency of the circular model (Girard & Nocca, 2017). The same authors propose that these circular models should follow the principles of sustainability, going even beyond analysis in the companies or sectors themselves and extrapolating it to environments or cities, thus considering economic, environmental, and social impacts. In fact, it is becoming increasingly important for governments to articulate the corresponding public policies in order to compensate for the economic costs of adopting circular measures that are less profitable. A good example could be the impact on generating qualified employment (Sulich & Sołoducho-Pelc, 2022). Additionally, it is going to be necessary to generate specific knowledge around the implementation of the Circular Economy in order to properly assess the impacts of circular practices on business activity as a whole in a way that enables strategic decision-making. Both considerations should be taken into account in the implementation of circular models.

3 Circularity Measurement

In this context, researchers from Valencian universities promoted the InnoEcoTur initiative, coordinated by researchers from the Department of Industrial Organization of the Universitat Politècnica de València and funded by the Valencian Innovation Agency (AVI). InnoEcoTur aims to promote the transition of the tourism sector in the Valencia Region towards circular models through, among other actions, the transfer of eco-innovations to companies in the sector.

In order to carry out this challenge, different activities were carried out. On the one hand, a dynamic map of the circular economy in the tourism sector in the Valencia Region was drawn up, analysing its situation, interactions, flows, and processes. Different circular economy solutions were also evaluated with the aim of creating a catalogue of good practices adapted to the needs of the sector.

On the other hand and applying a *participatory action research (PAR) methodology*, the needs, challenges, and points for improvement in the transition of companies towards the circular economy were analysed. Through various dynamics using the *focus group* technique with stakeholders in the tourism sector and using the implicative technique *of scenario matrix and flashcard toolkit*, the researchers worked together with representatives of public administrations, companies in the sector, and specialized consultants. The qualitative analysis software *QDAMiner v5* (needs, challenges, and barriers analysis) was used to analyse the information gathered. After several working sessions, feedback was obtained on the needs, problems, and concerns of those involved in the study. This has enabled feedback to be obtained by providing valuable information, e.g. on the importance or potential of a concept for the companies and objectives of the initiative.

With all the information generated, work has been carried out on the development of relevant and feasible sectoral circularity indicators to evaluate the degree of circularity of a hotel or restaurant, as well as methodologies and tools to facilitate this transition. The work carried out has materialized in a first version of an IT tool for the diagnosis of circularity for this type of company, whose model has been developed based on Law 3/2022 of the Balearic Islands. This tool includes utilities that make it easier for companies to evaluate actions and make decisions. The aim is that companies can assess the impact of their activity in terms of environmental footprint and define the best strategies in terms of cost-benefit.

As a result of the studies carried out by the InnoEcoTur (published at https://innoecotur.webs.upv.es/) and in line with different authors (Hopkinson et al., 2018), it has been established that the implementation of circular practices is a complex process. Through the analysis of barriers in the implementation of circular measures, ambiguities and doubts develop around the concept of circularity and how to introduce it in the business models of tourism companies beyond the R of "reduction" (raw materials, water, energy). Thus, apart from improving efficiency in the use of these resources throughout the project, the need to agree on specific sectoral indicators to measure the impact of circular actions to be implemented by companies has been noted, taking into account singular and regional issues for this sector, the legislative framework and cost-benefit objectives. Also, it is necessary not only to have adequate indicators but also tools and methodologies that protocolize aspects related to the measurement or monitoring of these indicators: what, how, for what, and when. This is the only way to have criteria to assess the impact of adopting circular measures in terms of cost/benefit (environmental, social, and economic). Without this information and the corresponding analysis, it is difficult to integrate circular principles into company business models and strategic management processes, which require the assessment of impacts on the company as a whole. Likewise, among the results of the InnoEcoTur project, it is concluded that public administrations should use these indicators to evaluate their plans and policies at a macro level for decision-making.

There are currently initiatives that attempt to quantify environmental impacts such as the environmental footprint. Although this reference may be useful, it would be convenient to analyse whether compliance with circularity objectives also implies optimization of the environmental footprint in terms of its reduction. Even going further, it would be appropriate to reflect on whether setting circularity indicators and targets obeys what should be their purpose, i.e. to achieve sustainability (Sandoval et al., 2017). This is not a trivial matter. Balas and Abson (2022) found in an analysis of heterogeneity of indicators and measurement contexts that have been developed. Furthermore, from the analysis of the case studies they carried out, they concluded that the indicators being applied should be better linked to sustainability objectives, as well as orienting the process of implementing sustainable models to generate information for decision-making. This implies extrapolating the circularity objectives at the company level to local or regional levels and analysing whether the objectives set and the circular practices implemented are really sustainable. Thus, it could be the case that a circular practice implemented at the company level to fulfil certain objectives may not be sustainable. For example, situations in which the recycling of a certain product would require transporting material a considerable distance due to the lack of adequate local infrastructure.

Therefore, the incorporation of sustainable circular models implies carrying out far-reaching analyses. At the company level, it is necessary to consider the entire value chain, involving suppliers and users (or consumers), incorporating as a strategic factor the generation of symbiotic relational capital with other companies, even from other sectors. All this must be done while considering at all times the impacts in terms of cost/benefit.

At the level of public policies and the articulation of norms that promote the incorporation of circular and sustainable models, it is necessary to consider sectoral particularities and other factors when establishing objectives or indicators. Among these particularities are the local and regional contexts, even more so when considering the three pillars of sustainability.

Another important aspect at the government level is the need to evaluate the policies and impacts of measures, both direct and indirect, at a sectoral or more global level. Generally, the laws of the market condition for the production of products should be considered so that production takes place where it is most profitable. Promoting the consumption of local products might seem to be a measure in favour of sustainability. However, if this is not adequately regulated, it could lead to a considerable increase in demand for these local products with the consequent increase in prices, making their products more attractive. At certain times and in certain circumstances, this could lead to more intensive use or unsustainable use of production factors, causing problems of overexploitation of resources. If the social pillar of sustainability is also taken into account, it could be the case that the implementation of circular measures could, in principle, have a high negative social impact on a region. Therefore, it is important that the process of transition to circular models is carried out in a planned manner over time, anticipating possible undesired consequences of micro-practices on the macro level and adopting corrective measures.

4 Conclusions

Currently, public administrations have published or are going to publish sectorial plans for the incorporation of sustainable and circular practices. Some governments, such as the Balearic Islands, have published a law that obliges companies in the tourism sector to implement circularity plans and their evaluation. Beyond the adoption of certain specific measures aimed at promoting circularity, such as recycling, the transition from a linear to a circular model may require the redefinition of business models and business management throughout the value chain of the product or service. It may also require planning and adaptation of the legislative framework by public administrations as well as policies that encourage and facilitate the incorporation of circular models from the perspective of sustainable development principles, including social awareness measures. This could involve carrying out a macro-level planning that takes into account regional objectives and particularities. In this way, and considering the characteristics of each economic sector, it could be possible to define the most suitable circular objectives or measures for it.

Research centres should not be oblivious to this evolution and should not only generate knowledge for the implementation in companies of circular models in an efficient and sustainable way but also provide profitable technological developments that facilitate the incorporation of competitive circular innovations in terms of cost-benefit. During the work developed in the InnoEcoTur project, several aspects related to the articulation and measurement of circular economy indicators in the tourism sector have been detected that should be considered in the implementation of circular models:

- The identification of appropriate indicators, including those necessary for strategic decision-making: The development of circular economy indicators for the tourism sector is a new topic. Specific indicators that are relevant and applicable to the tourism industry need to be further developed. A systematic review and analysis of the literature is needed to identify which indicators are most appropriate and effective.
- The development of measurement procedures and protocols: The implementation of appropriate measurement systems can facilitate companies' transition to circular economy models. It is not only important that the information recorded serves to identify opportunities for improvement, set clear objectives, and make informed strategic decisions, but also that it can be carried out in an economically viable way. In this way, circularity objectives can be achieved, and undesired negative impacts of tourism activity can be minimized. At the same time, the circularity plan and the adoption of circular measures can be profitable in terms of cost-benefit.
- Impact assessment: It is important to deepen the evaluation of the impacts of circular practices in the tourism sector at the micro, meso, and macro levels. This could require the consideration of multiple variables of analysis, especially if a sustainable economic model is also pursued. It is also important to evaluate the impact of the Circular Economy on the economic performance of tourism companies and the impacts in terms of cost-benefit.

- Consideration of specific local or regional aspects: The tourism sector may present unique and diverse characteristics depending on the region or even the destination locality. In the implementation of circular practices and indicators developed by companies and in the articulation of objectives and laws by public administrations, it is advisable to consider regional or even local contexts.
- Implementation and evaluation of measures and plans: Once sector and context-specific circular economy indicators have been developed and their impacts assessed, it is important to understand the factors that may affect the effective implementation of these practices in the tourism sector. This would entail the identification of barriers and/or facilitators and the role of public policies and decision-making in tourism enterprises.
- Support for innovation: In the transition to circular models, it is important to investigate how and where tourism companies can innovate as well as facilitate technological developments so that they can adopt circular economy practices to improve their environmental and economic performance. This includes not only the identification of best practices and the dissemination of information and knowledge among tourism companies but also generating dynamic environments that facilitate collaboration among all agents and from various disciplines.

Therefore, in order to adopt sustainable development models incorporating circular models, it will be essential to implement in this sector eco-innovative R&D&I results, concepts, and methodologies based on the principles of the Circular Economy that help to improve the efficiency and sustainability of this sector, while at the same time involving the end user and society in the implementation of circular models.

In the execution of the InnoEcoTur project, all these factors are being taken into account when it comes to deepening the generation of knowledge about the development of circularity indicators and their measurement and evaluation, with the aim of generating strategic information for the development of business models in terms of cost-benefit.

As a result, a self-assessment tool has been created to help companies in the sector to implement Circularity Plans and make strategic decisions.

It is the objective of the members of the project that this tool becomes a reference instrument, and, thanks to the InnoEcoTur project funded by the Valencian Agency for Innovation, it generates know-how that promotes a training programme around the figure of Circular Economy Manager that prepares professionals in the advice and implementation of circular models in companies.

In parallel, it will be necessary for companies to be able to monitor and demonstrate compliance with regulatory requirements, for example, by implementing systems to identify, measure, and manage consumption and waste. These and other aspects will be the focus of the continuation of the InnoEcoTur project over the next two years.

References

Andersen, M. S. (2007). An introductory note on the environmental economics of the circular economy. *Sustainability Science, 2*(1), 133–140.

Arzoumanidis, I., Walker, A., Petti, L., & Raggi, A. (2021). Life cycle-based sustainability and circularity indicators for the tourism industry: A literature review. *Sustainability, 13*(21), 11853.

Balas, M., & Abson, D. J. (2022). Characterising and identifying gaps in sustainability assessments of tourism—A review. *Tourism Management Perspectives, 43*, 101004.

Cayzer, S., Griffiths, P., & Beghetto, V. (2017). Design of indicators for measuring product performance in the circular economy. *International Journal of Sustainable Engineering, 10*(4–5), 289–298.

Chen, L. H., Hung, P., & Ma, H. W. (2020). Integrating circular business models and development tools in the circular economy transition process: A firm-level framework. *Business Strategy and the Environment, 29*(5), 1887–1898.

Ellen MacArthur Foundation. (2019). *Circularity indicators, an approach to measuring circularity*. https://emf.thirdlight.com/link/3jtevhlkbukz-9of4s4/@/preview/1?o

European Commission. (2013). *European Tourism Indicators System for sustainable destination management*. https://single-market-economy.ec.europa.eu/sectors/tourism/eu-funding-and-businesses/funded-projects/sustainable/indicators_en

European Commission. (2020). *New Circular Economy Action Plan for a cleaner and more competitive Europe.* https://www.miteco.gob.es/es/calidad-y-evaluacion-ambiental/temas/economiacircular/nuevoplandeaccionparalaeconomiacircular_tcm30-527275.pdf

Exceltur y Turisme Comunitat Valenciana. (2020). *IMPACTUR 2019. Estudio del impacto económico del turismo sobre la economía y el empleo.*

Demin, C. (2004). The essence of a recycling economy: Circular utilization of resources. *Chinese Journal of Population Resources and Environment, 2*(1), 18–23.

Geissdoerfer, M., Morioka, S. N., Monteiro de Carvalho, M., & Evans, S. (2018). Business models and supply chains for the circular economy. *Journal of Cleaner Production, 190*, 712–721.

Girard, L. F., & Nocca, F. (2017). From linear to circular tourism 1. *Aestimum, 70*, 51.

Glyptou, K., Amore, A., & Ashton Adie, B. (2022). From aspirations to applications: The SDGs and the role of indicators in the measurement of sustainable tourism. In *Planning and managing sustainability in tourism: Empirical studies, best-practice cases and theoretical insights* (pp. 13–25). Springer International Publishing.

Hopkinson, P., Zils, M., Hawkins, P., & Roper, S. (2018). Managing a complex global circular economy business model: Opportunities and challenges. *California Management Review, 60*(3), 71–94.

Ivars-Baidal, J. A., Celdrán-Bernabeu, M. A., Femenia-Serra, F., Perles-Ribes, J., & Giner-Sánchez, D. (2021). Measuring the progress of smart destinations: The use of indicators as a management tool. *Journal of Destination Marketing and Management, 19*, 100531.

Kirchherr, J., Reike, D., & Hekkert, M. (2017). Conceptualizing the circular economy: An analysis of 114 definitions. *Resources, Conservation and Recycling, 127*, 221–232.

Kristensen, H. S., & Mosgaard, M. A. (2020). A review of micro level indicators for a circular economy-moving away from the three dimensions of sustainability? *Journal of Cleaner Production, 243*, 118531.

Linder, M., Sarasini, S., & van Loon, P. (2017). A metric for quantifying product level circularity. *Journal of Industrial Ecology, 21*(3), 545–558.

Lüdeke-Freund, F., Gold, S., & Bocken, N. M. (2019). A review and typology of circular economy business model patterns. *Journal of Industrial Ecology, 23*(1), 36–61.

Ministry for Ecological Transition and the Demographic Challenge. (2020). *Spain Circular 2030*. Spanish Circular Economy Strategy. https://www.miteco.gob.es/es/calidad-y-evaluacion-ambiental/temas/economia-circular/espanacircular2030_def1_tcm30-509532_mod_tcm30-509532.pdf

Moon, C., Batle, J., & Morales, M. (2022). Implications of the New Balearic Islands circularity law for tourism practice and research. In *Proceedings of the 5th International Conference on Tourism Research, 2022*.

Murray, A., Skene, K., & Haynes, K. (2017). The circular economy: An interdisciplinary exploration of the concept and application in a global context. *Journal Business Ethics, 140*(3), 369–380.

Niero, M., & Kalbar, P. P. (2019). Coupling material circularity indicators and life cycle based indicators: A proposal to advance the assessment of circular economy strategies at the product level. *Resources, Conservation and Recycling, 140*, 305–312.

Pieroni, M. P., McAloone, T. C., & Pigosso, D. C. (2019). Business model innovation for circular economy and sustainability: A review of approaches. *Journal of Cleaner Production, 215*, 198–216.

Sandoval, V. P., García, M. C., & Ormazábal, M. (2017). Circular economy: Relationship with the evolution of the concept of sustainability and strategies for its implementation. *Memoria Investigaciones en Ingeniería, 15*, 85–95. ISSN 2301-1092, ISSN-e 2301-1106.

Sulich, A., & Sołoducho-Pelc, L. (2022). The circular economy and the Green Jobs creation. *Environmental Science Pollution Research, 29*, 14231–14247.

Tomassini, L., & Cavagnaro, E. (2022). Circular economy: A paradigm to critically rethink sustainability in tourism and hospitality. In *Planning and managing sustainability in tourism: Empirical studies, best-practice cases and theoretical insights* (pp. 1–12). Springer International Publishing.

Torres-Delgado, A., & Saarinen, J. (2014). Using indicators to assess sustainable tourism development: A review. *Tourism Geographies, 16*(1), 31–47.

Webster, K. (2021). A circular economy is about the economy. *Circular Economy and Sustainability, 1*, 115–126.

World Tourism Organization. (2004). *Indicators of sustainable development for tourism destinations: A guidebook*. https://doi.org/10.18111/9789284407262

Conclusions

Esther Poveda-Pareja, Bartolomé Marco-Lajara, Mercedes Úbeda-García, and Encarnación Manresa-Marhuenda

Considering that (CSR) and sustainability promotion by governments or institutions alone is not enough, a higher level of involvement is required from companies, as the main agents of economic development. For that reason, additional research is needed to analyse how the desired levels of sustainability can be achieved through each of the spheres (public and private) and by considering collaboration between both levels. This

E. Poveda-Pareja · B. Marco-Lajara (✉) · M. Úbeda-García · E. Manresa-Marhuenda
Business Administration Department, University of Alicante, Alicante, Spain
e-mail: bartolome.marco@ua.es

E. Poveda-Pareja
e-mail: esther.poveda@ua.es

M. Úbeda-García
e-mail: mercedes.ubeda@ua.es

E. Manresa-Marhuenda
e-mail: encarnacion.manresa@ua.es

E. Poveda-Pareja et al. (eds.), *The Strategic Paradigm of CSR and Sustainability*, Palgrave Studies in Governance, Leadership and Responsibility,
https://doi.org/10.1007/978-3-031-58889-1_11

book details the relevance of analysing (CSR) and sustainability from a strategic paradigm. In this sense, the actions of stakeholders belonging to both the private and public scopes have been considered, highlighting public–private collaboration to enable the formulation and implementation of CSR from a strategic perspective. Consequently, the book provides useful solutions for both private companies, and public institutions to overcome the main barriers when formulating their CSR strategies and scope, as well as to unveil the optimal mechanisms to bring public policies or laws in line with business philosophy.

The strength of this book is the provision of a diverse range of chapters that analyse the concepts of CSR and sustainability from a business strategy point of view, considering the different existing stakeholder groups. In addition to analysing the concepts from the two most relevant spheres (public–private), the book includes theoretical chapters, which allow for the renewal of academic knowledge on which topics or approaches are more interesting when studying the variables (main motivations, barriers, how the stage of the life cycle of companies influences them, among other aspects), as well as empirical chapters, which allow the theory to be contrasted in different sectors, giving a practical sense to the research and providing useful solutions for managers and public authorities in each of the sectors of activity under analysis, thus providing solutions adapted to each type of agent according to their activity or their position as a stakeholder in the company, overcoming the barriers that each group has experienced when it comes to making their CSR and sustainability strategies effective in their respective areas of activity.

Among the main conclusions derived from the book, we must differentiate between the conclusions provided in the first block, which analyses characteristics that affect companies when developing CSR and orienting their sustainable approach, such as the stage of the life cycle, recommendations regarding the role of certifications and the company's ethical behaviour, the degree of technological and innovation intensity, as well as the location in specialised environments conducive to the promotion of sustainable practices. Specifically, the first conclusion is that due to continuous economic and social environment changes, the format and content of CSR will also change; in other words, most companies may adopt different types of CSR strategies at different stages of their life cycle (evolutionary process of CSR). The second is that CSR and sustainability are vital in all sectors of activity, but it is obvious the existence of controversial sectors due to its negative impacts on society, such as mining activity, which result in a constant search for a social licence to operate. The third conclusion is related to the role played by technological intensity in the level of financial performance, green innovation, and sustainable performance achieved by industrial companies. The findings suggest that companies with higher technological intensity are more financially profitable, leading to increased investment in green innovation and, consequently, greater sustainability. The fourth conclusion highlights the positive effects that a cluster and a network of firms can have on the development of local communities, through bodies that coordinate CSR actions that are helpful in overcoming barriers to CSR, what is of special relevance to sectors integrated by SMEs, as is the case of tourism. Fifth, the idea emerges that circular practices not only consist significantly of recycling or reusing waste or materials but also the interference of topics not directly related but with significant impact, like transport; this conclusion emphasises the importance of transportation in the sustainability of all sectors of economy, although specifically in tourism, given that tourism cannot be understood without transportation, not only of people but also goods. In this way, all the chapters that make up the first block address topics of interest that could be developed by companies at a microeconomic level in order to address their CSR strategies appropriately and focus them towards the objectives of sustainable development, avoiding many of the barriers that companies in the sectors analysed have traditionally faced.

As for the second block, it is focused on highlighting useful solutions on the initiatives that can be carried out by public stakeholders in order to properly promote the development of responsible practices. Concretely, this section starts providing the sixth conclusion of the book, highlighting that the CSR practices adopted by the private sector depend on the institutional framework in which companies operate. The textile sector is often criticised for its environmental impacts and the social conditions of its workers. It is important to note that institutional influence is not only through stricter legislation but also through the indirect influence of other stakeholders and social actors.

It has been demonstrated that the media can influence social perceptions and indirectly affect the proposal of new sustainability regulations based on how they present information. Additionally, the public–private influence in promoting sustainable development is not unidirectional, as private initiatives also contribute to improving municipal management. The strategic planning of Sustainable Smart Cities demonstrates that improvements in municipal sustainability are the result of public–private cooperation. This cooperation involves the Public Administration, companies, and various stakeholders such as research institutes, universities, and the local population. This collaboration should be based on economic and social reality at any given time. Measures such as the creation of local action forums that promote citizen participation, transparency, and cooperation should be encouraged, if necessary. Finally, in addition to the implementation of public–private practices and measures that promote sustainable development, it is essential to have indicators, tools, guidelines, and measurement systems to evaluate the impact of actions and improve decision-making at the microeconomic and macroeconomic levels.

Index

E. Poveda-Pareja et al. (eds.), *The Strategic Paradigm of CSR and Sustainability*, Palgrave Studies in Governance, Leadership and Responsibility, https://doi.org/10.1007/978-3-031-58889-1

SPRINGER NATURE

GPSR Compliance

The European Union's (EU) General Product Safety Regulation (GPSR) is a set of rules that requires consumer products to be safe and our obligations to ensure this.

If you have any concerns about our products, you can contact us on ProductSafety@springernature.com

In case Publisher is established outside the EU, the EU authorized representative is:

Springer Nature Customer Service Center GmbH
Europaplatz 3
69115 Heidelberg, Germany

The manufacturer's authorised representative in the EU is Springer Nature Customer Service Centre GmbH, Europaplatz 3, 69115 Heidelberg, Germany. If you have any concerns regarding our products, please contact ProductSafety@springernature.com

Printed and bound by CPI Group (UK) Ltd, Croydon, CR0 4YY
01/10/2026
02225954-0006